THE VIETNAM CONNECTION

Isabel Molyneux

JANUS PUBLISHING COMPANY
London, England

First Published in Canada, 1991,
by Molyneux Books

Revised Edition published in Great Britain 1995
by Janus Publishing Company,
Edinburgh House, 19 Nassau Street,
London W1N 7RE

British Library Cataloguing-in-Publication Data.
A catalogue record for this book is available from the
British Library.

ISBN 1 85756 134 1

Cover design Linda Wade,
from a photograph by Michael J Gething

Printed & bound in England by
Antony Rowe Ltd,
Chippenham, Wiltshire

THE VIETNAM
CONNECTION

TABLE OF
CONTENTS

ILLUSTRATIONS & MAPS

ABBREVIATIONS

ARVN	Army of the Republic of Vietnam (South Vietnamese Army, pro-USA)
CIA	Central Intelligence Agency (USA)
CIDG	Civilian Irregular Defense Group
CINCPAC	Commander-in-Chief, Pacific (US commander for American forces in the Pacific, and SE Asia)
CORDS	Civilian Operations and Revolutionary Development Support
COSVN	Central Office for South Vietnam (communist)
DRV	Democratic Republic of Vietnam (communist)
GMI	Groupement Mixe D'Intervention Aeroporte (French airborne commandos)
MAAG	Military Assistance and Advisory Group (US)
MACV	Military Assistance Command, Vietnam (US)
NLF	National Liberation Front (South Vietnam, pro-communist)
NSC	National Security Council (USA)
OSS	Office of Strategic Services (USA)
PAC	Political Action Committee (USA)

PAVN	People's Army of Vietnam (communist)
PLAF	People's Liberation Armed Forces (the army of the NLF)
PRC	People's Republic of China
PRG	Provisional Revolutionary Government (South Vietnam)
PRU	Provincial Reconnaissance Unit (South Vietnamese paramilitary government agents)
SEALS	Sea, Air and Land Units (US Navy)
SMM	Saigon Military Mission (US)
SOG	Study and Observation Group
Vietcong	short for Viet Nam Cong San, or Vietnamese Communist
Vietminh	short for Viet Nam Doc Lap Dong Minh, or Vietnam Independence League. The term was not used after 1951, when the Vietminh was absorbed into a united party, mainly communist
VNQDD	short for Viet Nam Quoc Dan Dang, Vietnamese Nationalist Party, non-communist

PREFACE

The coming of some of the Vietnamese 'Boat People' to Western Canada first led me to study the history of their country. I have found that the tragic events which have taken place there, although they seem enigmatic, did not take place in a vacuum, but have a complex connection with cultural and historical factors, both oriental and western. Tracing this connection is the theme of the book.

As a short and fairly light 'read', I hope it fills the gap in the literature on Vietnam, between accounts of experiences in combat and longer, more detailed, histories and reference books. Some chapters, in the form of dialogues, are based on actual discussions, and it seemed natural to keep them in that form.

I would like to thank the staff of Edmonton Public Libraries for their help when I was preparing this book, and the staff of Bjarne's Books, Edmonton, for finding some out-of-print books for me.

I am indebted to friends, in Vietnam and in the west, who have encouraged me with their enthusiasm.

I.E.M., Edmonton, Alberta, Canada.

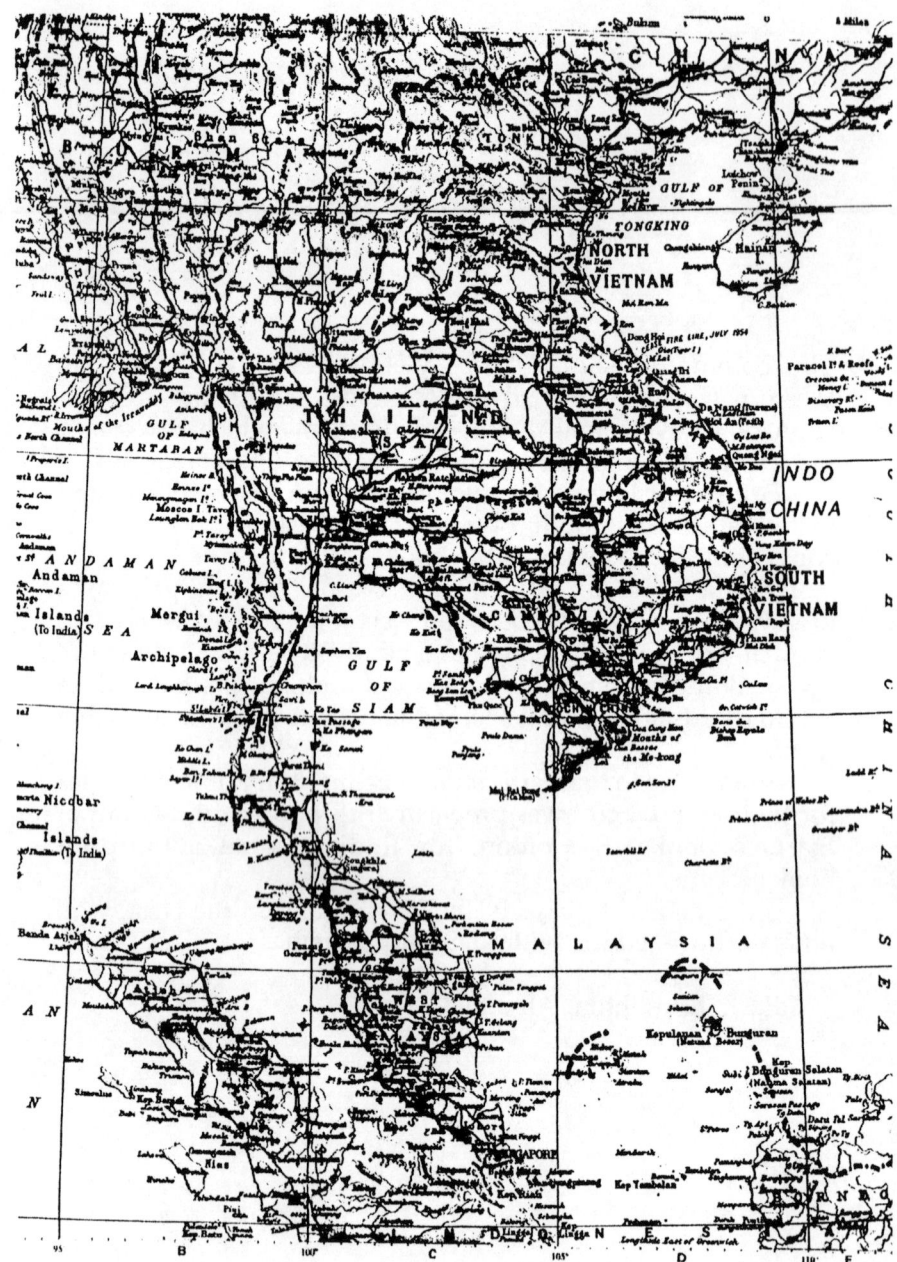

South-East Asia before 1975

INTRODUCTION

The Long Trail to My Lai 4

On the morning of 16th March, 1968, Lt W. Calley Jr, leading a platoon of the 20th US Infantry, 1st Battalion, Americal Division, entered the hamlet of My Lai 4, in Quang Ngai Province of South Vietnam. The platoon killed every person in the hamlet and burned the huts. Small children, babies at the breast, women, and old men were shot at close range, or bludgeoned to death. Their bodies were thrown into a ditch. Some little girls were raped before being murdered. Cattle were also slaughtered.

When Lt Calley found that there was no returning fire, could he have lowered his gun, given the orders to cease fire, and then just have walked away, through the bamboo grove and across the rice paddy? Or was he hardly more than a robot programmed for tragedy, unable to stop himself from compulsively killing, with no choice in the matter? Was determinism operating, or was some vestige of freewill left to him? Opinions differ still.

Much later, when he was court-martialled for his part in the massacre, some thought he was aware that what he was doing was wrong and he could have stopped, but others considered him a scapegoat for deep flaws in the US army system. '[It was] no big deal, sir,' he said when a senior officer asked him to describe what had happened at My Lai 4. To the public, however, the massacre expressed, in one swift, terrible climax, the mad, pointless cruelty of the war. One of many such incidents, just the tip of the iceberg as it were, it had overtones of bitter racism which came as a shock. People assumed that in fatigue and rage, after suffering many casualties during several gruelling days in the jungle, the members of the platoon had sought a 'high' and a release for their feelings through an outburst of violence.

This hypothesis one can accept, as far as it goes. But there were puzzling aspects to the incident, too, as it did not appear to be part of any overall military strategy. Called a 'Search and Destroy' operation, its connection with action elsewhere was hard to see. The members of the platoon shared with all levels of US troops in Vietnam a basic confusion as to the true nature of their task. Were they supposed to be 'nation-building', helping the South Vietnamese people to maintain law and order, and defending them against the communists, or were they meant to be 'nation-destroying', attacking and wiping out villages, whether or not communists had been sheltered in them?

The treatment the villagers got from the US troops was inconsistent. Each command had its own separate script; depending on what part of the military and pseudo-military forces a man was in, he could be doing any of the following: helping villagers get fresh water and medical supplies; arming them and assisting them in building a stockade; he might be dragging them all off to a 'Strategic Hamlet' just when their rice was ready to be harvested; he could be laying waste to their homes, on foot as at My Lai 4, or from the air, by dropping bombs or deadly chemicals on them.

Some villages were the object of more than one of these operations, which were carried out without any master plan, and in response, not to the imperatives of the actual conflict, but to the need of each separate service bureaucracy to prove its importance.

Two other aspects of the US military system which help to explain the behaviour of individuals in the US-Vietnam War were the systems of training, and those of promotion of individuals to officer status. The road from the brutalising experience of US army boot camps to the burning of My Lai 4 was an easy one: the lowering of the requisites for becoming an officer meant that some persons had commissions who were inadequate in a leadership role.

If we continue to look at the large military system of which the platoon at My Lai 4 was a tiny part, a natural question might be, 'Who was the Commander-in-Chief?'

The Constitution of the United States of America, ratified by some states in 1787, names the President as the Commander-in-Chief:

> The President shall be the Commander-in-Chief of the Army and Navy of the United States, and of the militia of the several states, when called into the actual service of the United States; he may require the opinion, in writing, of the principal officer in each of the Executive Departments upon any subject relating to the duties of their respective offices . . .
> (*Article Two, Section Two, Constitution of the United States of America*)

The short word 'may' in the phrase, 'he may require the opinion', affected the course of events long afterwards. It is permissive only; the president is not compelled, in the letter of the law, to consult anyone. But other clauses in the Constitution show that, if he kept to the spirit of the law, he would be consulting with Congress a lot. However, right there at the most supreme level of command ('Highest Authority in Land' – as the president was sometimes called in army memos), at the very top of the whole system is a fuzzy situation, a grey area, which has been the cause of a lot of grief.

According to the Constitution, it was also a prerogative of the office of the president for him to be able to appoint aides and consultants to assist him at the White House. They did not have to be elected, nor did they have to report regularly to Congress. They reported to the president. From a few hundred before the Second World War, their numbers grew to thousands between the 1940s and 1970s. They could not all be accommodated at the White House, and many had to be given offices elsewhere. Aides and consultants would have aides and consultants of their own, and their own specialists and public relations people. So extra layers of the government were created, with an inner sanctum, which gradually took over more and more of the Executive Branch of the US government. Thus, the increase in the power of the president, with the comparative weakening of the Congress, has had a major impact on the course of events.

So it came about that, during the US war with Vietnam, the military chiefs did not have consultations with the president on a regular basis. The process of consultation was diluted through several officials, who might be from various sections of government, e.g., Department of Defense, the National Security Council, or Department of State. Serving army and naval officers did not hold political office themselves.

Unity of command was an ideal never attained by the US forces in Vietnam. The strategic command headquarters were far away in Honolulu, under 'CINCPAC,' Commander-in-Chief, Pacific, while US MACV (Military Assistance Command, Vietnam) was based in Saigon.

Colonel Harry G. Summers, Jr, in his book, *On Strategy, A Critical Analysis of the Vietnam War*, commented that when General William C. Westmoreland was in command in Vietnam, he seldom received messages directly from the White House, as he was not the commander of the entire theatre of war, and technically only had authority within South Vietnam. Messages from Washington were relayed to him from Honolulu.

There was a marked contrast between this fragmented, tangential, rather *ad hoc* line of command and communication, and the system prevailing in North Vietnam. General Vo Nguyen Giap held both political office and military command. He was deputy Prime Minister, Minister of Defence in Hanoi, and Commander-in-Chief of the armed forces. He used to issue communiqués giving both political and military information to all local cadres, enabling everyone to feel part of the total plan for the DRV (Democratic Republic of Vietnam).

Many of the issues raised so far, such as the lack of unity of command in the US forces in Vietnam, and the growing bureaucratisation of the Executive Branch of the US government, are system matters, having to do with structural processes taking place in large organisations. In writing this book I have been influenced by system theory, finding that it adds another dimension to the study of history, providing a connection between seemingly unconnected events; very often this hidden relationship isn't revealed if historians limit themselves to writing biography – relating what an individual did – or chronology – relating 'what happened next?' Valuable though these two modes of writing history are, they seem to leave something unsaid.

Daniel E. Griffiths, an author of organisational studies, defined a system succinctly as 'a complex of elements in mutual interaction'. Using the term in a broad sense, I have regarded as systems not only the external ones such as armies, but also intangible groups of ideas (such as Confucian teaching and cold war theories), all of which have affected the course of history.

C. West Churchman, in his book *The Systems Approach*, said:

'Is there something essential about the concept of a system as a way of thinking? There surely is. Systems are made up of sets of components that work together for the overall objective of the whole. The systems approach is simply a way of thinking about these total systems and their components . . .'

Evidently seeing a systems approach as a dynamic, non-rigid, open-ended way of interpreting events, he wrote: 'The systems approach (in the end) really consists of a continuing debate between various attitudes of mind with respect to society'; and 'The systems approach begins when first you see the world through the eyes of another' (or, as the North American Indians put it, when you have marched in his moccasins).

If these comments seem daunting and hard to live up to, we could see how a systems approach can work in practice, by taking an analogy from a university department. Supposing a professor of history, baffled and frustrated by successive years of apparently dull, ill-prepared students, were to look at the educational and political system through which they percolated to his department, he might see their problems in a new light. For beyond the small system of his department lay other systems and sub-systems, in which changes might have taken place affecting the students. For instance, a new state administration may have cut down on funds for history teachers in high schools, drastically reducing the time, if any, allotted to the subject; or powerful corporations may have demanded greater emphasis on subjects such as computer science to prepare students for high-tech jobs in their service.

A very long-lasting group of ideas, or system-as-a-way-of-thinking, as Mr Churchman puts it, was the *Monroe Doctrine*. 'The Long Trail to My Lai 4', that is, the deep underlying causes of the massacre and the reasons why Lt Calley Jr and his men were there, had their origin in the assumptions which grew from it.

In 1823, when President Monroe, in his message to Congress for the year, expressed the policy later dubbed the Monroe Doctrine, he was politely telling the Russians and their European allies to keep out of the American continent, where he considered the United States' interests to be paramount:

> 'We owe it therefore to candour, and to the amicable relations existing between the United States and those powers, to declare, that we should consider any attempt on their part to extend their system to any portion of this hemisphere, as dangerous to our peace and safety . . .'
>
> *(President Monroe, 1823)*

What decades of grief have followed from these apparently innocuous words.

President Monroe, on the same theme, said the American continents were henceforth not to be considered as subjects for colonisation by any European powers, and any attempt to oppress Latin American states or control their destiny, would be regarded as acts of hostility to the US.

In the context of his time his statements were realistic. Russia was claiming territory south of Alaska down to the 51st parallel, and some of the European powers, in a congress at Verona in 1822, had planned to send troops to South America to get back some territories for Spain; France, too, hoped to acquire new lands there.

The flip side, as it were, of the Monroe Doctrine was the concept of an American geo-political area and sphere of influence in which it was legitimate for the US, and only the US, to intervene by force of arms in the affairs of sovereign nations. Although a *carte blanche* right to do this wasn't

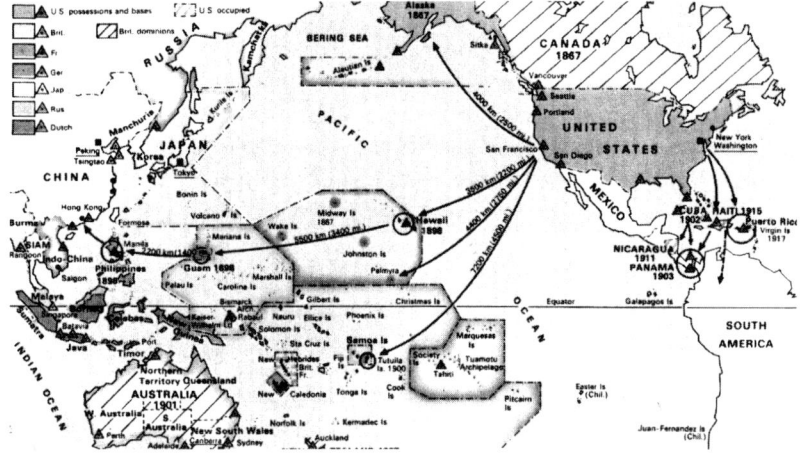

US expansionist policies from 1867

claimed in so many words by President Monroe, Americans inferred that the right was there by implication; to them it seemed that he had given a blessing to US expansionism, and to a habit of thinking that 'intervention' meant military action. Peaceful ways of solving problems were downplayed.

Lt Calley Jr could have found in history several precedents for the actions of his men at My Lai, for there had been My Lai-style massacres and village-burnings by US forces wherever American interests seemed to be threatened: in the Philippines at the turn of the century, and, nearer to the present, in Guatemala in the 1950s, and in the Dominicans in 1965.

Early in this century two corollaries, the 'Roosevelt Corollary' and the 'Wilson Corollary', added new dimensions to the Monroe Doctrine. President Theodore Roosevelt said, in effect, that if any nation in the western hemisphere got out of hand and behaved in an uncivilised way, the US, in accordance with the Monroe Doctrine, would act as an international police power. President Woodrow Wilson issued a 'Declaration' extending the Monroe Doctrine to include finance and business. For instance, he forbade European powers to get oil concessions in the neighbourhood of the Panama Canal; they were to go exclusively to American companies.

These corollaries set the stage for the development of the

curiously proprietary, 'holier-than-thou' attitude to small
nations (combined with shrewd attention to US business
interests), which has characterised American foreign policy
ever since, to the puzzlement of other nations. This attitude
was clearly expressed, for instance, in a report from General
Maxwell D. Taylor when he was the US Ambassador to South
Vietnam in 1964. Bemoaning the poor local support there for
US programmes, he said:

> 'It is most difficult to find adequate provincial chiefs and supporting
> administrative personnel to carry forward the complex programs
> which are required in the field for successful pacification. It is true
> that when one regards the limited background of the provincial
> chiefs and their associates one should perhaps be surprised by the
> results which they have accomplished . . .' (From *The Pentagon Papers*)

Cold war principles, such as the concept of the geo-political
Grand Area of US influence, 'Containment' to keep back a
constant threat of communist power, and the huge military-
industrial complex needed to do this, developed naturally
from the Monroe Doctrine and its Corollaries. They explain
some of the baffling aspects of the American presence in
Vietnam – which, if it fell to communism, was regarded as a
potential rotten apple in a barrel, contaminating all others
around it; or as a falling domino, causing a whole line of other
dominoes to fall. The choice of metaphor was a matter of
preference.

The cold war touched Vietnam with its chill hand as early
as the time of the First Indochina War, when the French forces
fought the Vietminh, from 1946-54, and in which the US paid
approximately 82% of French expenses. In September 1950 the
US got a foot in the door, as it were, in the process of
developing military intervention in Vietnam, by setting up US
MAAG (Military Assistance and Advisory Group), meant to
be involved with supplies only at first, but soon involved in
covert action.

Meanwhile, the People's Republic of China, waging its own
cold war from the oriental side, supported the Vietminh
against the French with massive supplies, thousands of
technical advisors, and training camps for Vietnamese troops

just across their border; so the war became proxy in nature. When the time came for peace talks in Geneva in 1954, the Vietnamese delegates were ignored while the representatives from the USSR, France and China haggled behind the scenes for concessions best suited to their own interests.

The Pentagon Papers, a big collection of documents outlining the steps by which the US became involved in Vietnam, show clearly that from 1949, when the People's Republic of China was proclaimed, US foreign policy was set to block the further spread of communism in Asia, by force of arms, if need be:

> 'It shall be US policy to accept nothing short of a military victory in Indochina.'
> *Report by the Special Committee on the Threat of Communism, April 5, 1954. From The Pentagon Papers.*

President Truman's reference (in his inaugural address in 1947) to helping free peoples who were resisting armed minorities, seemed to justify armed intervention by the US, in Greece at that time, and later in South Vietnam. President Kennedy echoed the same theme in his inaugural address in 1961, when he made it sound like a holy duty to fight the cold war. It must have been hard not to feel enthusiasm as he said:

> 'We shall pay any price, bear any burden, meet any hardship, support any friend, oppose any foes, in order to assure the survival and success of liberty.'

Several factors have made it hard for westerners to see the real Vietnam. In the 1950s McCarthyism made it dangerous in Washington to show any interest in a communist country. Joseph McCarthy was a Republican senator who ran a 'smear' campaign against leading Democrats by accusing them of belonging to communist front organisations. With scant evidence to back up his statements, he claimed that he knew many employees of the State Department were either 'card-carrying communists', or communist sympathisers. He created an atmosphere of fear and suspicion, preventing people from seeking information about any communist régime.

Even after the Declaration of Independence and Proclamation of the Democratic Republic of Vietnam in September 1945, the country was still regarded very much as a French colony. For administrative purposes the French had divided it into three parts: Tonkin, whose capital was Hanoi, in the north; Annam, whose capital was Hue, in the central region; and Cochinchina in the south, whose capital was Saigon. Communications with other governments used to be made in French by French officials. Expressions of Vietnamese nationalism went unheeded. When Ho Chi Minh tried to see President Woodrow Wilson at Versailles, and wrote several times to President Truman, one of his requests was that at international conferences Vietnam should be represented by Vietnamese delegates, not French ones. But he was rebuffed at Versailles and ignored by President Truman.

Ignored also was any feedback to the west about the insidious growth of Japanese power in Vietnam in the 1930s. The Japanese had a plan for a grand area of Japanese power and influence, called 'The Greater East Asian Co-Prosperity Sphere' whose slogan was 'Asia for the Asians'. Using their Kempei Tai, or Secret Service, they organised a very complex network of agents throughout Vietnam, gained control of the banks and mines, and obtained detailed data about ports and railroads; so that it was a pushover for Japanese troops to invade Vietnam in 1940 and set up bases, ready for their swift advance on Java and Sumatra in February 1942.

However, the greatest obstacle preventing Americans from understanding the local scene in Vietnam has been the practice of defining countries in terms of their place in the cold war hegemony, not as they are in reality. So US policy-makers did not notice the charisma that the personality of Ho Chi Minh had for the Vietnamese people; a legend in his own lifetime, he was 'Uncle Ho', who, though frail and tired himself, would turn aside on a long march to give the rice in his bowl to a dying woman. Even if the legend was carefully cultivated, as cynics suggest, still it had dynamic power in the hearts of the Vietnamese. When Ho Chi Minh died in September 1969 an estimated 100,000 people, dressed in white mourning clothes, filled the streets of Hanoi to observe his funeral rites.

The messages of history went unheeded, too. The

Vietnamese had had, before modern times, two thousand years in which to perfect the skills of fighting off invaders. (Legends relate that with ironic laughter, they used to send invaders home, graciously providing them with food and horses for their journey.)

The national reverence for ancestors, a tradition of centuries, was still powerful at the time of the war with the US, and could cause the Vietnamese to fight to the death for a place where their ancestors were buried, and return to retake it, even when there was nothing but scorched earth left there.

Presenting a mirror image to the history of the Vietnamese people, with several parallels, is the story of the indigenous races of central Vietnam; all grouped under the general term *montagnards*, in spite of their diversity, at various times they have been exposed to both French and Vietnamese colonising, and have been made use of by troops and then abandoned.

A chapter in this book is devoted to a description of Buddhist, Taoist and Confucian ideas, which have given the Vietnamese their background in thought, and mental furniture onto which they grafted their Marxism. The Buddhist Revolt of 1963, for instance, did not happen in a vacuum; it was loaded with ancestral memories and poignant regrets for an uncorrupted faith desperately at risk. Huge crowds demonstrated and wept and prayed aloud in the streets of Saigon, when a Buddhist monk, protesting against the persecution of Buddhists in the régime of President Ngo Dinh Diem, burned himself to death.

From this background of Marxism and oriental faiths, the leaders of the Vietnamese communists built up a comprehensive programme, called *Dau tranh* (meaning 'the struggle movement', or 'the people as creators of revolutionary warfare'). More dynamic than 'Containment', it inspired people, no one was left out, and it included all policies, training, and propaganda. It combined politics and fighting.

In 1944 General Vo Nguyen Giap started the huge, million-strong People's Army of Vietnam (PAVN) with 34 ragged persons, a few antique rifles and one machine gun. In my account of Giap's military philosophy I have included some description of the precepts of two writers on warfare who influenced him: General Sun Tzu, who wrote *The Art of War* in

China about 500 B.C.; and General von Clausewitz, a Prussian who wrote *On War (Vom Kriege)*, published in 1832. Both stressed the importance in wars of intangible factors, such as morale and planning, and enabled the reader to define the goals of a campaign, and to classify and analyse its various aspects. General von Clausewitz in particular made a careful distinction between strategy and tactics. (It was on this point that General Giap's theory of guerrilla war differed from that of Mao Tse-tung, Chairman of the People's Republic of China.) Clausewitz and Giap both considered war, not as an interruption in politics, but as a continuation of them; and they believed that, therefore, military leaders had to be submissive to the authority of the state. In an article published in 1965 in Hanoi, General Giap wrote: 'Because armed struggle is the continuation of political struggle, no powerful armed forces could be built without the people's mighty political strength'; and

> '. . . our military line is that followed by a small nation struggling against a much stronger enemy . . . relying on our absolute political superiority . . . on our people's unity in struggle, it is possible to use what is weak to fight what is strong, to defeat the most modern weapons with a revolutionary spirit.'
>
> (From *Vietnam and America: A Documented History;*
> [ed. Marvin E. Gettleman et al.])

General Giap's plans required intensive organisation. He was, in fact, no stranger to those large organisations which we call bureaucracies – once a neutral term but now having a negative connotation. They have been well known for centuries in the Orient: two hundred years before the birth of Christ a civil service was created in China, whose elite members wrote examinations in prescribed Confucian texts. (They used to send tax-collectors to Vietnam.) However, the First Indochina War showed that a bureaucratic government far away in Paris could not successfully run a war in Vietnam. President Truman realised that wars could be won or lost by bureaucracies, and created some new ones in 1947 to help wage the cold war: the Central Intelligence Agency; the National Military Establishment, which became the US

View of the Xang Canal from Phung Hiep Bridge, Hau Giang Province, Vietnam

Department of Defense; and the US National Security Council, which was really a bureaucracy inside another one, the Executive Branch of the US government.

When Max Weber, a German sociologist, first outlined his theories about bureaucracies at the turn of the century, he was optimistic about the benign effect they would have on society. He used the term 'bureaucracy' as a name for a certain type of organisation, whose main characteristics were the following: leadership was based on expertise in a certain function, not on charisma or on inherited rights; there was a graded hierarchy of officials who worked according to written instructions and fixed guidelines; and promotion was based on competence. However, as he observed the huge industrial firms of Germany grow ever more convoluted and top-heavy with their 'head office' mentality and structure, he began to feel that there was something inherently self-defeating about bureaucracies. With prophetic insight, he said that he believed that they would become a greater danger to democracy than either capitalism or communism would be. He saw already the signs of malfunction that are often visible today in large organisations: the infighting; the poor or non-existent communication between departments; and the preoccupation with internal politics, leading to the neglect of the true aims of the organisation. He observed situations in which the decision-making process was far away from the scene where the decisions had to be carried out, rendering the outcome ineffective, and where the process of bureaucratic self-perpetuation would then set in, covering up the failure so that no one would lose their job by pointing out their own department's total uselessness.

In this book I have tried to make a connection, or at least to raise questions about the connection between the recent and the remote past, and between events taking place far away from each other. What was the connection, for instance, between the teaching of Confucius and the obedience to death of the soldiers of the People's Army of Vietnam? And what linked the US soldier whose gun kept jamming in the jungle air of Vietnam, with the scams of the US military-industrial complex? A new line of questioning may be helpful, for as a modern poet has said:

'We know the answers, we know all the answers
It is the questions that we do not know.'

(Ascribed to *W.H. Auden*)

CHAPTER ONE

The Vietnam
of the Ancestors

This chapter is in the form of a dialogue, in which a student of the history of Vietnam is asking the author questions about it.

Question.
: Can you explain the very high morale, will to resist, and sheer toughness which the Vietnamese communists displayed in the US-Vietnam War? It's puzzling.

Answer.
: The answer to your question is very complex. There are many factors involved, and it takes us back a long way; I'm going to have you, for a start, think of the place we call Vietnam in prehistoric times.

Q. Yes, go ahead . . . what were the people's origins there?

A. Austro-Asiatic: nomadic tribes of Central Asiatic, Mongolian origin mixed with others of Malaysian and Melanesian origin.

Some objects found by archaeologists in digs near Hanoi, such as arrowheads, axes and sling stones, take us back, it's believed, 100,000 years, and fluted pottery has been found that is 10,000 years old. Nearer our time, things found between 3,000 and 4,000 years old show a rich variety: big bronze drums, lamps, bells for elephants and horses, pearls, and elaborately decorated pottery. They suggest a prosperous and lively society. A recurrent decorative pattern was a star (also shown on the modern Vietnamese flag) surrounded by cheery drawings of wild animals and of people dancing, fighting, harvesting and love-making.

Q.   Do the Vietnamese have a special feel for their ancestors?

A.   Yes, very much so; for them, their ancestors, the land, their homes, and themselves form a special unity.

Q.   Are there myths and legends handed down from early times?

A.   Yes, very many. One which symbolises a recurring *leitmotif* of Vietnamese history, the conquest of a strong nation by a weak one, was the story of Than Giong, which exists in many versions. Peter Weiss in his book *Notes on the Cultural Life of the Democratic Republic of Vietnam* describes how a woman who accidentally stepped in a giant's footprint became pregnant, and gave birth to a son who for three years never walked or spoke. One day messengers came to his mother's house to warn her of the coming of invaders. He got up, asked for an iron horse and sword, and rode off to drive out the enemy. His horse's hooves scorched the ground. (There is still a statue of him in Ho Chi Minh City.)

Dragons and demons also abounded in the old legends. The first name of Hanoi was Thanglong (Dragon Rising) as it was said that on the day the city was founded, a dragon was watching from the lake there.

Q.   Is there a particular time from which the Vietnamese date their sense of identity as a people?

A.   Some historians of the country consider their lineage goes back as a nation to the Bronze Age culture outlined above, but others only count themselves as the Vietnamese people since the time of a Chinese warlord called Trieu Da. In 196 BC – with the help of a traitor from within, or double agent who, according to legend, told him how to work the Vietnamese crossbows which could shoot ten arrows at once – he overran an ancient fortress near Hanoi. He declared himself emperor and called the country Nam Viet, meaning, Land in the South. His successors in their turn were crushed by another Chinese dynasty hostile to them, in 111 BC, and the land became a Chinese colony.

Q. So Vietnam has been fought over for hundreds and hundreds of years?

A. Yes; after nearly a thousand years of fighting invading Chinese and Mongols, with constant attacks and counter-attacks, a Vietnamese general defeated the Chinese in a battle near Haiphong in 938 AD, and Vietnam's right to be a sovereign nation was upheld. Sometimes they pursued the Chinese back to their own country, and fought them there. They used mountain caves as shelters and stores, as they have used tunnels in modern times.

Q. Did women fight beside the men?

A. Yes, frequently. There is a long tradition in Vietnamese history of women in combat. Women who were resistance leaders became national heroines, and, like their male counterparts, have streets named after them in modern Vietnamese cities.

In 43 AD two ladies called the Trung Sisters, whose husbands had been killed by the Chinese, put on the dead men's armour and gathered an army together. There were several women in the group. They drove away the Chinese and took power, but when the invaders returned in force two years later, the sisters realised to resist further was hopeless, and they drowned themselves in a river.

The Princess Trieu Au was another famous Vietnamese heroine. In 248 AD she led the troops against the Chinese, riding an elephant and clad in golden armour. But she was defeated, and killed herself.

Q. I've heard that Vietnam resisted invasion by the Mongols in the thirteenth century. How were they able to do this, when the armies of Kublai Khan were terrifying everyone and were considered invincible?

A. Your question leads us directly to the connection between events in ancient and modern Vietnam. For it was in these thirteenth-century campaigns, going on from 1257 to 1288, that the concepts and methods of people's warfare and guerilla fighting, which twentieth-century Vietnamese have used, were honed and practised repeatedly.

The number of men involved was utterly daunting: in 1284 the son of Kublai Khan advanced on Hanoi with an army of 500,000. The Vietnamese commander, General Tran Hung Dao, did not attempt to meet such a host in open battle, but he armed the village people, divided his army into small groups, and called it the 'Father-and-Son' army, meaning that they were a unity, and had to be of one mind, like father and son.

Q.   How did he deal with the enemy?

A.   The Mongolian leaders used watchtowers, or small forts, dotted across the land, holding between three and five hundred men each. They had spread themselves too thin, really, for the Vietnamese made surprise attacks on them by night like commandos, wiping many of them out.

When the Mongolians brought reinforcements up the mouth of the Bach Dang River, their junks were impaled by terrible sharp stakes placed in the riverbed. They were defeated in 1287 in battle.

Q.   Historically, did any other leaders develop these guerilla methods?

A.   Yes. A famous one was Le Loi, a well-to-do landowner who gathered together a partisan army to fight the Chinese early in the 15th century. In 1406 the Ming rulers had begun a reign of terror in Vietnam. Their occupying soldiers plundered and looted unchecked. All the rice was seized. Vietnamese writings, cults and language were suppressed. Chinese became the official language. The Vietnamese peasants had to go down into the mines for gold, which all went to China, along with other precious items such as pearls, rare woods, elephant tusks and rhinoceros horns. An apartheid system prevailed in which Vietnamese people had to have 'passes', or ID cards. (Described in *Vietnam: A History*, by Stanley Karnow.)

The methods Le Loi used to fight this tyranny had much in common with those of the modern Vietnamese Revolution: with the help of a friend who was a well-known poet, patriot, and military strategist – and therefore a good PR figure – he combined fighting with politics. Agents spreading disinformation and propaganda behind the enemy lines made the Chinese soldiers nervous. They were continually ambushed and murdered in surprise attacks.

Q. How long did the fighting go on?

A. Oh, for years and years, on and off, till 1426 when the Chinese were at last defeated in an open battle near Hanoi. Yet afterwards the Viets still paid tribute to the Chinese, in rice usually, in return for peace.

During the long years before his final victory, Le Loi established caches of food and arms at bases in the mountains, built up a huge army, cut the enemy's supply lines repeatedly, and gradually cleared the Chinese out, securing a small area at a time before moving on to another. In 1427 Le Loi proclaimed himself emperor; his dynasty lasted until 1778.

Q. You spoke of Le Loi as a landowner – how was land acquired in ancient Vietnam?

A. All land belonged to the emperor, who, like Le Loi, had claimed it in the first place by driving out the invaders; after all, people thought, 'the will of heaven' had decreed that he should be victorious, so his right to the land was accepted. The emperor used to keep large areas for himself before giving huge estates to favoured persons, such as generals, mandarins, and dignitaries who had been useful to him. Between these people and the villagers who owned no land at all, and who far outnumbered everyone else, was an ever-fluctuating group of small farmers and artisans, who sometimes had small holdings.

Q. Why d'you call them 'ever-fluctuating'?

A. I mean that their numbers rose or fell according to circumstance; among the favoured group mentioned, a lot of rivalry and 'keeping-up-with-the-Joneses' went on. Some spent extravagantly on luxury items and gambling, fell deep in debt and had to sell off parts of their estate, which could be bought by people who'd never owned any land before.

Unluckily, if taxes were raised or males in the family drafted, a small farmer might not be able to survive, and would sink back again into the landless group.

Q.   It sounds just like that modern game, 'Rat Race', doesn't it?

A.   Exactly; however, as Confucius had decreed, with the privileges of power went certain responsibilities. One of the duties of the emperor was to ensure, as much as he could, that the rice fields were irrigated, and flooding prevented. Canals, sluices and dykes were constructed, for instance, and ceremonies conducted to seek the blessing of the spirits of nature on these works.

There was a tradition that the emperor should grant land for Buddhist monasteries and pagodas, which is odd, really, like giving presents to the opposition, for the leading Buddhists were outspoken critics of the feudal establishment, in which the aristocrats paid no taxes, while the peasants were taxed exorbitantly.

Le Loi abolished serfdom, in which persons were regarded as part of the property if the estate on which they worked was sold or inherited. He helped youths who weren't aristocrats, but whose fathers owned a moderate area of land, to become mandarins. It doesn't sound like a big concession, but in the context of the time it was liberal, for it enabled them to enter what we might call the managerial class.

The emperor and his entourage did not, by tradition, interfere in village affairs. Behind their bamboo hedges the villages were little worlds of their own. Disputes were settled by the village elders, using their own judgement.

Q.   Do you think this pride in one's village, going back such a long way, partly explains the problems both the French and the Americans have had in this century, in 'pacifying' Vietnamese villagers, neutralising them – or whatever term you want to use for winning their hearts and minds?

A.   Oh yes, I'm sure there was a connection. The village, after all, was a sacred place, for not only did it hold the graves of the ancestors, the home shrines where they were revered, and maybe a pagoda; but as well, its groves and streams were believed to have their own particular spirits.

Later in the 15th century, however, there was an increase in the power of government officials to erode the independence of the villagers. One of Le Loi's successors, Le Thanh Tong, who ruled from 1460 to 1498, built up in his long reign a bureaucratic network of government officials, with regional headquarters, so that tax-collecting and drafting men for the huge standing army, could be effectively supervised.

The approach was very Confucian, stressing obedience to authority figures and the importance of knowing your place in the social hierarchy. You could write exams if you wanted to get a commission in the army, or wished to become a mandarin.

Q.   All very depressing, wasn't it?

A.   Well, yes; although defying a teacher or official could result in severe punishment, Le Thanh Tong's reign wasn't completely depressing. It had its positive side: he encouraged poets, people who recorded legends, made maps, and advanced the study of mathematics and science. A Vietnamese script called the Nom script was used, as well as Chinese. He made laws covering a wide range of affairs. For instance, he granted women property rights, and made regulations curbing mandarins' power to harass people. He made laws regarding the division of land, the payment of rent in kind with crops, and the rate of interest charged on debts.

Q.   Has the problem of not enough land for everyone ever been solved in Vietnam?

A.   I don't think a satisfactory solution has ever been found. There have been many attempts.

One solution, for instance, was to spread out and colonise fresh territories. A famous expedition of this kind in Le Thanh Tong's time was called 'The Great Trek South'. It continued for centuries afterwards. The reason was, the Red River Delta in northern Vietnam had become heavily populated. In 1471 about 50,000 men, mostly former soldiers and their families, marched south. They made settlements and planted rice, but used to be attacked by scattered gangs of bandits from hide-outs deep in the forest. Some of them, however, eventually built villages and planted crops.

Q.   It was very different from the orderly regime up north which you've described, wasn't it?

A.   Yes. In the spread southward, going on until 1773, one can see the rise of Vietnam as a conquering, colonizing power, and the beginning of the end of the hold of the mandarins over the people. In the social unrest of the migration south, the distant emperor became just a figurehead and was defied by aggressive warlords who seized vast areas for themselves – so the peasants still had no land – and set up their own private armies.

Q.   Were other nations living in the new land they went to?

A.   Oh yes; it wasn't empty by any means. In the coastal part of the central area of Vietnam there was once the kingdom of Champa. The Chams were a Hindu nation. They were good builders, and skilled fighters and sailors. Their capital, Indrapura, was destroyed by the Vietnamese, who, pressing ever further south, advanced far into the Mekong Delta, driving out the Khmers who were there at the time.

Q.   You mentioned 1773 as a turning point. What happened then?

A.   There was a big rebellion called the Tayson Revolt, led by three brothers from the area of that name.

Two families of warlords had seized power: the Trinh in the north, and the Nguyens in the south. They divided their territory at the 18th parallel, where the coastal plain was only forty miles wide. The feudal organisation of the country was falling apart; landowners neglected to repair irrigation systems and dykes, rents were raised, and thousands of hungry villagers fled to the cities. Merchants who had become prosperous in trade with visiting Dutch, Portuguese, French and English ships, joined them to protest against the impossible demands of the mandarins for forced labour and taxation. Their army numbered over 80,000.

Q.   Was it all soon over?

A.   Oh no, the fighting dragged on for years; till 1802 in fact.

TOP:
Playing shuttlecocks – polo – on horseback.
(Early Tra Kieu style, 7th century)

MIDDLE:
Kerchief dance [step of the My Son altar]
(My Son El style, 8th-9th centuries)

BOTTOM:
Dancing girl [one of the Apsaras, or
heavenly female dancers] (Late Tra Kieu
style, tenth century)

Designs on the friezes of statues in the
Museum of Cham Sculpture Da Nang,
Vietnam (From the museum handbook)

The Chinese invaded the north in the 1780s and had to be fought in addition to the Trinhs and Nguyens. They were all defeated after several years, and for a time the rebels were able to give out land to the destitute and make the taxation system fairer; but they were better at fighting than governing, and so were unable to sustain these improvements.

The Nguyens, through the intervention of a French priest, asked France for help in putting down the rebellion. King Louis XVI stalled and didn't help at first, but finally some troops were sent; and with them Nguyen Anh, the heir, marched into Hue in 1802, proclaimed himself emperor, and changed his name to Gia Long. He brutally suppressed the rebels.

Q.   Bringing in the French – wasn't that the kiss of death for Vietnamese nationalism?

A.   Yes, it was, for at least another hundred and forty years;

Böhnar children
(From *Minorities of Central Vietnam by J. Dournes*)

but to Gia Long it must have seemed a good idea at the time. He granted the French the port of Tourane (now Danang) and the island of Poulo Condor, and gave France 'most favoured nation' status in trade. He encouraged the study of French literature and history. Interestingly, he greatly admired the French missionary, Alexandre de Rhodes, who in the seventeenth century had transcribed the Vietnamese script into the Roman alphabet (the lettering was called *quoc ngu*). The mandarins disapproved of it because it seemed a ready tool for foreign, western influences, and made it easier for people to learn French.

Gia Long protected Roman Catholic missionaries, who seemed to many people to be subtle agents of the expansionist ambitions of France; not without reason, for with typically French pragmatism, the missionaries, the trading companies, and the French navy, all helped each other. Yet, with apparent inconsistency, Gia Long was ambivalent about the French, and was careful to build himself an impregnable oriental fortress at Hue. The long love-hate relationship between the French and Vietnamese people had begun its course through their histories.

Q.   Were the missionaries ever openly persecuted?

A.   Yes, and with them their Vietnamese converts, particularly after Gia Long's death in 1820. Of course anti-Catholic unrest gave the French the sanctified pretext they needed to bring troops to the country, and begin their long occupation; they wanted to get some of the rich trade with China before the British grabbed it all, and they hoped to find a way to southern China by means of the Mekong River, though its upper reaches proved to be unfit for large boats to navigate. However, they found an alternative way: to use the Red River and the port of Haiphong.

Q.   How long did the French occupation take?

A.   Not quite thirty years, 1859 to 1887. The French used their Legionnaires. They conquered the south first before spreading through central and northern Vietnam; Siam, Laos and Cambodia came under French influence too.

Q.   Did France have other colonies in this period?

A.   She had Senegal and parts of North Africa, but as an imperial power, was slipping elsewhere; she had lost her possessions in Canada and Louisiana, was humiliated in Mexico in the 1860s, and lost Alsace-Lorraine in 1871 after the Franco-Prussian War.

The search for a land route to China via the Mekong, and the need of the priests to find remote secure areas where they could build seminaries for natives, safe from persecution, led the French deep into the central highlands. Here they got to know the minority peoples of Vietnam. Although they recognised that they were very diverse, the French gave them all the name les montagnards, to avoid calling them savages or primitives. These people used to trade and barter with the Chams and the Viets; sometimes they used to take Vietnamese slaves, to exchange them in Laos for precious stones or elephants. They had and have many skills and are far from primitive. They have, for instance, houses of wood and bamboo raised on stilts, making them very healthy for a humid climate. Jacques Dournes, in his book *Minorities of Central Vietnam* described their mastery of several ingenious devices, such as a pneumatic lighter, a continuous screw mechanism to gin cotton, and a spinning wheel using reducing ratios.

Mr Dournes found that, when there was a wedding in a montagnard family, it was the custom for the bride-groom to go to live with his bride's family. The children would take her name. When he told the 'montagnards' that, on the contrary, it was the bride who moved in western countries, their reply was (as if to say): 'My God, how primitive the people out there must be.'

Q.   Touché . . . are the minority people Vietnamese?

A.   No. They have many different languages and tribes, within two large ethnic groups: the Austro-Asiatic, related to the Khmers; and the Austronesian, related to the Chams, Malays and Indonesians.

The French took land from them for big plantations of

rubber, tea, and coffee. But they also gave to them in many ways, by providing hospitals and caring for their lepers, and helping some of them learn how to write down their legends and poetry. The French hoped they would work on the plantations, but they had no work ethic, for they found all they needed in their surroundings, and had no conception of profit or saving. So the French brought in Vietnamese workers, who spread more and more into montagnard territory. This process of colonization within Vietnam itself is still continuing today.

Q.   I used to think of the minority people as quite isolated, but that's not really true, is it?

A.   No. Their history and that of the Viets is closely connected. They have figured in many of the events which were turning points in the nation's struggles. They were fighting with the Chams against the Vietnamese at the time of the Great Trek South. They fought side by side with the Tayson rebels in the 1770s. Some helped the French in the First Indochinese War, only to be abandoned far from home when things went wrong, just as, a generation later, they were recruited and then abandoned by the CIA and US Special Forces in Laos. They gave the Vietcong supplies from their food stores. From the ARVN in South Vietnam they deserted in droves, just as many Vietnamese youths did in the US-Vietnam War.

A poem quoted in translation by Mr Dournes provides an apt commentary. It was broadcast in the war by Radio Hanoi, in various minority languages:

O youth of our villages,
at the time of the French you were soldiering with them,
at the time of the Americans you were soldiers for them;
can't you see that is suicidal?
If we are attacked, let us give as good as we get
Let us turn back the weapons against the Americans
But let us not kill one another, as they would like.
(From J. Dournes, *Minorities of Central Vietnam.*)

Pavilions near Hue, Vietnam, built by the Emperor Tu Duc, Nguyen Dynasty, who ruled from 1848-83

CHAPTER TWO

Taoism, Confucianism, and Buddhism in the Vietnamese Destiny

Returning to one's roots is known as stillness.
This is what is meant by returning to one's destiny.
(*Lao Tzu*, from the *Tao Te Ching*, trans. D.C. Lau)

Three major systems of thought in the ancient oriental world, Taoism, Confucianism, and Buddhism, can throw some light on some of the baffling aspects of modern Vietnamese history: for instance, the choice of communism and the sustained high morale in North Vietnam.

Although the Vietnamese struggled over the centuries to avoid being ruled by the Chinese, they internalised much of Chinese philosophy, and adapted it to help themselves in their own circumstances. The words had a familiar ring to them, when no less a person than Mao Tse-tung stated that there was an identity between opposites, and that the law of unity of all opposites was the basic law of nature and of society. In one statement he was expressing both Taoist and Marxist ideas. The Chinese concept of *yang* and *yin*, symbolising the inter-connection between two apparently polar opposites, movement and stillness, was echoed in the work of Friedrich Engels, who described the law of the interpenetration of opposites as one of the basic principles of dialectical materialism.

When Ho Chi Minh first encountered the ideas of Engels and Marx in Paris, around 1917, he experienced, not the feeling of meeting new and strange ideas, but rather a shock of recognition. He was reading of something he had always known, a set of concepts absorbed long ago from his father and grandfather, but set out in such a way that it seemed to show a series of ideas through which nationalism could be achieved for his country. One reason for his choice of communism was its apparent familiarity, building on a value system which he already had. Whether it could ultimately bring happiness to his people was something he could not judge at the time. In his book *The Dialectics of Nature*, Friedrich Engels had expressed admiration for the Buddhists' grasp of dialectics; so it was not unnatural for Ho Chi Minh to select, as a means of overcoming colonialism, a political system whose philosophy looked as if it sprang spontaneously from ancient oriental thought. Hellenic democratic ideals would not have aroused the same resonance in his memory.

Georg Friedrich Hegel, a nineteenth-century philosopher, described the process of dialectics as a course of events characterised by the clash of opposing forces – thesis and antithesis – resulting in a new synthesis. He believed history should be interpreted in the light of this theory. The idea of progress was implicit in it, as he considered the synthesis of opposing forces would create a 'better' society than the one previously existing. Karl Marx used G.F. Hegel's theory to construct his own view of the course of history: the dialectic was economic (dialectical materialism), and the clash of thesis and antithesis, leading to a new and better synthesis, described the clash between classes resolving itself into a classless society.

To Ho Chi Minh in 1917 this was heady stuff. While Karl Marx applied G.F. Hegel's theories to society, Friedrich Engels extended them to cover the whole of life, and made communism seem to be in line with the 'law of nature'; and the idea that the synthesis resulting from the clash between the thesis and antithesis in society would always result in a better society enabled its adherents to give to communism a high moral tone. Its quasi-religious hold on people is well understood by the Chinese, who, as if to indicate its links with ancient religious thought, have made Taoism a state religion in The People's Republic, and founded the China Taoist Association in 1957.

This recently acquired respectability is surprising, considering that in China Taoist sects had a long history of association with anti-government rebels, secret societies, and nature cults. In Vietnam, however, Taoism was not a separate, clear-cut discipline, but was, rather, a set of luminous ideas which blended with Buddhism, Confucianism, ancestor-worship and animism to form the mental attitude of the Vietnamese. There was not any definite reference to belief in God, so to speak of the 'Vietnamese religion' would be misleading; but a concept closer to the western idea of the Godhead was described. The Buddha declared: 'There is, O monks, an Unborn, neither become nor created nor formed.' Similarly, the Taoists believed that: 'The Tao which can be conceived is not the real Tao.' The term 'Tao' was used to mean a transcendent spiritual power, or the basic law of nature, or a way of life in tune with natural law.

Over the centuries, magical and superstitious practices were carried out in the name of Taoism, but they had nothing in common with the philosophy and values of true Taoism, as taught by its founder Lao Tzu (or Lao-tse) who is believed to have lived about five centuries before Christ. He summarised his precepts in one short book called *Tao Te Ching (The Way and Its Power)*. Some scholars wonder if Lao Tzu was a real person, and whether the book was not by written him, but compiled later. Legend has it that Confucius visited Lao Tzu for some instruction, but no one knows for sure. However, the simplicity and realism of the *Tao Te Ching* still comes through in modern translations, and after close to twenty-five hundred years, its cheery debunking of officialdom is as fresh as ever:

> Exterminate the sage, discard the wise,
> And the people will benefit a hundredfold . . .
> Exterminate benevolence, discard rectitude,
> And the people will again be filial . . .
> Governing a large state is like boiling a small fish.
> I take no action and the people are transformed of themselves.
> (*Tao Te Ching*, trans. D.C. Lau)

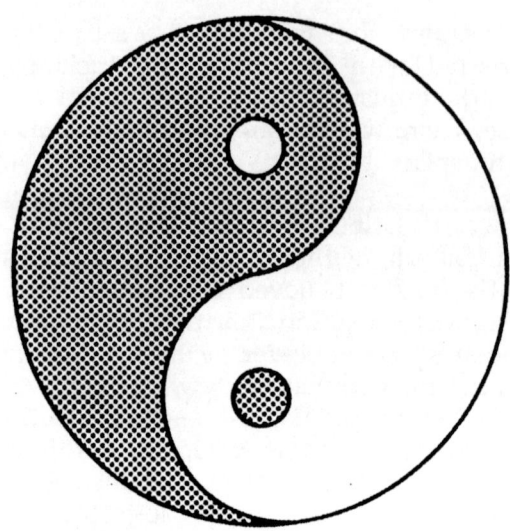

This diagram is the Taoist symbol of *Yin and Yang*, or the dynamic unity of polar opposites. The two dots in the diagram represent the idea that each time one of the two forces reaches its extreme, it contains in itself already a tiny part of its opposite. In the end both are resolved in an all-embracing circle.

The Taoists believed that there was a hidden unity in apparent opposites such as good and evil, active and passive, negative and positive, and that they really complemented each other. So, if one tried too hard to achieve a certain result, 'the law of reversed effort' would start to operate, and the effect would be the exact opposite of the desired outcome. An illustration in modern times was provided in the US by Prohibition (1920 to 1933); the intention was to abolish alcohol consumption, but most of the time there was a non-stop binge going on, with illicit spirits, bootlegging, rum-running, and gang warfare on a massive scale.

Robert Ardrey, in his book *The Territorial Imperative* (1966), calls the law of reversed effort 'The Amity-Enmity Complex'. He considers it to be the basic reason why the intention of the US in Vietnam, to contain communism, resulted, on the contrary, in its spread; he also links this result with the primeval impulse to defend one's territory, which the Vietnamese were obeying.

A basic Taoist tenet was that transformation and change were going on all the time in the natural world, so it was not hard to regard the transforming of society by revolution as part of a natural process. The Taoists encouraged simplicity in manner and dress instead of pomp and ceremony; nature and all her creatures were to be cherished and carefully preserved; and one should try to develop for oneself the practice of creative stillness. Called 'Wu-wei' in Taoist philosophy, this quality has sometimes been misunderstood as just doing nothing about anything, but what it was meant to convey was more like an absence of over-fussy busybody activity. Competing and being self-assertive were deprecated and considered counter-productive, and people were asked to take care of the crippled and handicapped, who personified lowliness and helplessness. Thus the strength inherent in weakness was perceived, in the sense that when a person realises his weakness and stops talking about his power, he can then be receptive to The Way, that is, to the deepest spontaneous impulses of his own nature, and to the spiritual meaning of the natural world.

> The submissive and weak will overcome the hard and strong . . .
> Limpid and still,
> One can be a leader in the empire.
> (*Tao Te Ching*, translated by D.C. Lau)

Intuition was considered by the Taoists to be a safer guide than logic. They distrusted systems and plans, and discouraged people from thinking in terms of dichotomies or clear-cut moral distinctions. Life was not simple like an old western movie, with good guys on one side and bad guys on the other, clearly marked out as the sheriff's posse or the robbers' gang.

For many centuries, Taoists in China rebelled against the common practice of killing infant girls who were unwanted, and they objected to the slave-like state of women in old China. So they had many women among their followers, some of whom became leaders. This fitted the national traditions of Vietnam, whose heroines were women who had been leaders in their old wars of resistance. Some Taoist groups held their goods communally. In the *Tao Te Ching*, the author, or authors, advise rulers not to cramp the living space of workers, nor to deprive them of their means of livelihood. Hunger and poverty was seen as the direct result of the greed of the prevailing bureaucracy:

> The people are hungry:
> It is because those in authority eat up too much in taxes
> That the people are hungry.
> (*Tao Te Ching*, translated by D.C. Lau)

If the ideas of the Taoists seemed to point the way to a new concept of society, and made revolution appear to have continuity with the past because it was like a new Tao and in tune with the laws of nature, the influence of Confucius, on the contrary, appeared weighted on the side of the reactionary and the elitist. Confucius was born around 551 BC in the Shantung province of China. About two hundred years before the birth of Christ, his teaching became a state religion, and in

Traditional Portrait of Confucius

130 BC it was adopted as the main training for officials of the government. Advancement was based on success in examinations on Confucian texts, and eligibility to take the exams in the first place depended on family prestige, though in theory the road to advancement was open to anyone. There were thirteen texts in all, some dealing with history; some philosophy, poetry, and ancient rites; some, such as *The Analects of Confucius,* describing wise and correct behaviour. Many of the texts were not actually written by Confucius, but were compiled and edited by him and his followers; *The Analects* were considered to be a record of the actual sayings of Confucius himself.

Some Vietnamese families sent sons to follow this Chinese route to success, and a few who also had acquired wealth or land by trade became mandarin landlords, or worked as official tax collectors. So, when the French organised their administration of Tonkin, Annam, and Cochinchina in the 1880s, a small nucleus, as it were, of a bureaucracy was already in place. This was not so clearly true in the south because some of the mandarins fled to the north at that time; but some did not mind the change of masters, and if they were civil servants they went on being civil servants regardless of a change in management. To their way of thinking this showed no disloyalty to their country, only a shrewd awareness of which way power lay, and, as the Chinese put it, that the 'will of Heaven' now favoured the French. But as the French took over more and more trade and business, they lost their own power and wealth, and became ciphers in the French administrative system.

In 'The Scholars' Revolt' of 1885 at Hue, some mandarins tried unsuccessfully to rebel against the French. One of their number, a civil servant named Nguyen Sinh Huy, was dismissed from his job as a result. He was the father of Ho Chi Minh.

Confucius' concept of government by a group of civil servants on behalf of a supreme ruler was, in his era, an attempt to provide an alternative to the anarchy and bloodshed prevailing then in the warring feudal states of China. Hence his insistence on moderation and self-control, and on negotiation and compromise rather than confrontation, in both personal and governmental affairs; he expressed the idea of the person not as a being living in a vacuum, but as always impinging on other people's lives, as, in fact, a social being, with social duties. One duty he stressed above all was that of obedience: of the son to the father, the wife to the husband, younger brother to older brother, and the subject to the ruler. To western individualists there is no harder duty than obedience, and it requires at times considerable pride-swallowing; but in the Confucian scheme of things it is seen as part of a role, so it does not appear humiliating personally. Fate has given a certain role to everyone.

However, Confucius did not expect that people's obedience out of their strong sense of duty, could always be totally uncritical. Embedded in the tradition-bound facade of Confucian teaching are some ideas, like small blades of grass pushing up and cracking a stone, which had the potential to help the growth of a nationalist movement. Confucius and his followers, when one first considers their work, seem to lead the reader back to think about the past; about the ancestors; about keeping up the *status quo*, always behaving graciously, and never rocking the boat. There was a correct procedure laid down for every situation.

At the same time, Confucius was careful to stress the responsibility that comes with power. He believed that the personality of the leader, in the last analysis, determines whether a society will live according to moral values and by the rule of law, or whether it will give way to greed, selfish ambition, and anarchy. He said:

'If you rule the people by a code of manners and duties, they will become more and more well-mannered and dutiful; if you rule them by punishments, you will need more and more punishments. If punishments multiply, the people will resent it and rebel . . .'
(*Confucius, Rites of the Elder Tai*, trans. A.C. Graham)

Confucius stated that the three vital matters for successful government were to have enough money; sufficient arms; and the trust of the people. The last-named was the most important, because, he believed, if the government lacked the spontaneous consent and confidence of the people it could not stand. Power rested, when the chips were down, in the will of the people, even in the most elitist system; and Confucius added, by implication, that rebellion, not obedience, could have moral sanction, if the head of state was evil, or very incompetent.

The young North Vietnamese recruits who fought in the National Liberation Front in the twentieth century received instructions on their duties towards civilians, which faithfully echoed Confucian teaching. They were to be polite and fair, earning the respect of the civilians, and if they were billeted in a civilian's house, they were to look after it as well as they would their own. The advice of Confucius was:

> 'What you do not wish done to yourself, do not do to others.
> Feel kindly towards everyone, but be intimate only with the virtuous.'
> (*Confucius, The Analects*, trans. by Arthur Waley)

In training North Vietnamese troops, very careful attention was given to their indoctrination, and to exposing them to wholly new concepts; in his era, Confucius believed that a long period of orientation into the required value system should be provided, before men could be expected to take up arms on behalf of their ruler. So the Chinese internalised moral values by means of fables, proverbs, plays, festivals, and historical accounts, presented again and again. With shrewd psychological insight, Confucius saw that music and liturgy had cathartic power; to him, that power was most effective if kept within a controlling structure of prescribed etiquette.

After many centuries, Confucius' conviction that anyone, of however lowly a background, could be receptive to the civilising influence of education, was vindicated. In the five hundred years before the Chinese Revolution, admission rules for the bureaucratic examinations were gradually relaxed, enabling a small but persistent number of sons of peasants and merchants to enter the civil service and possibly reach a managerial level. The potential for social change was there, paradoxically, within the system designed to prevent it.

The overwhelming importance which Confucius attached to family ties led him to condone the practice of 'covering up' for relatives. To him it was more dutiful, even in court, to conceal part of the truth, or even lie, rather than to tell the truth, if because of the truth a family member lost face. The journalist Ms Oriana Fallaci, in response to an ambiguous statement from President Nguyen Van Thieu (whom she interviewed January 1973), teasing him, said: 'Then it's true your 'no' is a 'no' '*à la vietnamienne*'. That is, a 'no' could mean 'yes'.'

By the same token, nepotism was a fact of life. The Americans in Vietnam, who for the most part were unaware of these age-old traditions, found it deeply puzzling that, where the ARVN (Army of the Republic of Vietnam, that is, of South Vietnam) was involved, very often it was hard to find out what really happened in a given situation; and the criterion for promotion was not efficiency, or skill with arms, but the prestige of a man's uncle. However, in President Kennedy's time some wag quipped that 'success is relative' in his régime in the US; promotion through the family networks in South Vietnam should not have been surprising.

In 1964 an estimate was made of the numbers of adherents, either active or only nominal, of the various religious groups and sects in South Vietnam. Dr Vu Duy-Tu, of the University of Hamburg, and Dr Heinz Bechert, of the University of Göttingen, analysed the figures as follows:

The Hoa Hao sect claimed two and a half million followers, another, the Cao Dai had two million; there were slightly more than two million Roman Catholics, and 400,000 Protestant Christians. About a million people of the more isolated mountain areas had their own folk religions. In a population of about fourteen million, thus, there would remain roughly six million persons, claiming to be Buddhists; so Buddhism was regarded at the time, if not exactly the national religion, at least, the dominant group of religious concepts. There were Taoist ideas in it too.[1]

In the twenty years between 1935 and 1955 the Cao Dai and the Hoa Hao sects, with their subsects and internal factions, achieved enormous power, until they were finally outwitted

---

1   From *Buddhism In The Modern World*, Heinrich Dumoulin, ed. (New York: Macmillan and Collier-Macmillan, 1976).

and defeated in street fighting in Saigon by the forces of President Ngo Dinh Diem, who also annexed their lands. Politically, the sect leaders cunningly played both sides against the middle ; in the 1930s the French supported them as means of obstructing communist influence in South Vietnam, only to find, in the 1940s, that they were collaborating with the Japanese secret police during the time of the Japanese occupation of Vietnam, 1940-45.

Another group defeated in 1955 by President Diem was the Binh Xuyen. It was sometimes thought of as a sect because of its pseudo-religious front, and because its members colluded for a short time with the people of the Cao Dai and Hoa Hao sects: but in reality the Binh Xuyen was a band of thugs and river pirates, who took sides with the Japanese for a cash return and, from time to time, allied themselves with the French, too, making deals with them to gain control of the lucrative drug, prostitution, and gambling operations of the Saigon area.

The Cao Dai and its associated subsects practised a mixed, rather eerie kind of 'religion', with overtones of spiritualism and emotional 'born again' characteristics. In 1930 it was estimated to have more than 500,000 followers. It had a tremendous hold on people, and while it was usually regarded as a religion for the uneducated, rural poor, in fact educated city-dwellers were drawn into it too. Its founder, Nguyen Van Chieu, claimed that through a medium, God had told him that He had granted to mankind pardon on three successive occasions: the 'First Amnesty' was given to western peoples through Moses and Jesus Christ; the 'Second Amnesty' came to the Orient by means of the Buddha and the Tao of Lao Tzu; while the 'Third Amnesty' was to be obtained through spiritualist practices. At Tay Ninh, about fifty miles from Saigon, near the border with Cambodia, the Cao Dai had a huge building, like a pagoda, a mosque, and a cathedral all in one, with a mixture of religious statues, such as figures representing Confucius, Lao Tzu, Christ, Vishnu, and the Buddha: something for everyone, as it were. It is worth noting that these cults and intelligence work were related. Such varied persons as Joan of Arc and the poet Victor Hugo, were invoked in spiritualistic sessions by the sect. Its symbol was a large eye, meant to represent the eye of God. Predictably, the

Roman Catholics considered the sect satanic. Finally, it is apparent that the Vietnamese became very familiar with the practice of pursuing politics with religious fervour and politicising religion.

Like the members of the Cao Dai sect, the followers of the Hoa Hao sect supported the Japanese during the 1940s in their efforts to gain power over all South-East Asia. The Japanese used the sects to spread anti-white and anti-western propaganda, through a programme of expansion called 'The Greater East Asia Co-Prosperity Sphere.' Both sects, until 1955, ruled large areas in South Vietnam, and had armies in excess of twenty thousand men.

The founder of the Hoa Hao was named Huynh Phu So; he came from a village of the same name. Chronically in poor health, he stated that in May 1939 he had had a profoundly religious experience during which his sickly condition was cured by faith healing. After this charismatic experience, Huynh Phu So, who had been a conservative Buddhist, was transformed into a person with a radically different approach to others; as a wandering monk he travelled the country, preaching to the desperately poor, and telling them that they needed no priest or pagodas, but could practise their religion themselves, out-of-doors, without any professional help. A western version of the same ideas appeared in the twelfth century in Languedoc, France, when the Cathars rebelled against the official Roman Catholic Church, and were wiped out in bitter fighting by the papal armies.

When Huynh Phu So's preaching began to have a political and anti-French message rather than a solely religious one, he aroused mob emotions against the French, who then declared him insane, and had him committed to a psychiatric hospital. This subversion of psychiatry for use as a political weapon was neatly foiled by the patient, however, who converted his psychiatrist to his own beliefs and got himself released.

Although he had been protected by the Japanese, in 1947 Huynh Phu So was executed by the Viet Minh. At one time he had been their friend, but proved to be a turncoat as he tried to keep his own Hoa Hao army and would not give up his considerable power to the nationalist cause. Then his followers, based on large land holdings southwest of Saigon,

Interior of Cao Dai Temple at Tay Ninh, Vietnam

made terrorist attacks on the French and anyone who supported them, until President Ngo Dinh Diem disbanded them in 1955, executing their leader in 1956.

In the 1940s a group called 'The Buddhist Home Contemplation Movement' with about five hundred thousand members, many of Chinese origin, believed, like the Hoa Hao members, that religion could be self-taught. The best and purest meditation could be done in the solitude and privacy of one's home. But they never became violent like the Hoa Hao people. They were not in favour of the communists. Among many devout Vietnamese Buddhists, there was a feeling of 'A plague on both your houses!' They felt that the only truly Buddhist path through the jungle of politics was a course of strict non-alignment; they felt, in fact, that both conservative and communist groups, the Vietminh, the French, and later, President Diem and his US-supported henchmen, all represented deeply corrupting Western influences. They experienced a fierce nationalism and wanted Vietnam for the Vietnamese.

While leading Buddhists did not feel they could go all the way with the communists, as it were, yet many of them in South-East Asia perceived much in common between

Buddhism and Marxism. Dr U Ba Swe, a Burmese statesman of the 1950s, believed that Marxist and Buddhist ideas on organizing society were in agreement; in addition, Buddhist teaching gave guidance to individuals for the ordering of personal matters. It was no chance occurrence, but part of a long-term plan, that in the late 1920s, Ho Chi Minh spent two years in a Buddhist monastery in Thailand, telling the monks of his point of view on human rights and of his hopes for the liberation of his country from colonial rule. It was not his expectation or intention that the monks should become communists, but he knew that when they had finished their time of preparation in the monastery, they would be the ones through whom values and concepts would be passed on. They could influence people's thinking.

However, it has not been communism, but rather a broad humanism and growing awareness of social needs which has characterised the practice of Buddhism in countries of South-East Asia in the twentieth century. The Buddhists in many countries, such as Burma and Sri Lanka, have identified closely with their own nationalist movements, and have worked actively to support a drive to have dialogue with Buddhists of other countries, and of different traditions from their own. The age-old, other-worldly, private, meditative side of Buddhism is still there, but is complemented by an outgoing modern reform movement. Since the 1930s Buddhism in South-East Asia has developed a powerful interconnecting structure of universities, study and retreat centres, conferences, and publications, which all reinforce and give continuity to Buddhist ideas.

Thailand, Korea, Taiwan and Japan have many centres for the study of Buddhism. At Rangoon, Tokyo, Colombo, and other cities of the Far East, modern Buddhists have held conferences and conventions, some attended by delegates from Vietnam. In the 1950s, there were large gatherings of Buddhists in many parts of South-East Asia, in recognition of the 2500th anniversary of the death of the Buddha. In 1950 the World Fellowship of Buddhists was founded in Colombo. So, in spite of great differences in the history and political situation of the various nations involved, Buddhism has provided a supporting network for its followers of several countries.

The Buddhist Wheel of Law.

One of the hallmarks of the Buddha's teaching, from the very beginning, was the emphasis on simplicity. Buddhism began as a reaction against the Hindu system of caste, privilege, and fixed elaborate ritual into which the Buddha (whose name was Siddhartha Gautama) was born. The son of an Indian prince, it was foretold at his birth that he would either be a great king, or would be a mystic who would redeem the world. On the soles of his feet at birth was stamped the outline of the symbolic 'Wheel of Law'. The Buddha's father hoped that he would become a king, brought him up in luxury, and shielded him from every ugly sight or disturbing experience. If he went out on horseback, the route he took was cleared beforehand of unwashed or deformed persons. However, according to legend, this plan did not work, and on four different rides, the youthful Gautama saw by the roadside the 'Four Passing Sights'.

The first of the 'Four Passing Sights' was a very old man, gaunt and crippled; the second, a very sick man lying by the roadside; the third, a dead man; the fourth was a monk who had nothing but his staff, his bowl, and his robe. Symbolically, the story describes how the Buddha became aware that nothing in his previous experience had prepared him for the reality of suffering and death, and no one had ever told him that it was possible to withdraw from the world and live without luxury, as the monk he met was doing. Soon after he saw the 'Four Passing Sights', he left his palace and spent about seven years in the solitude of the forests, meditating on, and contemplating, the meaning of suffering and death, until he achieved a spiritual experience in which he became the Buddha, that is, the 'Awakened One', or, the 'Enlightened One'. Then he spent the succeeding forty-five years travelling through India, establishing monasteries, training monks, and teaching about suffering and death and how to come to terms with them.

The Buddha summed up his practical teaching for daily life in four statements, called the 'Four Noble Truths', and in eight commands, known as the 'Eightfold Path'.

The Four Noble Truths, as stated by the Buddha, express a new vision of true reality, by which suffering and transience can be transcended; the Eightfold Path leads on from the Four Noble Truths to show this new vision can be attained if eight specific courses of action, or self-direction, are carefully followed.

The Four Noble Truths are:

1.   Suffering and frustration are universal because people cannot accept the fact that everything changes and is impermanent.
2.   Suffering arises from a grasping attitude as people cling to materialistic satisfaction.
3.   There is a way to break through the unreality of materialism and attain a higher reality.
4.   That way is the Eightfold Path.

The guidelines laid down in the Eightfold Path cover three areas of self-development: increasing one's knowledge; practising right actions and eliminating wrong ones; and attaining greater awareness. The first two guidelines ask the follower to pursue knowledge of the faith, and to do so with total commitment, showing that cognition has an important place in the life of the spirit. It is important to study one's faith, the Buddha stated; one of the best ways of doing this, he said, is by 'right association', that is, spending time with people who have trained themselves in the faith, after learning it from others, as an apprentice spends time with a master of his trade.

The succeeding four recommendations in the Eightfold Path describe practising self-restraint in speech and action, refraining from unloving comments and violent self-indulgent behaviour, being persistent in these efforts and pursuing a constructive livelihood, not one that involves harming other people or degrading oneself. Some of the occupations which the Buddha considered to be incompatible with true self-development were: poison peddler; tax-gatherer; slave dealer; prostitute; and, with prophetic insight, arms manufacturer and merchant.

The seventh and eighth steps of The Eightfold Path describe first, the process of self-examination and analysis of the self's own motives and attitudes as the underlying causes of prevailing suffering and lack of harmony: and, finally, how to achieve heightened awareness by practising meditation and contemplation in solitude.

The Dhammapada, a collection of sayings believed to have been made by the Buddha himself, begins with the statement that:

> What we are today comes from our thoughts of yesterday, and our present thoughts build our life of tomorrow: our life is the creation of our mind. (From *The Dhammapada*, trans. Juan Mascaro).

With sayings such as this the Buddha continually led his followers on to see the law of cause and effect working in their own attitudes and prejudices, hostility breeding hostility, and love creating harmony. He saw the mechanism of blame as a handy tool with which people rationalise away their discomfort about their own behaviour:

> Think not of the faults of others, of what they have done or not done. Think rather of your own sins, of the things you have done or not done.
> (From *The Dhammapada*, trans. Juan Mascaro).

The title *Dhammapada* means 'Path of Truth', or 'Way of Enlightenment'.

There are several links between Buddhist teaching and

Statues in the Museum Park, Vung Tau, Vietnam: animals pay homage to the Buddha after he had received enlightenment

modern thought. The Buddha's concern for people feeling grief and pain, his efforts to help them come to terms with suffering and to understand their own hidden, unconscious drives, all reveal him as a master of psychotherapy. The Buddhist concept of the material world, seen not as a solid, static affair, but as a dynamic creation of processes, functions, and forces, interpenetrating and always in flux, bears an uncanny likeness to the findings of modern physicists on the nature of matter. Friedrich Engels (1820-1895), who in 1848 had been a co-author with Karl Marx of *The Communist Manifesto*, towards the end of his life claimed Buddhist lineage for his dialectics, which he defined as 'the science of interconnectedness.'

Following oral tradition, the Buddhists made no written record of the Buddha's sayings for more than four hundred years after his death. However, during those years, Buddhist monks held several councils and conferences, in which they checked over with each other, again and again, the essential details of the Buddha's teaching. When they did embark on the task of recording, the writing stretched to several long *sutras*, as they were called: that is, volumes of religious and philosophical documents.

The oldest of these works is known as the Pali Canon, as it was written in the Pali language, a branch of Sanskrit. In the succeeding two centuries other sutras were compiled, the most famous being the Avatamsaka Sutra. It was inevitable that, over the centuries, variations and shifts of emphasis would develop within Buddhism, according to individual temperament or national culture. Gradually two main schools of thought defined themselves: the 'Theravada' and the 'Mahayana' Buddhists. The term 'Theravada' meant 'Way of the Elders'; its followers are orthodox Buddhists who keep very closely to the Pali Canon, which they believe was passed on by the elders, or in fact most ancient Buddhists, who actually knew Buddha himself. Another name for them is the 'Hinayana', meaning 'the little raft', whereas 'Mahayana' means 'the big raft' (continuing the figure of speech, as in The Eightfold Path, by which the faith is defined as a means of leaving one spiritual space, as it were, and attaining another). The Mahayana Buddhists are regarded as the more liberal group, accepting more variations; they follow the Avatamsaka Sutra. One group complements the other.

The Buddhists of Sri Lanka, Burma, Cambodia, and Thailand have been dominated by the Theravada approach; further to the north, in China, Tibet, Nepal, Japan, Korea, and Taiwan, the teaching of the Mahayana Buddhists has been prominent. The Vietnamese might follow either group, as both have been represented in their country. The influence of the Theravada monks has been greater in the deep south of Vietnam, where people of Khmer origin lived for centuries.

The genius of the Buddhists of the Theravada school has lain in structuring and in administration. They established huge monasteries containing thousands of monks, educated and organised in hierarchies, following canon law closely. They saw Buddhism as a faith expressed and led by professionals, not laymen; yet they stressed the importance of self-reliance, and recalled that the Buddha had said, in effect:

Be ye lamps unto yourselves. Work out your own salvation with

diligence.
(From E.A. Burtt, *The Teachings of the Compassionate Buddha*).

The Buddha had once stated that 'Compassion is the law of laws'; and compassion was stressed in the teaching of the Buddhists of the Mahayana school. Their most characteristic figure was, and still is, the Bodhisattva, a person religious by profession, often a monk, or in some instances a nun who, though yearning to devote himself or herself to contemplation withdrawn from the world, lives in the crowded poor villages in order to be of service. The importance of the laity was emphasised. A Buddhist of the Mahayan school could not be truly living his or her religion by himself, but only as a social being involved in other people's joys and sorrows; 'compassion', for instance, is meaningless in abstract, until it is expressed in the feelings or actions of one person towards another. The ideal Bodhisattva most frequently venerated in Vietnamese pagodas, 'Quan Am', is shown in figurines and statues as a goddess of mercy and wisdom.

Buddhism was brought to China in 67 AD and, by tradition, from China to Vietnam in 189 AD. It did not supersede ancestor worship and animist beliefs in the spirits of, for instance, the trees or river of a place, but took its place in the Vietnamese consciousness beside them; the Festival of the Dead, called Trung Nguyen was a national holiday, like our Memorial or Remembrance Days. In villages or towns which had a pagoda, there were rituals and prayers daily at set hours, as the Buddhists of the Mahayana school made use of ritual and petitionary prayer, unlike those of the Theravada school, who concentrated on meditation. Most of all, the bodhisattvas endeared themselves to the Vietnamese people, and gave the faith its lasting dynamism and influence. Often they were lay people, as well as monks, who spent their time in serving in whatever way was needed; as counsellors, helpers in time of harvest, male nurses in sickness, or comforters in times of grief. Naturally they identified with the poor against the mandarin tax-gatherers, who tried from time to time to get rid of them by closing the pagodas or forbidding instruction in the Buddhist texts, but after going underground for a while they would continue their work in remote villages. The monasteries, far away from large cities, were natural centres of peasant revolt, and were not as aloof from local society as the English word suggests. The Buddhists felt their faith went deeper and had a more universal application than Confucianism, which was intended for a particular culture and society only.

The modernist movement in Buddhism spread to Vietnam from other Buddhist countries in the 1920s and 1930s. In 1931 the Union for the Study of Buddhism was founded in Saigon, and another based in Hanoi started in 1934, while the Bao-Quoc Seminar, an institute of learning, opened in Hue in 1932. These groups interpreted and modernised texts, educated monks, built hospitals, began lay and youth movements, and laid the foundation for organizing Buddhists on a regional basis, under the United Buddhist Congregation of Vietnam (inaugurated in 1964). The soldiers of the ARVN (Army of the Republic of Vietnam – South Vietnam) deserted in droves during the US-Vietnamese War, carrying much American arms and equipment with them to North Vietnam; one of their reasons was that they were mostly Buddhists, and did not want to fight their Buddhist compatriots.

A very ancient tradition of Vietnamese Buddhism, based on texts brought through China from India, was the practice of religious suicide and self-immolation. It became a political weapon when, on 11th June 1963, an elderly Buddhist monk, Thich Quang Duc, a member of the 'Begging Sangha Community', sat down crosslegged at a busy crossroads in Saigon, and allowed one companion to pour gasoline over him and another to set fire to him. His action was a protest against the persecution of Buddhists under the regime of President Ngo Dinh Diem. The reaction of the Vietnamese public was deeply emotional. In crowds they demonstrated and knelt and wept in the streets.

Some Buddhists were shot in the pagodas at this time, though the American advisors had particularly asked President Diem not to allow this. Some were driven into exile and starvation in the Cambodian jungle. Some were imprisoned in the terrible cages in the penal colony on the island of Poulo Condor, where they were so cramped they lost the use of their legs, and for lack of water had to drink their own urine. Under a French law which had never been repealed, Buddhist processions were forbidden, though in practice the French had not been too strict about it. Diem forbade the Buddhists to have a procession to honour the 2,500th anniversary of the birth of the Buddha.

Statue of Quan Am, Goddess of Mercy and Compassion, in the Museum Park, Vung Tau, Vietnam

Diem was a very aloof autocratic man who alienated himself from the people more and more. He was a devout Catholic and very hard on himself; his catholicism seemed more akin to that of the Spanish Inquisition than to the Sermon on the Mount. He set up the Agrovilles and Strategic Hamlets, driving people away from their homes on the pretext of getting rid of hidden communist agents. Secret police were very powerful in his time. With his brother he was assassinated on 2nd Nov. 1963, allegedly with the agreement of the CIA representatives in Vietnam at the time.

CHAPTER THREE

French Rule in Indochina and the Rise of the Vietnamese Revolution

The hero Jason, having slain a dragon, sowed its teeth, and there sprang up armed men. (Greek legend)

The ancient myth of the hero Jason, sowing the dragon's teeth, unaware that the resulting crop would be armed men, ready to fight him and each other, is a symbol of the unconscious origins of conflict. The French who were part of the ruling administration in Indochina between the 1880s and the 1950s had the same Jason-like blank unawareness of consequences, and were puzzled by passionate rebellions, because according to their perception they were bringing to Vietnam the priceless gifts of French civilisation and culture. They could point to many 'improvements' in the land – roads, railways, hospitals, schools, all French-built – and cite many tireless French doctors and nuns who toiled to try to save their Vietnamese patients from dying of malaria; and there were many Francophile Vietnamese, particularly in the south, who tried to become as French as possible, were Roman Catholic, and felt more at home in Paris than in Saigon. Ho Chi Minh himself, who had studied French classical literature, once said that he felt torn between admiration and hatred for the French people, summing up his own feelings as a member of a country of divided loyalties, caught between east and west.

In the period between the closing years of the nineteenth century and the early 1940s, when France fell to Germany and the Japanese invaded Indochina, French power and influence reached into every aspect of life in Vietnam. Trade and industry, education, the law courts, and banking were all controlled by the French. The mandarins were supplanted by French-appointed minor officials, collecting taxes and settling disputes in the villages. There was much corruption. Villagers could be press-ganged to serve in the Legion anywhere in the world, or, during the First World War, be sent to dig trenches in France.

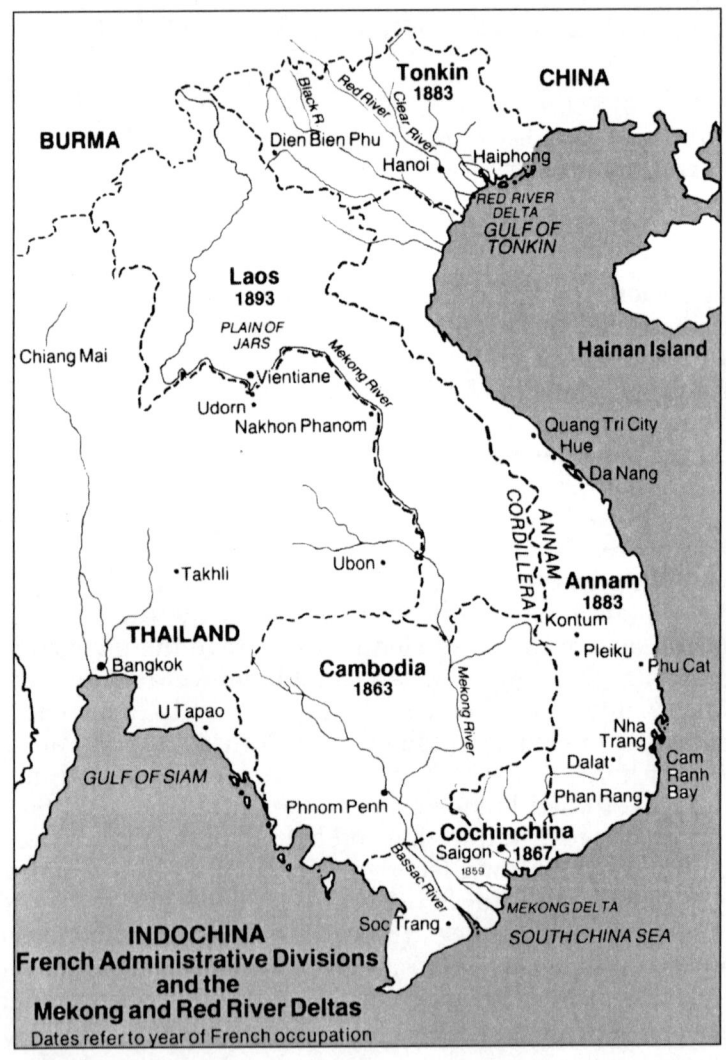

INDOCHINA
French Administrative Divisions
and the
Mekong and Red River Deltas
Dates refer to year of French occupation

In a memo to Cordell Hull in 1944, referring to the idea of setting up an international trusteeship for Vietnam, President F.D. Roosevelt of the US stated that:

> France has had the country – thirty million inhabitants – for nearly one hundred years, and the people are worse off than they were at the beginning . . . the case of Indochina is perfectly clear. France has milked it for one hundred years. The people of Indochina are entitled to something better than that. *(Vietnam, A History in Documents*, ed. Gareth Porter)

Vietnam was perceived by the French as a boundless source of much-needed raw materials and of profits, which all flowed to France. Thousands and thousands of tons of rice and coal were exported. Other exports from Vietnam enriched the economy of France. They included: tin, iron ore, manganese, zinc, tea, coffee, silk, and rare woods. For the year 1939 the value of exports from Vietnam to France was estimated at three and a half billion francs. To keep such a volume of goods moving the French created an efficient transport system of roads, railways, dock and harbour facilities, and built expensive dykes to prevent flooding along the Red River and in the Mekong Delta, undertaking much dredging and canal making. Finally, to further increase profits, many Vietnamese were virtual slaves on the great plantations.

There was a government monopoly on alcohol and opium, and profits were large. The use of opium among the Vietnamese increased greatly under French rule. The legal system used by the French was that of the Code Napoléon or Code Civil des Français, proclaimed in 1804. This was satisfactory if the protagonists were Frenchmen, as it promised personal freedom and equality before the law; but it did not work for Vietnamese persons, who on the one hand could not win if they brought a charge against a Frenchman in a French court, and on the other they could be imprisoned without trial. The French did not understand that there had been in Vietnam a tradition of settling disputes unofficially, in informal dialogue; and the tacit oriental agreement to refrain from giving evidence against a friend or relative was lost on the French, who just inferred that there was no evidence to give. Women, least of all Vietnamese women, got little help from the Code, which stated that they could not plead in their own names without the authority of their husbands, to whom they had to be obedient.

French was the official language; instruction at the University of Hanoi, and in the schools founded by the French, was in the French language. The history taught was primarily French history. In writing it was compulsory to use western lettering, and the use of Chinese characters was forbidden. There were some unofficial schools where Vietnamese was the language of instruction, but these were regarded with suspicion by the French, who thought they would encourage sedition and revolt (this was, of course, true in some cases), but the truth was an alternative point of view could not be tolerated, and if possible some pretext was found to close such schools and imprison their principals.

For the purpose of governing a small country the French administration was very top-heavy, with many thousands of officials. Turnover at the upper levels was very high, so many individuals with a lot of power never got to know and understand the Vietnamese people. The governor-general resided in Hanoi and was represented by his lieutenant-governors in other major cities. Vietnamese employees only obtained government jobs that were poorly paid and low down on the totem pole, as it were. Even Vietnamese scholars educated at the Sorbonne could not find work in their own country at a level appropriate to their qualifications.

With regard to religion, the French did not actively persecute any followers of native creeds, but on the other hand Vietnamese who were Roman Catholics were more likely to find a job (albeit a lowly one) in a government office than people of other faiths. Although Buddhists continued their worship in the pagodas, public assemblies and processions to celebrate Buddhist festivals were banned under French rule. Roman Catholic processions were legitimate, however.

Rebellions were cruelly suppressed with executions, use of the stocks, and imprisonment in the penal colony on the island of Poulo Condor or in any of several French prisons, such as those at Yen Bay and Cao Bang. Many leaders of the various revolutionary groups had long prison sentences, and told of being tortured while in prison. Ho Chi Minh stated that 'They [the French] have built more prisons than schools', when he was giving his speech at the Declaration of Independence of the Democratic Republic of Vietnam, on 2nd September 1945.

Yet such is the complexity of the relationship between the conquered and the conquerors, there were, during the French regime, many acts of mercy being performed by the French for the Vietnamese patients in their hospitals. (By a terrible irony, some of these hospitals, built with two or more storeys, European style, decades later become obvious targets for bombing raids by France's own allies, the Americans.)

If most of the time the French régime in Vietnam was short on human rights and the values going with the concept, it was long on values beloved by the business world, and for many years was satisfactory to French politicians, too. The Bank of Indochina, operating at exchange rates highly favourable to the franc and disastrous for the piaster, in spite of rake-offs and corruption by dishonest officials on the spot, siphoned off vast sums of money to the French government. Thus criticism at home of French colonial policy, and complaints about the expenses of maintaining legionnaires and French soldiers in Vietnam, were neutralised. The system worked; it did what it was meant to do: that is, it brought prestige and profit to France (for a time) but down the road a terrible price would be paid in the agony of the Siege of Dien Bien Phu.

The story goes that Ho Chi Minh as a teenager was asked to leave his high school because he used to ask awkward questions, such as why it was that the buzzwords of the French Revolution – liberty, equality, and fraternity – evidently did not apply to Vietnamese persons. Born in 1890 on 19th May at the village of Kim Lien in central Annam, he was a child of the new, only partly modernised French Vietnam; but at the same time his background was in the old Vietnam of mandarin power over impoverished villagers. Central Annam had areas of desperate poverty, where to have a piece of rancid fish to eat with one's rice was luxury. Ho Chi Minh's father was Nguyen Sinh Huy, a Confucian scholar, who had been a secretary at the Imperial palace at Hue; forced to leave his job because of his anti-French views, he became a wandering scribe.

Ho Chi Minh's name at birth was Nguyen That Thanh, meaning 'He who will be victorious'. He used many aliases over the years. When he was living in Paris during the First World War and the time just after it, for instance, he took the name 'Nguyen Ai Quoc' ('the patriot'); and he did not become well-known to everyone in North Vietnam as Ho Chi Minh – 'He who brings light' – until much later, in 1945, when he proclaimed the independence of his country. He was fifty-six years of age by then, having spent more than thirty years away from Vietnam. He had travelled around the world, and had been imprisoned several times, yet had never wavered in his long-term purpose to build up the nationalist movement of Vietnam.

Giving an impression of charm and simplicity, he used to wander through the country in old clothes, with his trousers rolled up like a paddy worker's, holding meetings in streets and factories. His advice to North Vietnamese recruits was given in simplicity: they were to learn to read, and if they lodged in someone's house, they were not to damage the garden or furniture, nor bring live fowl into the house. He used to tell the young soldiers that victory would come through the efforts of the people, not solely because of the work of their leaders.

Once dubbed 'The Gandhi of Indochina', Ho Chi Minh inspired passionate admiration and reverence in the Vietnamese, who, after he had become famous, would often carry a small picture of him with them, or would have a plaster cast of him at home. His unassuming manner, however, gave no outward clue to his iron resolve and brilliant organisation skills, which enabled him to persist for more than three decades in laying the groundwork for the eventual establishment of the Democratic Republic of Vietnam; incessantly studying, writing, and travelling back and forth between east and west, he built up support for his work outside his own country. He became fluent in Russian, English, and Cantonese in addition to the French he had learned at home.

Ho Chi Minh was twenty-one when he first left Vietnam, working as a galley-hand on a French ship. He visited the US briefly, and in 1913 went to Britain. It was there that he was addressed as 'Sir' for the first time ever, to his astonishment.

He was surprised too at the extreme poverty he saw in Britain. He made contact with the Fabians, whose society was the forerunner of the British Labour Party. They believed that socialism would triumph, not by extreme revolutionary measures, but only after universal suffrage had brought in a long period of political education and development. It is possible that Ho Chi Minh was influenced by Sidney Webb's view that gradual change in a people's political outlook was more favourable than a sudden switch; this would tie in with his knowledge of the advice of Confucius to rulers who expected men to rally to their cause: he said a nation would require many years of political education before such a result could be achieved. So the idea of gradualism was readily acceptable to him. While he was in England, Ho Chi Minh worked as an apprentice chef in a large London hotel, and, never forgetting his resolve to struggle against imperialism, helped to found an anti-colonial group called 'The Association of Overseas Workers'.

In 1917 he moved to Paris, where he worked at various times as a laundryman, gardener, and assistant photographer. Again, he was surprised to find that the poor of France were hardly less wretched than their counterparts in Vietnam. It has been estimated that there were at that time up to sixty thousand Vietnamese persons in Paris alone, and in the course of the First World War 140,000 Vietnamese men were conscripted to dig trenches and perform many other hard and menial tasks. Yet their time in France brought them into contact with other desperate people, enabled them to see different ways of living, and added to their longing for independence.

Ho Chi Minh found that the French of metropolitan France were more liberal and sympathetic towards the Vietnamese than the Frenchmen were in the colony. He wrote a treatise called 'The Process of French Colonisation', studied Marx and Engels, and wrote articles for left wing papers. When he first read Lenin's 'Thesis on the National and Colonial Questions', he felt that it made all his previous studies of revolutionary writings come together for him. He felt exultation and elation such as the poet Wordsworth experienced at the beginning of the French Revolution, when he exclaimed:

> Bliss was it in that dawn to be alive,
> But to be young was very heaven!
> (*W. Wordsworth, Book 10, The Prelude, 1805*)

(The sense of revelation was real enough at the time, although the new era of freedom and joy which the poet expected, did not come into being.)

In the Thesis, Lenin stated that socialists everywhere should support the struggles of oppressed nations fighting for emancipation from their colonial state. In the Far East, Lenin thought that revolution should take on a nationalist form, developing in phases until a completely socialist society could be created. In imperialism he perceived capitalism at its most extreme and most ruthless; literally, capital was exported to 'backward' countries where land and labour were cheap, or even free for the taking, and where raw materials were plentiful. Then through government monopolies the capital was returned a hundred thousandfold to the dominant country, leaving the colonised people more wretched than they had been formerly, when they had produced food and goods simply for their own use. This empire-building was essentially an exploiting enterprise, polarising the world along fault lines between 'have' and 'have-not' countries.

Like Lenin, Ho Chi Minh thought of revolution as developing in phases. His concept of these phases as they would appear in Vietnam was the following: that the first phase would be taken up with the expulsion of the French; the second would be a period in which a middle-class democratic republic would be created; and the third phase would bring in a truly socialist society. He drew up a list of plans by which the aims of the revolution could be achieved and which became the basis of his political platform. The plans were as follows:

1. To overcome the French imperialists and their Vietnamese collaborators.
2. To make Indochina independent.
3. To establish a people's government.
4. To confiscate the banks and other large French-owned enterprises.

5. To take over the plantations and divide them up among the peasants.
6. To set up an eight-hour working day in Vietnam.
7. To abolish unjust taxes and government loans at exorbitant interest.
8. To give 'freedom to the masses' – universal suffrage, freedom of assembly, freedom of movement, and fair hearings before the law – and freedom of the press and of speech.
9. To provide universal education.
10. To bring about equality between men and women.

In *The Communist Manifesto* of 1848 Karl Marx and Friedrich Engels had also drawn up a list of measures to bring about a communist revolution, and Ho Chi Minh's list echoes theirs to some extent, but not completely. It is more positive in its outlook, and is tailored to the particular situation in Vietnam. Unlike Marx and Engels, for instance, he did not spell out that rights of inheritance had to be abolished, along with the right to hold property in land, for he found that he needed to keep the support of many thousands of people who had small-holdings. Even so, his list, which now comes across as more moderate than expected, was about as accessible as the other side of the moon to most of the Vietnamese between the two world wars, as the basic freedoms and rights he outlined, such as the eight-hour working day and equality before the law, were denied to them.

In 1919 Ho Chi Minh went to Versailles, hoping to gain an audience with Woodrow Wilson, who was at that time the president of the United States of America. Wilson was taking part in the Peace Conference which led to the Treaty of Versailles. Ho Chi Minh submitted to him a request for democratic rights, including full legal rights, for the Annamite people. Ho Chi Minh was not allowed to see the president, but at least by attempting to do so he had publicised and set on record the claim of his people for justice and freedom.

Becoming a co-founder of the French Communist Party in 1920, Ho Chi Minh was selected in 1922 for leadership training at the International School of Marxism in Moscow. Then he went to Canton to be an aide in the USSR consulate there, and after setting up the Communist International Bureau in Shanghai, returned to Moscow and taught in the Asiatic Department of the Lenin Institute.

Even then, Ho Chi Minh did not consider himself as a communist per se, but more as a patriot and a socialist. He found western left wing groups did not feel a pressing concern about people oppressed under colonial rule, although they were sympathetic towards them; and some of the French socialists were hesitant to be outspoken in criticising their own government's colonial policy.

On his return to Canton in 1925, Ho Chi Minh took up the long and complex task of building a nationalist party along communist lines. It was a rocky road he had to follow. In the 1920s and 1930s there was in Vietnam a medley of political factions fighting among themselves. Their platforms ranged from far right of right, to middling liberal, to extreme, militant left. Some gave a very plausible show of true concern for their national destiny, but were really only fronts and puppets for other nations to gain power in Vietnam. Others appeared as look-alike revolutionaries on the surface, seeming to be true patriots and socialists, yet revealed in their teaching doctrinaire inconsistency which would later destroy them.

Ho Chi Minh's chief rivals in the latter group were the Vietnamese Trotskyites. There were two chief branches who often could not agree among themselves: the 'October' group in Hanoi, and the 'Struggle' group in Saigon. They published illicit papers by these names, 'October' and 'Struggle' (La Lutte) respectively. Their rise and fall are significant in that they illustrate, already very early in the Vietnamese revolution, three problems common to communist governments anywhere, and still not solved. These are: the problem of how to reconcile the need for obedience to a central controlling elite with the danger of creating a suffocating bureaucracy; the problem of too much use of violence; the problem of finding ways to adapt basic communist tenets to local conditions without compromising unduly.

These ongoing built-in dilemmas had been perceived by Leon Trotsky himself, who was a founding member of the Polit-Buro, along with Lenin and Stalin, in the Russian Revolution of 1917. He was Commissar for War and created the Red Army. He believed in the theory of 'Permanent Revolution' which could only be achieved by the proletariat, who would have to become more and more radical and violent. They could only succeed with the support of their counterparts in other countries.

Trotsky became more and more alienated from Stalin, who believed in the concept of 'Socialism in One Country', intending the opposite of Trotsky's theory. Trotsky thought that the success of the revolution in Russia would depend on backing from revolutionary movements in other countries, but Stalin planned the reverse: that the USSR would become the chief power for revolution, and the revolutionary forces in other countries would be dependent on it. For the internal structure of the government he planned along the lines of 'Revolution From Above', that is, by gradual change, revolution would evolve through the rule of the party elite, with the support of the proletariat from below. He created the basis of the bureaucratic government of the USSR, with its still-characteristic secrecy, centralism and exclusiveness. In the 1930s he eliminated rivals to his power among the older revolutionaries by execution or murder. There were thousands killed or sent to hard labour in the 'Yezhovshina' or purges, named after Yezhov, the head of the Soviet secret police at the time.

In the decade before the First World War Lenin and Trotsky had gone along with the idea that a central commanding group was necessary for the revolution to succeed, but by 1920, finding that even then, the state offices had no less than six million employees, they became more and more critical of Stalin's 'Revolution from Above'. They saw that the country could have a dictatorship of bureaucrats, not a 'dictatorship of the proletariat' as they had imagined formerly. Lenin died in 1924 and Stalin denounced the views of Trotsky, who was expelled from the party in 1927, banished in 1929, and murdered in 1940 in Mexico by a Stalinist agent.

Trotsky was realistic and foresaw that the revolutionary government in Russia would inevitably turn into a police state, as he wrote in the work, *The Revolution Betrayed*, because of chronic shortages of food and basic necessities, and the backwardness of the peasants. Yet the term 'Trotskyite' in spite of his insight, came to mean a person who was very militant and unreasonably radical, and revolutionary in the sense of wanting to overthrow the old order, but having no commitment to the development of a better system in its place.

Collectively, the Vietnamese Trotskyite movement followed to an uncanny degree the pattern of the career of Trotsky himself, passing from enthusiastic agreement with other communists, to bitter dissidence, ending in the violent death of their leading members in 1945. Founded in 1930, they worked for a while with friends of Ho Chi Minh, who had studied with him in Moscow under followers of Stalin, and jointly produced the paper *La Lutte*. But they soon split into several factions quarrelling among themselves, and with Ho Chi Minh's followers, polarising communist partisans in Vietnam between the 'Stalinists' on the one hand, and themselves, the Trotskyites, on the other. They were bitterly critical of Ho Chi Minh's efforts to conciliate the French and the nationalist Chinese, and considered him a traitor, although actually his policy was a means of survival until his party was ready to

A boatman on the Mekong River, Vietnam

confront these powers. They took the theory of 'Permanent Revolution' to mean that unlimited violence was justified any time. They were trouble makers continually stirring up fights, revolts, strikes and demonstrations, regardless of timing, and never waiting to consider whether they had enough support at the grassroots to be effective. In 1932 the French police arrested thirty-two of their leaders, and in September 1939 around six thousand followers, many of them in the Saigon district of Cholon, were rounded up and jailed.

The Vietnamese Trotskyites were more numerous and popular in the southern part of the country than they were in Tonkin or Annam. Many of their leaders were intellectual people educated at French universities and influenced by French Trotskyites. They illustrated the diversity of Vietnamese society, as, accustomed to French analytical thought, they had little in common with the mystical bodhisattvas of the poor Buddhist villages; and though in theory they believed that the peasants should be armed and should take possession of the land, they had no clear plan on just exactly how a group of people could achieve such a goal, when most of them had no money, no transport, could not read or tell the time, might even speak a non-Vietnamese minority language, and were separated from the next hamlet by an expanse of water.

It was in fact the issue of the role of the peasants in the revolution which caused the split between the Trotskyites and the other Vietnamese Marxist-oriented groups, who in 1930 joined forces and formed the Indo-chinese Communist Party under the leadership – often in absentia – of Ho Chi Minh. The Trotskyites gave a narrow interpretation to Trotsky's teaching: that only the proletariat could bring about the revolution, as by 'the proletariat' they meant the industrial workers. (Lenin had defined the term to mean the sum total of persons forced by necessity to sell their labour power.) In Vietnam the theory that industrial workers would create a revolutionary society was doctrinaire and unrealistic, because their number was very small. It is thought to have been in 1918, for instance, only around 100,000. Ninety percent of the population were peasants. In 1929 it was estimated that in Annam and Tonkin only about 4% of the people lived in towns, and in Cochinchina to the south, about 14%. It was even artificial in Vietnam to divide people into industrial workers and peasants; often the distinction was blurred because many persons who worked in the cities used to return frequently to their family homes in the villages, to get rice or help with the harvest. The wretched plantation workers did not fit easily into the Trotskyites' scheme of things either, forming a huge oriental rural subclass.

Ho Chi Minh's acceptance in the party of persons owning a small (usually pitifully small) piece of land caused the extremists among the Trotskyites to accuse him of making too many concessions to 'bourgeois' aspirations. They did not agree with his view that a large part of the task of the party was to build up peasant support by working continually with small groups in the villages. What was needed from them was some indication, which they evidently could not give, of their ability to be loyal; changing as the wind changed, they made friends on and off with various non-communist groups, and with the powerful Hoa Hao, Cao Dai and Binh Xuyen sects. There was some ambivalence among them and doubt as to whether they really did totally oppose French rule in Vietnam. Some had friends among the French communists, and some supported Prince Bao Dai, the hereditary 'Emperor of Annam', who had no real power but was a native figurehead set up by the French for cosmetic purposes; if he spent most of his time in holiday resorts, who can blame him? He was shrewd, and a patriot as much as was possible in his situation.

One of the Trotskyite leaders who had served Bao Dai as his nominal prime minister was killed, with six other Trotskyite leaders, by agents of Ho Chi Minh in a period from late 1945 to early 1946. Although Ho Chi Minh advised his followers that terrorism was not the best course, he also said that all those who would not follow the line he had laid down would be broken. (There was a terrible resonance echoing down the years, set up by the words of Marx when, as if to rationalise the use of violence, he stated that in the historical process of a revolution some individuals would have to be sacrificed.)

Another non-communist nationalist murdered at the time many of the Trotskyite leaders were killed, was a professor named Bui Quang Chieu who had been the founder of the Constitutionalist Party. This party was one of those in the category previously mentioned which, while appearing truly patriotic, was really serving the interest of a foreign power. The members believed that liberation could be achieved, not by revolution but by keeping within the framework of French rule, and they hoped to be able to share the business of governing with the French by sitting with them on civic and regional councils. They wanted the French to stay in Vietnam. They hoped for French citizenship with full legal rights for the Vietnamese, and extra government subsidies for rice growers.

The party had a large following in Cochinchina among Roman Catholics who were educated either in French-directed schools in Vietnam, or in France; some members were fairly cosmopolitan government officials who really did not want any drastic change in the status quo. Their way of thinking may have sounded reasonable, but proved to be only a pipe dream. When by the mid-thirties it became clear that there would be no liberalising of the French official attitude toward the Vietnamese, the members who could not agree among themselves drifted away to other groups. Some joined the Cao Dai.

Another political party in Vietnam which was the tool of a foreign power was the 'Viet Nam Quoc Dan Dang', the Vietnamese Nationalist Party (known as the VNQDD). Founded in 1927, it was non-communist and was basically inconsistent because it was supposed to be nationalist, yet was pro-Chinese and totally dominated, and funded generously, by the Kuomintang.

The ties between the VNQDD and Nationalist China were of long standing. The Kuomintang had been founded in 1891 by Dr Sun Yat-sen to encourage social reform and democratic government; in 1898, in fact, Dr Sun Yat-sen made a proclamation entitled 'Three Principles for the People', which Ho Chi Minh translated into Vietnamese in 1943. Under his successor, Chiang Kai-shek, however, it became corrupt and anything but democratic. Dr Sun Yat-sen was trained as a doctor in Hong Kong, and was a Christian and an American citizen. After the Chinese Revolution of 1911, in 1913, when the Manchu dynasty was overthrown, he was elected 'President of the United Provinces of China', but he resigned a few months later, hoping by doing so to help his party members settle their disputes. He went to Canton, and was popular and influential there in the early 1920s.

In the Canton area at that time there was a large settlement of Vietnamese emigrés, whose families in some cases had been there before the turn of the century. Dr Sun Yat-sen allowed communists to be members of the Kuomintang in order to get help from the USSR, who sent advisors and arms. So Canton became a natural base for the origin of communism in South-East Asia. Dr Sun Yat-sen died in 1925, and ironically, both Nationalist and Communist Chinese claimed him as a political patriarch. The VNQDD published literature about his life and teachings, but worked against the Vietnamese communists.

The VNQDD, whose very name was a Vietnamese version of the word 'Kuomintang', had an elaborately structured plan drawn up for a possible provisional government, ready for the time when they would seize power. It was a carbon copy of the Kuomintang bureaucracy, with a central executive section and sub-departments of finance, propaganda, foreign affairs, and so forth. At the lower levels they organised themselves into small groups according to the model of communist cells. From these they evidently received unduly optimistic feedback on the amount of popular support they would get if they decided on an armed uprising. Violence and terrorism became their hallmark.

In February 1929 a hated French recruiting officer for plantation workers was murdered by the VNQDD. Of an estimated 1500 members at that time, 225 were arrested. The survivors killed whoever they thought had betrayed them, and mutilated their bodies. In February 1930, instigated by the NVQDD some rebel Vietnamese soldiers from the colonial forces entered the Red River French army base of Yen Bay by night, killed a few of the six hundred Frenchmen there, but were overwhelmed. They set some bombs in Hanoi, and led demonstrations in other centres. They were brutally suppressed by the French; who, over the next two years or so, arrested their leading figures, with the unintended result of eliminating the greatest threat to the dominance of the communists under Ho Chi Minh.

A violent minority group of VNQDD members survived, however, and vowed to cause the death of French officials and their Vietnamese collaborators. To obtain funds they used to rob the train that ran between Tonkin and Yunnan, where there was an army training school which some of them attended, and an arsenal where they learned to make explosives and hand grenades. In September 1945 they helped the Chinese looting in North Vietnam.

They suffered, however, from poor leadership and the lack of a strong clear-cut plan which could appeal to the rural population of Vietnam. There was a lot of infighting; one faction allied with the Japanese, and another group wanted joint intervention in the French Indochina War by the US, China and the United Nations. The divisions caused by these opposing views proved insurmountable and the party folded in the late 1940s, really having no further raison d'être.

Another political party which at first might have appeared to have credibility as a nationalist party because of its links with the 'Rebel Scholars' of Ho Chi Minh's father's time, was the 'Phuc Quoc' or Vietnam Restoration League. It was founded in 1912 in Canton by Phan Boi Chau, a Vietnamese patriot who had a lot of influence in seminating the idea of resisting the French and gaining national independence. He was arrested in 1925 and confined to house arrest in Hue, and did not take any active part in politics afterwards. The Restoration League was a royalist group whose members believed that Prince Cuong De, an exiled descendant of the old Nguyen ruling family, should return and take his rightful place as ruler of Annam. He had many followers among Vietnamese people living abroad, whose forbears, from the 1860s through the 1880s when the French were establishing their rule in Indochina, had left to settle in China, Thailand, Formosa, and Japan. The prince set up his base for anti-French activities in Tokyo and became an obvious tool for Japanese ambitions in South-East Asia.

Prince Cuong De was a personal friend of Matusita, who was an agent, under cover of the Japanese consulate, working in Indochina for the Japanese army intelligence network. He became its director in 1941, and worked at the same time with the Kempei Tai, the Japanese secret police and espionage organisation. He became the real power in the Phuc Quoc, provided the party with money from the banks and industries in which the Japanese had controlling interests, and brought the Hoa Hao and Cao Dai sects into the act as well, to work for Japan against the French, as part of the programme of the

'Greater East Asia Co-Prosperity Sphere'.

This was the name given by the Japanese to a propaganda movement based on the hypothesis that there was a vast area, in which most of the resources and wealth were held by white men, but which should be controlled by the Japanese. The area they had in mind ranged across South-East Asia, from Burma through Thailand and Cochinchina to Singapore and the Dutch East Indies, and then north to the Philippines and Hong Kong. Indochina was perceived as a marvellous base from which to control the whole zone, and a source of much-needed raw materials. The Japanese slogan in Vietnam for the 'Greater East Asia Co-Prosperity Sphere' was 'Asia for the Asians', and thus they were able to stir up anti-French feeling, particularly among discontented native troops recruited by the French.

The Phuc Quoc members were used by the Japanese Kempei Tai to provide themselves with allies among the Vietnamese, to infiltrate themselves everywhere, and to gain information valuable to them in preparation for the Japanese occupation of northern Indochina in September 1940. The Japanese always were interested in amassing information. It would be hard to exaggerate the power of the Kempei Tai, and the terror they could arouse. Founded in 1881, they really had a much older ancestry going back to many centuries of Japanese intelligence work, and in the nineteenth century to members of Japanese secret societies, who vowed to seek knowledge abroad for the greater honour of Japan. So it was a matter of great patriotic pride to gain membership in the Kempei Tai, not something to be slightly ashamed about, as western people might feel about their spying activities. The Kempei Tai had almost unlimited funds and was a semi-independent body answerable only to the emperor. Its members were allowed considerable freedom, and could arrest army officers three ranks above their own. They could wear uniforms, with a special badge showing a star surrounded by leaves, but mostly they worked in plain-clothes, both abroad and in Japan.

In Vietnam the Kempei Tai members often merged with the crowds in the cities, and listened unobtrusively to casual conversations in the bars, brothels, and market places. They got permission from the French authorities to obtain data about mines, harbours, troop positions, and bases, and openly took photographs and made maps and diagrams, so their swift occupation of the country in 1940 was carefully prepared in every detail. After Japan's surrender to the Allies in September 1945 following the dropping of the atomic bombs on Hiroshima and Nagasaki, the Phuc Quoc people who had been so pro-Japanese were discredited and some joined Ho Chi Minh's followers.

Though they went down false trails and culs-de-sac, the many different political factions in Vietnam between 1920 and 1940 each represented a point of view on how to reach a nationalist solution for their country. In any decision-making process, to find out what not to do is as important as making one's mind up on the best course to choose. The Trotskyites, the VNQDD, the Constitutionalist Party and the Phuc Quoc, though passionately nationalist in their own way, gave Ho Chi Minh object lessons in what to avoid in forming a political party: being too doctrinaire; indulging in in-fighting; failing to gain the support of the peasants or provide them with a positive program; and being used by a foreign power. These options all came under the scrutiny of Ho Chi Minh's logic as he built up the Indochinese Communist Party in the decades between 1925 and 1945.

The party was formally founded in 1930, but Ho Chi Minh had by then spent several years in laying its groundwork. At Canton in 1925 he founded the Vietnam Revolutionary Youth League, whose members included students, professional people, workers, and small business or modest property owners. Trying to keep up links with both the Kuomintang and with Moscow, Ho Chi Minh sent some members to the Chinese Military Academy at Whampoa, and some to Russia for training. At first the members numbered only a few hundred, but in a few years had risen to an estimated 1700 in Vietnam and China in 1929. There were thousands of unofficial sympathisers. Ho Chi Minh set up leadership training and courses for members. He published a weekly paper called *Youth* (or *Thanh Nien* in Vietnamese), which began to express the blend of patriotism, Marxism, and Confucian moral loftiness which would give to the Vietnamese Revolution its unique atmosphere. In the paper he reminded

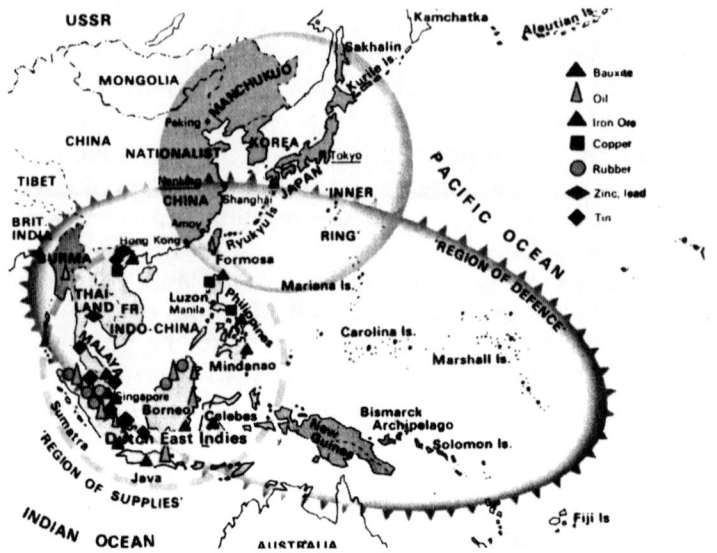

The East Asian Sphere of Prosperity

the readers of the glorious exploits of the Vietnamese national heroes and heroines of ancient times, and stated that League members would have to put the first aim of the League (namely, to overthrow the French in Vietnam), before any personal wishes or plans of their own; and that it was necessary to have a well-prepared party strategy and stick to it, instead of, for instance, starting a demonstration or revolt on impulse.

In 1926 he elaborated on these themes in a pamphlet called *Road to Revolution*, in which he stressed the need for careful organisation combined with devotion and hard work from every member at the grassroots. This pamphlet became a set book, as it were, for revolutionaries. In it Ho Chi Minh acknowledged the influence of Lenin, and so made it clear that the party was a communist one. He established regional party committees in Tonkin, Annam, and Cochinchina, and municipal ones in large centres. From the beginning he emphasised work with peasants, and with women of all levels, pointing out the slave-like and exploited state of Vietnamese women under French rule. Throughout the country he used the 'cell' method of teaching in small discussion groups, and set up peasants' co-operatives, trade unions and women's groups. He stressed the importance of communication skills. If people could not read or tell the time, they were taught to do so. The cadres and leaders were urged to learn minority languages and dialects and work with isolated communities, and were asked to seek work among the proletariat in the factories, mines, and on the railways and plantations. An armchair revolution was regarded as a contradiction in terms; there could be no such thing.

One of the early members of the Indochinese Communist Party was a Vietnamese writer named Truong Chinh who, after many years in prison, held office in the party, and was a leading exponent of its principles. He saw that there were three aspects to the task of leading the people into the revolutionary movement: to teach them to resolve to overcome the imperialists; to educate them politically; and to help them found partisan forces. Men, women, and children would all take part. They would be told about international communism and the party objectives as outlined in Ho Chi Minh's ten-point plan, and there would be strikes, demonstrations, semi-legal protests and appeals against injustice, and illicit leaflets circulated. But there would be no general, organised rebellion until the ideas of the revolution had had time to sink in.

Facilitating this process was indeed the tough and subtle part of the task of winning over the peasants: how to get people who thought in experiential terms to conceptualise and begin to analyse what happened to them; and to link cause and effect. Another Vietnamese author, Nguyen Dinh Thi, speaking of the concept of individualism, said that many persons who had not learned to read until they were adults could not imagine what it meant to be an individualist. They wondered if it was like being a cannibal, trying to put a general expression in terms of a specific action or situation; they had always lived communally and shared everything, and had no keen sense of separateness. It was as if, before they could be true revolutionaries, not just superficial ones echoing jargon, they needed some consciousness-raising and what is called today assertiveness-training.

Peter Weiss, in his book *Notes on the Cultural Life of the*

Democratic Republic of Vietnam, translated from the German, recounted an incident told to him by Nguyen Dinh Thi. He said that once while visiting a village, Ho Chi Minh noticed how arrogant the local party secretary was. Instead of just saying in general that officiousness and greed in party leaders should not be tolerated, he made the point much more vividly by asking the villagers, if they killed a pig to celebrate the party secretary's birthday, what parts would he receive? When they replied that he would get some choice cuts of ham, pork and bacon, he asked them 'And what parts would you get?' Then they all broke into laughter when they had to admit that they only got the tripe.

Among the Vietnamese there had existed for centuries before the revolution a traditional comic theatre, in whose sketches stereotypes of authority and grandeur, such as the brutal tax-collector and the pompous prince, would be defied and humiliated again and again. The hero was always a poor man, who would add to the dialogue some extempore references to local personages or events, or, advancing to the front of the space (usually outside the pagoda) which served as a stage, would ask the audience what he ought to do. They would call out their replies. The wandering players who acted the stories and sketches were sometimes banned because of their potential for stirring up rebellion. So, in symbolic form, the origins of the revolution were very ancient, but leadership and planning were needed to make it come about.

Ho Chi Minh combined remarkably in one person both the ability to tune in to the feelings of poor rural people, and the diplomatic skills needed to unite members of all levels and build up a strongly organised party. In 1930 the task must have appeared almost hopeless. Because of jailings and executions there were only a few hundred official communists in Vietnam, although there were many unofficial supporters in the country and in Thailand and Canton. There were three main groups of members, each with their own slant, who were unable to work together and agree. The emigrés were more radical and followed Moscow's lead more closely than the others, while the peasant members from impoverished Tonkin did not have much in common with the lawyers, teachers, and other professional people in the party in the south.

However, in February 1930 Ho Chi Minh managed to get representatives from each group to sit down together around a conference table in Hong Kong. The title 'Vietnam Communist Party' ('Vietnam Cong San Dang') was chosen and the party was officially founded; Ho Chi Minh's ten-point plan was discussed and made the basic outline of party policy, and a nine-member central committee was formed. In October 1930 their talks resumed in Saigon, and there the name 'Indochinese Communist Party' ('Dang Cong San Dong Duong') was chosen. Their Russian advisors thought this was a more truly representative name, and they officially recognised it the following year. Details of organisation were discussed and explained in detail.

In the early thirties, in fact, the planning and leadership of the party was very good and many peasant associations and soviets were formed, whose members held demonstrations, refused to pay taxes, gathered stores of rice which they distributed: all in the face of stepped-up persecution by the French. Thousands were imprisoned, yet the number of supporters grew by thousands, too. In September 1930 a peasant demonstration near the city of Vinh was broken up by bombs dropped by aircraft. This was a time of incredible poverty and hardship. Thousands were starving. After the Depression of 1929 the price obtainable for exported rice and rubber fell, and so did the workers' already pitiful wages, while taxes went up, and natural disasters such as floods and droughts alternated and added to the misery.

In June 1931 Ho Chi Minh was arrested in Hong Kong by the British, who though they thought he might be an agent for the USSR, would not let him be extradited into the hands of the French, who probably would have executed him. After many appeals and a long bout with his old enemy, tuberculosis, he was released in December 1932 and went to Moscow.

So he was not present when the First National Congress of the Indochinese Communist Party was held in Macao in March 1935. But he soon communicated with the party members through a well-known Vietnamese communist, Le Hong Phong, who returned to his country from Moscow shortly after the Congress in Macao. He was the Comintern representative and secretary-general of the party until 1938, when he was arrested. (He died in prison in 1942.)

In 1935 the Vietnamese communists had to try to come to terms with their conflicting emotions about being good nationalists, yet good international communists, too. Ho Chi Minh, who perceived even then the ambitions of the Japanese in Vietnam, asked the party members to slow down for the time being their open defiance of French rule, in order not to play into the hands of the Japanese. At the same time the USSR, which was subsidising the party in Vietnam with about 5000 francs a month, wanted them to support the French communists, and to model their party structure on the Comintern, keeping Moscow in the lead always. Basically the ideas were those of Stalin's 'Revolution from Above', and 'Socialism in One Country'.

Ho Chi Minh advised the members to work on making progress on the home front by pressing for democratic rights, such as freedom of the press and of assembly, and amnesty for political prisoners. He asked them to try to win over two categories of people they had not considered before: liberal or discontented persons in the French forces, and small shopkeepers and entrepreneurs.

The members did a lot of agonising over these commands; how much, they wondered, did they have to toe Moscow's line? They were Vietnamese after all, not Russian. Hadn't the main thrust of their party been to overthrow the French? It was galling to have to go along with the French communists, who thought the Vietnamese ought to have some home rule, but only within the framework of French administration. This would not be the total independence they longed for. They queried Ho Chi Minh's shrewd offering of party membership to small property owners, though many of them were downtrodden by tax-collectors.

However, they did comply for the time being. They set up an office in Shanghai where the USSR also had a base. They built up a network of fellowship and leadership linking small groups of members in villages and factories with regional and city committees. The authority of the Central Committee of Nine was re-affirmed. The members again proclaimed the ten-point plan of 1930 as the basic party platform, and although they talked of the need in the future for armed rebellion, they agreed for a while to avoid direct confrontation with the French authorities.

For a while this paid off, for following the election of the Popular Front government in France under Léon Blum in 1936, there was a short honeymoon of increased tolerance for Vietnamese aspirations: the eight-hour work-day was introduced; from 1936 to 1937 many thousands of political prisoners were released; and the publication of radical literature in the Vietnamese tongue was made legal. The ICP members were able to become more visible and better known as some assemblies, such as ones on May Day, formerly only allowed in the south, were made legal in the north too; and they were able to take part in local elections.

Several Vietnamese communists who had spent a long time in prison and later became famous leaders worked together at that time to produce a big outpouring of party literature such as *Dan Chung* (The Masses), *Gia Phong* (Liberation), and many others. They produced *Le peuple* and *Le Travail* in French too. Among leaders working on the papers were Le Duan, Pham Van Dong, Truong Chinh, and Vo Nguyen Giap. After being released from Poulo Condor in 1936 Le Duan set up a bookshop in Hue which was an outlet for the party literature and propaganda.

The interior of the Tomb of Kai Dinh, father of Prince Bao Dai, near Hue, Vietnam (he ruled from 1916-25)

CHAPTER FOUR

War and Independence in Vietnam, 1937-45

In 1937 Truong Chinh and Vo Nguyen Giap jointly authored an essay entitled *The Peasant Question,* describing the plight of the Vietnamese peasants and outlining the party's policy for them. Ho Chi Minh asked Vo Nguyen Giap to train the first guerrilla fighters of the party in 1941, and after the proclamation of independence he became Minister of the Interior, then Minister of Defence, and master-minded the organisation and campaigns of the revolutionary armed forces.

Vo Nguyen Giap endured more than his share of personal tragedy. Born in 1912, his father, like Ho Chi Minh's, had taken part in the Scholars' Revolt of 1880 against French rule, and he was introduced early to revolutionary ideas. He attended the French school in Hue where Ho Chi Minh had been a pupil many years senior to him, but in 1927 he was expelled for stirring up student unrest. In the purge of communists after the rebellion at Yen Bay in 1930, Giap was sent to prison for organising a student protest at the Lycée Albert Sarraut, and at the University of Hanoi, where he received a law degree and a doctorate in political science.

While he was teaching history in Hanoi to support himself Giap lodged at the home of a well-known professor, and fell in love with his daughter, Nguyen Thi Minh Giang. They were married and had a son. Minh Giang's sister was the wife of the communist Le Hong Phong.

In 1939 after the Popular Front Government in France was defeated, the French Communist Party was dissolved, and there was a renewed crackdown on the communists in Vietnam. Minh Giang and her sister went to Vinh, hoping to lead the French police on a false trail away from Giap, who had fled with Pham Van Dong to Kunming, China. The sisters were captured, Minh Giang was sentenced to fifteen years' hard labour, and her sister was guillotined. Some historians say that Minh Giang died fighting off the rats in her cell. Her baby also died.

In spite of the arrests of many leaders and being forced to become an underground organisation again, in the World War II years events both at home and abroad gave the Vietnamese communists their unique opportunity to mobilise, increase the popular backing of their movement, and at last reach the point when they were ready to proclaim independence in September 1945.

After the Stalin-Hitler Pact of August 1939 was announced they refused to collaborate with the French by agreeing to fight abroad or work extra hours for the French war effort, and refused to pay increased taxes. There were more arrests than ever. The shrivelled heads of executed communists were on display in market places, and many party members had to hide and live secretly in caves in remote parts of the country, moving constantly. There were large rewards offered for informing on them.

In June 1940 France fell to the Germans, and Ho Chi Minh realised that this was the time to take command of the party and begin to organise and train their guerrilla fighters at bases in the north near the border with China. The Vichy government in France hoped still to hang on to power in Vietnam, but in August 1940 the Japanese began their takeover of the country by demanding the right to close the railroad to Yunnan, to set up their own controlling headquarters and station 6,000 troops in Tonkin, and to construct airfields. There was little the French could do about the situation. However, in the south they were more powerful, and in November successfully put down a large uprising near Saigon. At that rebellion the flag of the party, now the national flag, with a gold star on a red background, was first displayed.

At this time in the early 1940s the situation of the people of Tonkin was desperate. Many died of starvation. Periodic droughts depleted the rice stores, which were raided by the Japanese troops, who expected to live off the land. After a time the communists were able to seize some supplies of rice, seed, and clothing, and distribute them.

In May 1941, Ho Chi Minh, who had been staying at various points just north of the border for safety, crossed it from China and set up his headquarters in the caves of Pac Bo in Cao Bang province, only a very short distance south of the border. Here the fateful decision to arm and fight was made.

A conference of the Central Committee was held and the Viet Minh Front was formed, combining propaganda with guerrilla training. Soon the term 'Viet Minh', short for Vietnam Independence League, passed into general use, meaning the revolutionary movement as a whole. During the four years following the conference at Pac Bo, the Viet Minh were able to make many surprise attacks on French and Japanese outposts and strongholds, and by May 1945 had created the 'Liberated Zone' of six northern provinces. The driving force in organising the armed resistance was Nguyen Vo Giap, who led a group of crack guerrillas, called the Vietnam Liberation Army Propaganda Unit; this was the origin of the highly disciplined People's Army which he developed afterwards.

Communications and information were not neglected in the total plan. After the meeting at which the Viet Minh was created, Ho Chi Minh, who had again crossed the border into southern China, sent his famous *Letter from Abroad* to his countrymen, and it was distributed to many people by the party members. In the Letter he reminded everyone of their national heroes and heroines who had resisted oppression in the past, linking them with their modern successors, the martyrs of the Revolution. The French, he wrote, have become more cruel than ever in their exploitation and repression of the Vietnamese, while shamelessly giving up the country to the Japanese; so they were caught in the middle.

'As a result our people are writhing under a double yoke of oppression. They serve not only as beasts of burden to the French bandits but also as slaves to the Japanese robbers.' (*Ho Chi Minh, Letter from Abroad, June 6 1941*, from *Vietnam, A History in Documents*, ed. Gareth Porter)

However, he continued, even in this terrible situation lay their chance to bring about the revolution; with France defeated at home and the Japanese fighting both the Allies and the

Chinese, the moment would come when, taking advantage of the vacuum of power as the authority of both France and Japan slipped, they would be able to step in and proclaim independence. He wrote:

> 'The sacred call of the Fatherland is resounding in our ears; the ardent blood of our heroic predecessors is seething in our hearts! Let us unite . . . to overthrow the Japanese and the French.
> The Vietnamese revolution will certainly triumph!
> The world revolution will certainly triumph!'
> (Ho Chi Minh, Letter From Abroad. Ibid.)

Making the connection between the ancestors and the modern revolutionaries was a masterstroke. It enabled people to feel an almost religious zeal for the movement, giving it a mystique; for 'the will of heaven' or a divine purpose was endowing it with impetus and power as part of the timeless cycle of war and peace.

So the revolution developed its own mythology. Peter Weiss, in Notes on the Cultural Life of the Democratic Republic of Vietnam described two poems by Ho Chi Minh. The first one was written in 1941 when he was living in the caves of Pac Bo. He said that he had maize soup and bamboo shoots to eat and used a stone for a plate:

> 'How splendid is the life of a revolutionary . . .
> You do not need much for your well-being!
> There the Marxist peak, here the Leninist river;
> Bare hands will build up the land.'

Twenty years later he went back to Pac Bo, and wrote:

> 'Twenty years ago I lived in this cave.
> After each step I smoothed the grass to hide my tracks.
> From here started the battles
> Against the French and Japanese.
> The revolution has conquered.
> How splendid today are the mountains and streams.'[1]

---

1   The Translation of this poetry by Ho Chi Minh is included with kind permission from Marion Boyars Publishers Ltd, 24 Lacy Road, London SW15 1NL, UK.

There were many Vietnamese writers who expressed nationalist and revolutionary ideas, usually partly disguised in allegorical stories or poems. Most of them did not become well-known until the 1950s, when literacy had greatly increased in the land. However, in 1941 from the Pac Bo region, Vo Nguyen Giap, Pham Van Dong and Ho Chi Minh sent out a journal called *Viet Lap (Independent Vietnam)*. Training, indoctrination, and education were carefully carried out throughout the Liberated Zone.

In September 1941 Truong Chinh, who was the Secretary-General and a leading planner for the party, distributed among the members a *Study Document*, outlining their position in relation to the rapidly changing international balance of power. He realised that the fortunes of the Vietnamese Revolution would be very closely linked with world affairs. He described how the French, bitterly divided between the Vichy and Gaullist factions, had given in to the Japanese, who, exploiting the weakness of the French, not only had overrun the country but had taken over the economy, gaining mastery of the banks as well. Small merchants and landowners were ruined because the piastre was devalued, yet speculation and hoarding drove prices up, and both the French and the Japanese demanded large payments towards their war efforts. However, Truong Chinh said that:

> 'The world situation will change unexpectedly, creating a favourable opportunity for the Indochinese revolution. With our own subjective efforts, the conditions for the armed uprising of the Indochinese people will rapidly ripen.'
> (From *Vietnam, A History in Documents*, ed. Gareth Porter)

Truong Chinh emphasised his belief that only careful preparation would enable the communists to seize the coming opportunity. He advised the party leaders to establish a united front against Japanese and French fascism by politically educating not only their own followers but foreign members of the imperialist forces, such as legionnaires and troops from French colonies elsewhere. He asked them to study guerrilla fighting in China and the experiences of the revolutionaries in Russia; and to analyse carefully the course of events in their own uprisings, in order to deduce from them which plans of action would lead to failure and which to success. He asked for the preparation of guerrilla and self-defence units linked by an intelligence network of runners, village committees to provide for the fighters, and 'national salvation bases'. The latter were hide-outs along strategic communication routes, where troops could get rest, food, and clothing. Later they were extended along the Ho Chi Minh Trail to form an elaborate chain invisible under the thick jungle foliage.

In August 1942 the party met with an apparent setback which Ho Chi Minh was able to turn to his advantage. On his way to meet some of the Chinese communists just north of the Sino-Vietnamese border, he was arrested and imprisoned under conditions of terrible hardship by the secret police of the Kuomintang. His friends thought him dead until they received a fragment of a poem, scribbled by him on a scrap of newspaper, describing his sadness as he looked continually to the mountains to the south and yearned for his old friends. In September 1943 he was set free in return for agreeing to set up two bases for Vietminh guerrillas in the Viet Bac area for the purpose of harassing the Japanese troops there. Ho Chi Minh pointed out that he would need arms and money, and was given a $50,000 monthly subsidy by the Kuomintang, but did not receive the thousand rifles, four thousand hand grenades, and machine guns he had asked for. However, he had succeeded in causing the anti-communist Nationalist Chinese to subsidise the Vietnamese communists.

When Vo Nguyen Giap first set up the Vietnam Liberation Army in December 1944, it only had thirty-four members – three women and thirty-one men – with one machine gun and hardly an antique rifle apiece. After a year, there were three thousand of them, and an estimated 170,000 towards the end of the decade, with around a hundred thousand back-up people working with the village groups and national salvation committees. When he addressed the founding members in 1944, while arousing their emotions by urging them to be worthy of their ancestors, and 'under the red flag with the five-pointed gold star' to advance on the road of armed struggle, at the same time he pointed out that at that time their role was one of preparation:

'Comrades,
The mission which the Organisation has entrusted to us is an important mission, a heavy mission. Politics is more important than military activities, propaganda more important than combat; that mission has the characteristic of being the mission of a transitional period: employ propaganda to appeal . . . [to all] to stand up, preparing political and military bases for the general uprising later on.'

(*Vo Nguyen Giap*, 22nd Dec. 1944,
from *Vietnam, A History in Documents*, ed. Gareth Porter)

During the first four and a half years of the 1940s, while the Vietnamese communists were successfully establishing their Liberated Zone in the northern provinces, they were unable to make similar headway in the south, largely because of the huge private armies of the Cao Dai, Hoa Hao and Binh Xuyen sects, who were infiltrated and armed by the Japanese Kempei Tai, thus becoming collaborators with the invaders. This was the period when the Japanese reached the peak of their power in the Pacific, and the control of Vietnam was crucial to their strategy. It was an ideal supply base and launching pad for the invasion of Thailand, Malaya, Burma, and the Dutch East Indies, where there was plenty of oil; Japan desperately needed oil and petroleum products. In July 1941 the US placed an embargo on export of oil to Japan, in August Japanese funds and assets in the US were frozen, and it was forbidden to export any petroleum products used for aviation fuel to Japan. On December 7 1941 Pearl Harbor, the main naval base in Hawaii, was attacked by Japanese aircraft which had taken off from carriers that had secretly sailed from the Kurile Islands twelve days earlier. In the attack five battleships, fourteen smaller vessels, and one hundred and twenty planes were demolished and over two thousand people were killed.

Meanwhile in Vietnam, the Japanese, already having troops in Tonkin, demanded the right to have troops anywhere in the country in unlimited numbers, to use eight airfields in the south and the naval facilities at Cam Ranh Bay and at Saigon. It was thus easy for them to launch their invasion of Java and Sumatra from South Vietnam in February 1942. There was a three-pronged, incredibly rapid, advance southward: the western one from Cam Ranh Bay, and two others from bases

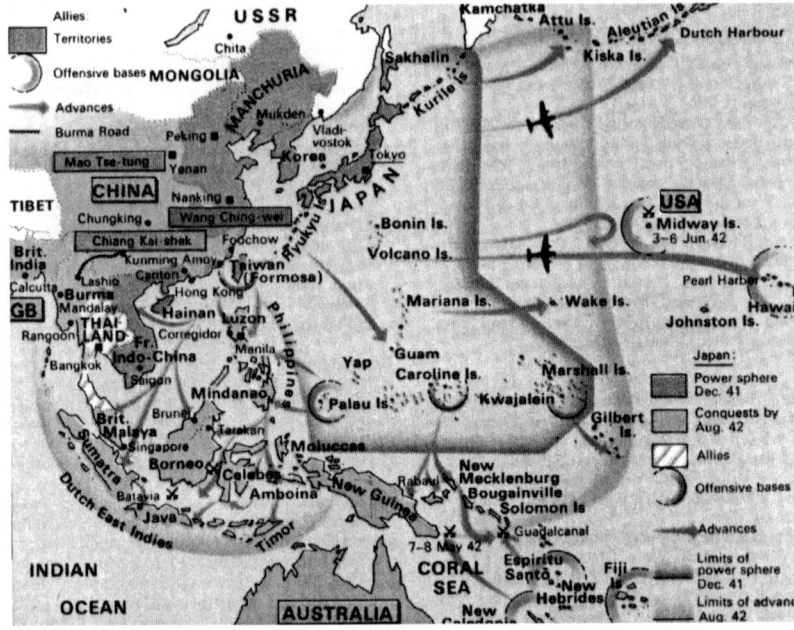

Japanese Offensive Operations, 1941-2

in the Philippines. The Japanese were able to set up a string of captured airfields in the Dutch East Indies, each one not more than three hundred miles from the next.

Although the Vichy French had collaborated for expedience with the Japanese in Vietnam, the de Gaullists were not willing to do so, and believed that French authority could be restored there completely after the war. So they began to plan a counter-attack against the Japanese, and stockpiled arms parachuted in by a British group of commandos. But they were not very good at keeping their plans clandestine; the Kempei Tai found out about them and the Japanese decided to annihilate French forces in a lightning strike. In the night of March 9 1945 they attacked hundreds of army bases and administrative head-quarters all at once. The Legionnaires afterwards called it 'the Night of the Samurai', as thousands were slaughtered or imprisoned. At Lang Son, northeast of Hanoi, the huge garrison of over twelve thousand French troops fought for two days but all were killed in the end; in many places, however, they did not resist at all.

The Japanese declared martial law, set up a curfew and travel restriction, removed all French flags from public buildings, and took over government offices. They appointed the Vietnamese Prince Bao Dai as titular head of state, thus bringing French rule to an end. (But the de Gaullists still hoped they could return).

The lack of the will to resist shown by the French in the Japanese onslaught seems puzzling, as they had well-stocked arsenals. The remoteness of the country and the infighting between the Pétainists and the de Gaullists added to their problems. What they found hardest in their situation was the lack of clear central direction and organisation. In France the systems of the army, of local government, and of education had all been centralised for generations – part of the legacy of Napoleon – to a stifling degree. In the 1930s education was so tightly controlled that a government official in Paris could tell at once from his schedules, what lesson any class in a school in the remotest small town, was receiving at any given time; many Frenchmen liked this state of affairs. So the habit of waiting for orders before doing anything was very deeply ingrained. The Buddhist precept 'Be ye lamps unto yourselves', was quite alien to their way of thinking.

Another factor in the failure to resist could have been the large proportion of non-French soldiers among the French forces. Besides the regular French troops there were many thousands of native soldiers, and legionnaires from other European nations and from North Africa, with mixed loyalties preventing them from feeling inspired to fight to the death defending a distant citadel for the sake of France.

There was another presence: that of the staff of the American Office of Strategic Services, or OSS, who besides the Nationalist Chinese and the Japanese, inadvertently and without really trying, as it were, helped the communist cause in North Vietnam. They had a base near the border of Vietnam at Kunming, Yunnan Province in southern China. It was because of Pearl Harbor that they had come there. The American intelligence service for Hawaii had been split between the FBI, the Army and the Navy, with obviously disastrous results. There was also a civilian intelligence organisation, the Office of the Co-ordinator for Information, with which the forces people did not co-ordinate very well because they disapproved of the highly unconventional methods used by the director, William Donovan, nicknamed 'Wild Bill'. He was not so wild, however, that he could not see the importance of planning: he laid down a basic structure for an intelligence agency, with an executive main office, a research and analysis division, and a special operations department. He sought out skilled and knowledgeable people for staff.

During the war the officers in the forces came around to agreeing that an intelligence agency under one head would be more effective than the existing disjointed operation. So in June 1942 President F.D. Roosevelt changed the name of the Office of the Co-ordinator of Information to the Office of Strategic Services, which was the precursor of the Central Intelligence Agency, or CIA. He placed the OSS under the jurisdiction of the Joint Chiefs of Staff, so that it was no longer civilian, and made Bill Donovan Director with the rank of Major General.

With regard to the Vietnamese, the mandate of the OSS staff at Kunming was ambiguous and ambivalent. Major Donovan had advised them to work with any group who would assist them in resisting the Japanese, but to avoid getting involved in any political machinations between the French and the Vietnamese. In Vietnam in 1945 this was rather like telling someone it was all right to go for a swim if he did not get wet; however, after the sudden Japanese attack on March 9th 1945 on French bases and government centres, they were given permission to provide arms and other supplies to any native resistance group prepared to contribute, by providing intelligence or sabotage and guerrilla fighters, to the ultimate victory of the Allies over the Japanese. But they were still treading on eggshells, as they were asked to refrain from any course of action which would either align them with the French, or on the contrary, would antagonise them.

The conflicting messages from Washington came into an area where the Allies were already bedevilled by confused and overlapping lines of authority, with several separate unco-ordinated intelligence networks. Although the French disapproved of their liaison, relations between the OSS staff and the Vietminh became cordial, as the latter offered a well-organised intelligence service, providing valuable information about Japanese troop movements. The OSS provided Ho Chi Minh with life-saving medicine when he was very ill with malaria, and the communists rescued and sheltered some downed American airmen.

The communists agreed to provide, in addition to intelligence, a thousand guerrilla fighters for anti-Japanese operations in return for arms, supplies, and training. So in July 1945 a group of five men sent by the OSS under Major Allison K. Thomas parachuted into the communists' headquarters in the Viet Bac area north of Hanoi, in deep forest, and stayed there for over two months. Their expedition was given the code name 'Deer Mission'. They slept in a bamboo shelter with a roof of palm leaves, and except for the first night, when they drank captured beer and ate beef from a cow slaughtered specially for them, they lived on rice and bamboo shoots, as their hosts did. From their accounts it sounds as if the young Americans thought it all a good lark, rather like camping in Sherwood Forest with an oriental Robin Hood; Major Thomas referred in a report to 'Our friend in the forest, Mr C.M. Hoo, now Mr Ho Chi Minh', and 'another friend of the forest, Mr Van, now Vo Nguyen Giap', and a sense of warm friendship prevailed. The Deer team trained two hundred of Giap's elite troops in expert commando tactics, provided field radio equipment and clothing for them, and gave them up-to-date sub-machine guns, mortars, and bazookas to replace their antiquated weapons. They were not supposed to use them against the French, according to official instructions, but the OSS thought they probably would, sooner or later.

Although the rapport set up between the Vietminh and the Deer team was very good, they were all whistling in the dark. President F.D. Roosevelt (who once said that he was concerned about 'the brown people in the East' as there were 1,100,000,000 of them ruled by a handful of whites, whom they resented) was unwilling to help the French regain their colonial status quo before the war unless they could see themselves as trustees, helping the Vietnamese achieve independence. But he died on April 1945, and was succeeded by President Harry S. Truman. More hawkish opinions prevailed, American foreign policy switched to an anti-communist attitude, and Ho Chi Minh's famous eight letters to President Truman were never answered. The OSS staff at Kunming were recalled at the end of September 1945, and the agency disbanded. In 1949 the Chinese communists were victorious in their struggle against the Nationalists, and in 1950 McCarthyism spread like a black cloud through Washington, and no one dared mention communists or show even the faintest interest in them, or knowledge of communism, for fear of being thought a traitor and 'one of them'. Truman himself was accused of being soft with them. So the liaison the OSS staff had made with the Vietminh was cut off and its marvellous potential for peaceful dialogue was wasted. The brief happy interlude of the Deer Mission was to be one of the saddest lost opportunities of history.

In July 1945 at the Potsdam Conference, with regard to Indochina the Allies agreed that Chiang Kai-shek would take charge of the surrender of Japanese troops north of the 16th parallel, while British troops under Mountbatten would occupy Vietnam south of that line. This was done in order to settle a dispute between the British and Americans over theatre boundaries. On 6th August the first atomic bomb was dropped on Hiroshima; then two days later the USSR declared war on Japan; another bomb was dropped on 9th August on Nagasaki, and Japan agreed to surrender on 15th August.

Ho Chi Minh realised that he only had about six weeks' grace, as it were, to establish his Provisional Government before the advent of Kuomintang armies in the north and a British one – probably accompanied by French forces returning – in the south. He guessed that the Allies' chief interest in being there would be the restoration of their colonial power in South-East Asia, while the Chinese would jump at the chance to invade North Vietnam.

During the spring of 1945 the Vietminh had formed the National Liberation Committee as the basis for the Provisional Government, and had organised the armed forces into three main groups: a permanent army with a leadership role towards a middle-level group of fighting people; and a militia made up of everyone else, so that it was literally a People's Army, and there were no civilians or non-participants, except very small children and invalids. A ten-point program was laid down for the Liberated Zone, namely to:

1. Drive out the Japanese and all who collaborated with them.

2. Seize their goods and give them to the starving.

3. Proclaim votes for all and basic democratic rights.

4. Arm everyone, urging them to support the troops.

5. Work towards a self-supporting economy by encouraging production and land reclamation.

6. Regulate hours of work, and provide some social insurance.

7. Share out communal land previously confiscated, and reduce land rents and debts.

8. Reduce taxes and abolish the corvée system, i.e. forced labour on the plantations and in the mines.

9. Give everyone the chance to learn to read, to be taught how to fight in the People's Army, and to receive some political education.

10. Work towards equality for women and for ethnic minority groups.

Two courses of action which made the ordinary people feel that 'the will of Heaven' and the power it brought, were now flowing in the communists' favour, were the setting up of military bases to resist the Japanese, and, most of all, their taking control of the rice stocks in the Liberated Zone. The people were desperate because the French and the Japanese used to commandeer large quantities of rice, not only for their own consumption as food, but for export, and for the manufacture of alcohol. If the crop had been poor and the peasants could not produce the amount demanded, they had to go and buy more at an inflated price to make up the difference. So they were ruined and starving.

On August 13 1945 Ho Chi Minh called for a Party Convention at Tan Trao, a village in the jungle in the Liberated Zone of the Viet Bac north of Hanoi. At this meeting vital decisions were made which had a long-term effect on party policy, and contributed much to its ultimate victory. Not all the delegates were keen about him as leader as some hardly knew him, owing to his prolonged absences; but he won them over through his charm and enthusiasm.

At the convention a National Insurrection Committee was formed under the leadership of Giap and Truong Chinh, who at once proclaimed 'Military Order No. 1', which called for an immediate uprising. Then the Committee set out a 'Plan of Action' which placed all programs, whether political or military, and all supporting persons, whether in the army or in their homes, under one command only; and channels of communication with the leadership were made clear.

After this in-group meeting a larger one was immediately held. It was 'The First People's National Congress', which began on 16th August 1945. It was led by Ho Chi Minh, and provided him with an opportunity to gain publicity and to explain his intention to form a provisional government and seize power from the Japanese before the Allied troops could take over. More than sixty people attended, not all communists by any means, but representatives of other nationalist parties, religious groups, organizations, and ethnic minorities.

At the Congress the delegates accepted the ten-point program which had been laid out in the spring, and agreed that the National Liberation Committee headed by Ho Chi Minh, should be the provisional government until such time as elections could be held. To help create a sense of belonging and of unity, they gave people a flag to wave and a song to sing, officially adopting the red flag with the gold star as the national flag, and making the song 'Tien Quan Ca' (Marching to the Front) the national anthem.

The delegates were impressed and a little mystified by the signs of Allied support shown by the presence of the 'Deer' team, and troops of the Liberation Army neatly clothed and provided with arms by US aid. The implication seemed to be that the provisional government would be recognised by the Allies.

This was a vain hope. However, after all the long years of struggle, in the last few days of August 1945 the Vietnamese Revolution gathered momentum at last, and with incredible speed on a tide of mass euphoria, reached its climax on

Independence Day, 2nd September. During these days there were demonstrations and processions in all the large cities. The singing, flag-waving crowds numbered in the hundreds of thousands, and it was estimated that Ho Chi Minh addressed more than half a million people in the crowded streets of Hanoi on 2nd September. (It was not so much fun in Saigon, though, where fighting, instigated allegedly by the French, broke out between rival political groups and sects.)

Major Archimedes L.A. Patti, who was in charge of the OSS Secret Intelligence operations for Indochina in 1945, was based at Kunming, and was in Hanoi on Independence Day. In his book *Why Vietnam? Prelude to America's Albatross*, his description of the crowds that day brings out the diversity of Vietnamese society. There were the entire populations of nearby villages in festive clothes, mountain people in distinctive dress, peasants with yellow turbans and green sashes, and many officials who were not particularly pro-communist:

> 'Waiting for the arrival of Ho and his entourage, I observed a group of Catholic prelates in dark blue and black cassocks, several with the red piping and sashes denoting ranking church officials. Not far from them I saw Buddhist bonzes in orange and white shrouds and Caodaist dignitaries in their white robes, embroidered turbans, and coloured sashes.'
>
> (From *Why Vietnam? Prelude to America's Albatross*,
> by Archimedes L.A. Patti)

For Roman Catholics, Independence Day fell on the Feast of the Vietnamese Martyrs, and a mass was said in their honour at the cathedral. Giap's troops, smartly turned out, accompanied by members of the US Deer Team, had marched into the city. Some of them formed an honour guard for Ho Chi Minh and other leading party members as, exactly at noon, they took their places on a platform set up in the open air. A whistle blew and the troops were commanded to present arms.

Ho began his speech by quoting directly from the Virginia Declaration of Rights of June 1776:

'We hold these Truths to be self-evident, that all Men are created
equal, that they are endowed by their Creator with certain
unalienable Rights, that among these are Life, Liberty, and the
Pursuit of Happiness . . .'

When he paused to ask if everyone could hear him the crowd
roared their assent. Men and women from local militia and
self-defence groups waved scimitars and clubs taken from
pagodas or shrines at home, while others brandished placards
on which were written slogans such as 'Vietnam for the
Vietnamese', and 'Death to the Oppressors'.

Then Ho Chi Minh stated that in September 1791, during
the French Revolution, under the new French Constitution it
was proclaimed that every man is born equal and enjoys equal
rights. But in Vietnam the French imperialists had abused the
basic principles of their own revolution: 'Liberty, Equality, and
Fraternity'. Speaking for over two hours, he gave a detailed
description of French rule in Indochina. Misery had been
widespread, he said, as the French demanded virtual slave
labour in the mines and plantations, annexed rice supplies,
imposed heavy taxes, and controlled the banks.

He stated that the French had 'arrogated to themselves the
privilege of issuing banknotes'; had built more prisons than
schools; silenced dissent by torture, imprisonment, and murder; forced opium and alcohol upon the people to weaken
them; and set up three separate political régimes in Northern,
Central, and Southern Vietnam in an effort to divide and
disrupt the nation. Yet, he said, when the Japanese invaded the
country in 1940 to set up bases in Indochina from which they
could launch their attacks on the Allies, the French did not
protect the Vietnamese, but gave in on bended knee to the
Japanese, and handed the country over to them; so, since the
summer of 1940 it had ceased to be a French colony and had
become a Japanese possession. When the Japanese
surrendered, the French fled, Emperor Bao Dai abdicated, and
the moment came to overthrow both the ancient hereditary
rulers and the power of the French, and to proclaim Vietnam
an independent country.

Then Ho Chi Minh stated that the Provisional Government
then formed declared that its members ceased to have any

connection with imperialist France, whose privileges and treaties regarding Vietnam were now null and void. Any attacks by the French would be resisted to the death. He considered that the Allies should recognise the independence of the Vietnamese, who, having doggedly opposed French domination for more than eighty years, had also courageously fought on the Allied side against Fascism. Then he ended his speech by declaring the independence of the Democratic Republic of Vietnam under its Provisional Government, and said:

> 'The people of Vietnam decide to mobilise all their spiritual and material forces and to sacrifice their lives and property, in order to safeguard their right of Liberty and Independence.'
>
> (From *Vietnam, A History in Documents*)

After Ho Chi Minh had concluded his speech, Vo Nguyen Giap addressed the people. He was pessimistic about de Gaulle's attitude towards Vietnamese aspirations for independence, and said the French government was already scheming to reinstate French civil servants in administrative offices in Vietnam, but, he said, 'We swear that we will defend our nation against them to the death.'

Ho Chi Minh proclaiming Independence 2nd September 1945

He quoted sayings of Chiang Kai-shek and President F.D. Roosevelt, evidently hoping that China and the US would be allies against imperialism. He drew attention to the many positive advances already made by the party, in establishing law and order in the Liberated Zone, distributing food supplies, organising an armed force and local defence units, and providing education. He warned his audience that there would be tough times ahead, that they could not rely on anyone for help, and would achieve success only through united support of their government. Reminding his listeners of the heroic resistance of their ancestors against their oppressors, he said that the Vietnamese people demanded independence, freedom, and equality, and if diplomacy and moderation did not work they would fight. He said:

'Under the leadership of the Provisional Government and Chairman Ho Chi Minh, our people will give all their wealth, their bones and blood to build and beautify the fatherland, to make our beloved Vietnam bright, wealthy and powerful after so many years of misery and exhaustion.'

(From *Vietnam: A History in Documents*,
ed. Gareth Porter)

At the close of Giap's speech the members of the Provisional Government were presented to the people, and each swore an oath of allegiance. Giap himself was chosen to be Minister of the Interior, while Pham Van Dong (who became Prime Minister in 1955) was Minister of Finance. In an effort to make the Provisional Government as truly representative of the people as possible, Ho Chi Minh had arranged that half its fourteen members were not communists. They were well-known Roman Catholics or leading nationalists from moderate groups.

Until late in the evening of Independence Day the streets of Hanoi remained packed with people, waving their flags and at intervals taking up the chant of 'Doc Lap' ('Independence'). So the crowd celebrated the birth of the Democratic Republic of Vietnam.

Appendix to Chapter Four
International Events
Affecting the Vietnamese Revolution
(1937-50)

1937-8
Japan, having signed the Anti-Comintern Pact with Germany, invaded China and held the coastline.

September 1939
Outbreak of World War II.

June 1940
Fall of France. (General de Gaulle fled to Britain and set up the Free French to resist the Germans. Marshal Pétain ruled unoccupied France from Vichy, collaborating with the Germans when they invaded the whole country in November 1942. De Gaullists and Pétainists competed with each other for power in the Far East.)

September 1940
The Japanese occupied Indochina.

June 1941
Germany invaded Russia.

December 7th 1941
The Japanese attacked the US fleet at Pearl Harbor, Hawaii. Next day the US declared war on Japan, and three days later Germany and Italy declared war on the US. By the following April (1942), the Japanese had seized Singapore, and invaded Java, Burma, and the Philippines, accepting the surrender of the US forces on the Bataan Peninsula.

1943-5
Beginning with the invasion of Guadalcanal, British Solomon Islands, the Allies mounted a counter-offensive against Japan, and retook the Philippines and Burma, and US Marines took Iwo Jima, though with heavy losses.(March 1945.)

August 1944
Meantime, in Europe, following the invasion of Normandy, Paris was liberated. In Russia, Germany had to retreat (surrendered officially in May 1945).

February 1945
At the second wartime summit meeting of Stalin, Churchill, and President Roosevelt, the last named gained Stalin's agreement for the USSR to join in the war against Japan. This meeting was at Yalta in the Crimea.

12th April 1945
President F.D. Roosevelt died, and was succeeded in the US presidency by Harry S. Truman, his vice-president. The change in administration marked a shift in US foreign policy away from tolerance of Vietnamese aspirations to a pro-French stance.

July-August 1945
At the Potsdam Conference, with regard to Indochina, the Allies agreed that Chiang Kai-shek would take charge of the surrender of Japanese troops north of the 16th parallel, while British troops under Admiral Mountbatten would occupy Vietnam south of that line.

6th August 1945
First atomic bomb was dropped on Hiroshima. Two days later, the USSR declared war on Japan, and the next day another atomic bomb was dropped, this time on Nagasaki.

August 15 1945
Japan agreed to surrender unconditionally.

September 1949
People's Republic of China proclaimed in Peking, recognising the DRV in January 1950.

CHAPTER FIVE

French Shadows on the Grass

The decision at Potsdam with regard to Indochina, giving Nationalist China a mandate to supervise the departure of the Japanese north of the 16th parallel, while Britain was to perform the same role south of that line, was convenient for the Allies; but it brought instant grief to the Vietnamese.

On September 14 1945 General Lu Han, with the vanguard of the Chinese army of occupation, arrived in Hanoi. Over the course of the following thirteen months more than 180,000 of his Chinese troops came to North Vietnam, for the purpose of arranging the exodus of only about 35,000 Japanese. The General regarded the time of occupation as a chance for systematic looting: the troops lived off the land. Exceeding their mandate they invaded the Laotian Highlands as well as the Red River Delta, in order to seize the opium harvest.

Many Vietnamese, besides being robbed of their food stores, were ruined because Lu Han's followers included many swindlers and carpetbaggers, who forced them to sell their property at rock bottom prices. They gave them almost worthless Chinese paper money and devaluated the piaster. Some of the Chinese formed syndicates and bought mines, plantations, and factories, or a large controlling interest in them, for prices far below their real value. Some of them stayed in Vietnam, and their descendants 'the boat people' experienced the communist backlash for this plundering.

Meanwhile in the south, patriotic emotion ran high and outbursts of violence increased rapidly. On the 13th of September General Sir Douglas Gracey, Commander, Allied Land Forces for Indochina South of the 16th Parallel, arrived in Saigon with the vanguard of 20,000 British Gurkhas of the

20th Indian Army. General Gracey's mandate was to restrict himself to disarming Japanese troops; but with puzzling insensitivity he ordered that all Vietminh be disarmed and be 'pacified' with all other Vietnamese, by the Japanese. When everyone went on strike as a result, he declared martial law. Then he freed French troops who had been interned by the Japanese: his mistake was to free all 1400 of them at once. They went on a rampage through the city, beating up or murdering anyone they happened to meet who was Vietnamese. Three divisions of French troops disembarked at Saigon during the ensuing month, and the communists and many other nationalists fled into the country, and joined the Binh Xuyen, Hoa Hao, and Cao Dai and their guerrilla fighters; the Binh Xuyen had already murdered many French in Saigon. Mistaken for a Frenchman, an OSS officer called Major Dewey was killed by a sniper near Saigon on 25th September. The first American to be killed in Vietnam, he had protested against General Gracey's tactless handling of the tricky political situation in Saigon. At the end of February 1946 the French and Chinese signed an agreement whereby, in return for giving up their bases in China, the French could bring in their troops north of the 16th parallel, and the Chinese would withdraw theirs (when they had had time to grab the opium harvest again).

As soon as the agreement was signed, the first instalments of a French force of 15,000 with 10,000 Vietnamese soldiers, began disembarking at Haiphong. Ho Chi Minh had been in France for several months, playing for time and trying to work out a compromise with the French, but getting the runaround. Meantime his next-in-command, Vo Nguyen Giap, had been consolidating the Vietminh control of the north and building up the army, so that when Ho returned in October 1946 there was a force of 60,000 waiting to fight the French.

Inevitably the chance came soon. After intercepting a Chinese junk bringing guns to the Vietminh, the French demanded that all the Vietnamese be disarmed; they refused, and street fighting broke out. From ships in the harbour the French shelled the residential parts of Haiphong, and about 6,000 people were killed, on 23rd November. In Hanoi more civilians were killed in the next few days by the French, who occupied some of the public buildings, and were evidently pushing for a confrontation. On 19th December Vietminh sappers blew up the city power station, and in the house-to-house fighting with French troops in the dark, some were killed but many were able to escape through a secret underground tunnel. Then fighting broke out in other parts of the country as well, and the French-Indochina War had begun.

On the same night Vo Nguyen Giap issued an order for a nationwide call to arms. Stating that the French had provoked hostilities in Hanoi, that the Fatherland was in danger and the time to fight had come, he went on to say:

'In accordance with the order of Chairman Ho and the Government, as Minister of National Defense, I order all soldiers of the National Guard and Self-defense militia in the Center, South and North to:
    Stand up in unison,
    Dash into battle,
    Destroy the invaders and save the country,
    Sacrifice to the last drop of blood in the struggle for the Independence and Unification of the Fatherland.
    The resistance will be long and extremely hard, but the just cause is on our side and we will definitely be victorious . . .'
    (From *Giap, Orders of the Day,* translated by Gareth Porter).

The French-Indochina War, which dragged on for eight years from 1946 to 1954, with terrible casualties on both sides, on first impression has such an archaic ambience that it is hard to realise that it took place after World War II, not at some time before it. It seems to belong to a much earlier era. Pictures of the soldiers of the French Foreign Legion marching immaculately and pointlessly down dusty Vietnamese roads, their white kepis gleaming, recall the romantic image of Beau Geste; and the same idea of the romance of life in the Legion is shown in a poem by Alan Seeger, beginning:

       'I have a rendezvous with Death
       At some disputed barricade,
       When Spring comes back with rustling shade,
       And apple-blossoms fill the air . . .'

(Alan Seeger was an American who joined the Legion in 1912 and died in 1916 in the First World War, leading a charge against a German stronghold.)

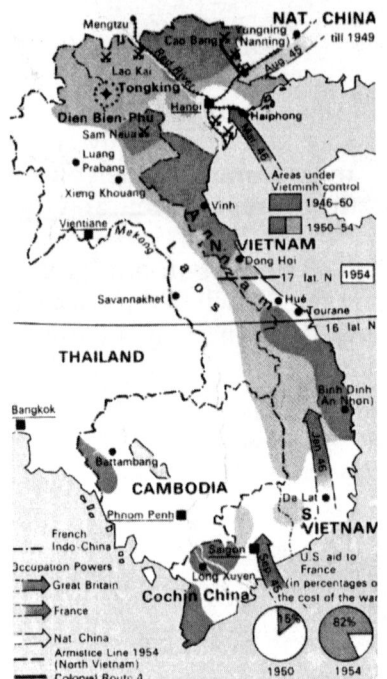

First Indochina War, 1945-54

The fighting on the side of the communists too seems at first to be happening in some long-gone period, as they employed ancestral hunting techniques with pitfalls, bows and arrows, and bamboo panji sticks to booby-trap the French, giving a false impression of backwardness.

In reality, however, something essentially modern was going on: the slow death of an old system and the agonising birth of a new one. The French anachronism lay not only in the legionnaires' uniforms, but in the cause for which they were fighting a rearguard action, and which was becoming an embarrassment to their friends: old-style autocratic colonialism. Meanwhile, the Vietnamese communists, making a connection between the past and the present, synthesised theories of war learnt from both oriental and European writers, and worked out a new dynamic of war for themselves, calling it 'dau tranh' ('the struggle movement'). Defined also as 'the people as instrument of war', 'dau tranh' presented a total way of life for everyone, adding psychological and semi-religious dimensions to a political and military plan.

During the war a pattern developed in which the French sought continually to confront the communists in formal open battle at which they excelled, and which Giap, after some terrible defeats, learned to avoid. Where there was an open plain, as around the town of Ninh Binh in the delta of the Day River, the French had a clear field of fire and in June 1951 inflicted severe losses on the Vietminh; after several such catastrophes Giap tried different tactics, as at Hoa Binh in November 1951, when his troops surrounded the French instead of meeting them head-on in a textbook-style battle. Gradually the Vietminh were more and more often able to be the ones to choose the time and place to fight.

The French never gave up a rather static concept of warfare, and would defend a post to the bitter end, long after it had lost whatever strategic importance, if any, it had had in the first place. With the lesson of the futility of the Maginot Line[1] still evidently unlearned, General Jean de Lattre de Tassigny, who took command of the French forces in Indochina in December 1950, set up more than 900 strongholds in the northern Red River Delta, to intercept the flow of arms coming to the communists from China, and to stop them from advancing south. Some of the strongholds were large complexes with bunkers and trenches, but many were like small old-fashioned movie set forts. As well as requiring men inside them, the forts needed mobile troops around them to guard them, but there were never enough; so the communists easily infiltrated them and slipped past the forts, which caused the French to be always on the defensive. The line of forts was dubbed the *de Lattre Line*. In contrast to the French idea of the importance of standing and defending a particular place, the Vietminh developed very rapid mobility, and a sense of the importance

---

1 Regarded as a symbol of the defensive thinking of the French military command, the Maginot Line was constructed in the time from 1929-34, and was named after André Maginot, French war minister of the period. It was a series of fortifications with extensive ramifications underground, stretching along the Franco-German border. The Germans bypassed it and invaded France via Belgium in May 1940.

of not being attached to any particular place when losses had become too great to make its defence worthwhile. They used to employ the 'human wave' technique in fighting, swarming in thousands over the French tanks and dropping hand grenades inside them. The daunting jungle terrain of the remote areas made surprise attacks and ambushes by the Vietminh guerrillas easy, and the French would often lose more men in convoys than there actually were in the outpost to which they were trying to bring supplies.

The French had a lot of faith in the effectiveness of their dinassauts. These were groups of fortified rivercraft, both large and small, carrying troops and supplies. Usually there were around twelve boats in the group, but there could be as many as twenty. Men lived aboard the boats, which were mostly modified World War II landing craft, made in Britain or the US. They had tank turrets, armour plating and artillery pieces. The trouble was that they presented a very vulnerable target, unless they were moored at the bank and hidden by overhanging foliage. There were ten dinassauts in all, eight used in the south and only two in the north. In planning to use them the assumption was made that the men in the boats would know where the enemy forces were in the jungle along the river banks, and could see them and fire on them, or make an informed decision as to whether to land or not. But usually they could not see them. Sometimes, however, a dinassaut was in the right place at the right time, and the men on board were able to make a surprise attack by night on an enemy stronghold, and could give support to other troops on shore; but often it was difficult to co-ordinate their movements with those of other detachments. (Later, in the US-Vietnam War, the US troops used helicopters to solve the co-ordination problems of rivercraft, but in the French Indochina War very few helicopters were available – only two in 1950, ten in 1952, and twenty-eight by the end of the war.)

The soldiers manning the dinassauts, in common with all other French troops, in spite of their individual valour, laboured under a system malaise emanating from top command. It was in essence a conceptual problem, a fuzziness over strategy and tactics. It was as if the French troops were never fully decided on their true aim: were they supposed to be holding an area, maintaining order and control and bringing in supplies, or was their main raison d'étre to launch assaults on enemy positions? The fundamentally conflicting demands of the tasks of maintaining long supply lines, while meantime luring the enemy into open battle, created a weakness in the French campaign which Giap perceived and was quick to exploit. Thousands of French troops were tied down along the de Lattre Line trying to stop the activities of about 80,000 communist guerrilla fighters, who clandestinely intercepted transport and supplies, blew up ammunition stores, and sabotaged motorised equipment, so that an estimated 40% arrived at its destination useless or badly damaged.

Like the dinassauts crews, other sections of the French forces suffered from system uncertainties and inconsistency at the top level of command. General de Lattre organised very efficient army units called groupes mobiles. These were regimental combat teams with up to two thousand men including commandos, heavily mechanised, with armoured scout cars, ranks, and artillery. They were terrifying and often successful, and individuals showed much bravery and dash. Collectively, however, the effects were inconclusive, and unless victory in combat at a particular location was co-ordinated with action elsewhere it often made little difference to the overall picture.

The communists knew, too, that they would have to find some way of solving the co-ordination problems on their side. Theoretical planning of communications, based on the assumption that it would be possible for groups of men to keep in touch with each other, never worked in Vietnam. Triple canopy jungle, impassable mountains or vast river deltas, kept people apart.

The French troops used 'crabs', which were light amphibious vehicles suited to wetlands. Unfortunately their tracks were fragile, so they often had to be carried, by dinassaut if one was at hand, or by two-and-a-half-ton trucks, to the spot where it was intended that the action should take place. But what if the enemy had other ideas, and did not attack where official paperwork had indicated that he would? The crabs would be useless if the trucks got bogged down or ran out of

Patrol Boats of the French 4th Dragoons in the Mekong Delta, 1952

fuel. So sometimes mechanised equipment created more problems than it solved.

In the film based on the book *The Guns of Navarone*, David Niven, in the role of a commando pilot, said as he was protesting against the order to go on yet another dangerous raid: 'I've been on dozens of 'parties' [special commando missions] and none of them made the slightest difference to the war'. The many thousands of French troops engaged in commando-type operations in Vietnam from 1946-54 must often have felt as he did. Many were very brave fighters parachuting deep into enemy country. Several units were merged under the general name of Groupement Mixte d'Intervention Aéroporte, usually called GMIs for short. By 1953 about 20,000 of them had spread through remote areas of Vietnam and over the border into Laos, along the upper reaches of the Mekong River. On the Chinese border in the north there was a large Vietminh base at Lao-Kay, where supplies and arms from China were stored. The GMIs made a successful raid there, destroying large quantities of goods and killing more than 150 of the enemy. They might have altered the course of the war if they had not been held back, for just as they were getting their act together and becoming successful, the French high command made a change of plan and ordered their materiél to be diverted to the area of Dien Bien Phu in readiness for the action there. The GMIs were relegated to a minor supportive role.

The GMIs worked a lot with natives, as many of them were assigned duties which came under the general term of pacification. Defined as 'clearing a given area of insurgents', the word acquired later very cynical overtones. How pacific it really was depended very much on the skill and personality of the Frenchman in charge, or French representative, in any particular place. There were instances of village huts being burned, and the chief killed if the people would not co-operate. Even before the war had officially begun, the legionnaires employed a technique called 'oilspot', radiating out in an ever-widening circle from a central hamlet which they had cleared by force, to flush out any communists believed to be hidden there. But hundreds of French officers made friends with the natives and were able to persuade them to fight for them, and to act as guides and go on reconnoitering expeditions for them. This was a remarkable achievement, for the retaliation from the communists for any collaboration with the French was violent: villages were burned down and heads impaled along the jungle paths. Some GMIs lived for months with the remote peoples of Vietnam and would take a wife from among them in order to gain their trust. This was, of course, not entirely for the native's benefit, but often was necessary to gain survival techniques in unfamiliar surroundings. The extreme daytime heat in the jungle highlands could change to bitter cold at night. Eerie disorienting mists would suddenly come down. The loneliness and constant fear were terribly hard on the French soldiers. Some became physically ill and some went mad.

The native peoples of the remote areas of Indochina were grouped together by the French under the general term of les montagnards. But there were big differences between the various tribes. Some were used to white men, and served the French out of hatred for the Vietnamese and their condescending ways towards them (but that did not necessarily mean that

'Crabs' of the French 1st Legion Regiment in Vietnam, 1950

they liked the French) but there were many others, about 700,000 aborigines, who had never heard of the Vietnamese, let alone the French. They had Malayan and Polynesian ancestors. Naked, silent, and dignified before strangers, they could easily slip away into the forest and avoid further contact.

From an anthropological standpoint the French made some glib assumptions about the natives' perceptions of themselves and of the fighting they were asking them to assist in. Their conception of events was magical, for they were animists; every tree and stream had its spirit, and surely if a white man emerged from the forest or dropped from the sky, in strange attire, he must be a spirit too and should be obeyed. Supposing, for instance, a tribe had no word for 'enemy' because they never had one, and had never thought in adversarial terms, then what would they make of the French request for help in fighting 'their enemies'? A lack of first names or of a word for 'I' would indicate too a fundamentally different way of thinking from that of western individualism.

After the fall of Dien Bien Phu in May 1954, when the French forces in the north were ordered to withdraw and fall back on Hanoi, the indigenous soldiers who had fought loyally beside them were abandoned and left behind by order of the French high command, overriding the protests of the officers who had trained them. Some managed to return to their home areas, but many never got back.

When open battles were fought in the French-Indochina War the number of casualties on either side were often in the thousands, though usually many more Vietminh died than French. At home the French got little sympathy for their suffering, or praise for their endurance and valour. Between 1946 and 1950 such was the instability of the French government that it changed hands no less than twelve times. There was constant criticism of the huge cost of the war, which failed to restore prestige France had lost to the Germans in World War II.

By means of politics as well as through force of arms, the French hoped to regain control in Vietnam. Except for a coastal area of Tonkin, where there were Catholic villages loyal to the French, the communists were much stronger in the north than in Cochinchina; so instead of negotiating with Ho Chi Minh, the French named Bao Dai as the official ruler. His ancestry gave him a legitimate claim, as he was a descendant of former emperors. However, general support for him never became very strong, for while many people in the south were anti-communists they were still nationalists and were anti-French too. Even Bao Dai himself was aware that 'the Bao Dai Solution' (to the country's conflict) was really a French solution, and that the French fully intended to take over the administration of the country again.

The real power, however, in Saigon and the surrounding area lay neither with the French nor the communists, but in the hands of the huge private armies, of about 10,000 men in all, belonging to the sects of the Hoa Hao, the Cao Dai, and the Binh Xuyen. The last named had very little claim to any religious qualities, but was more like a secret society, controlling the criminal underworld, and the gambling dens and brothels of Saigon, as well as the opium traffic. People were terrified of them. Each 'sect' had its own territory, with absolutely autocratic leaders like medieval warlords, and a hierarchy of army officers. Bao Dai gave them big concessions in return for cash and protection, and for the most part they sided with the French.

To this land of unpredictable guerrilla fighting, confusing divided loyalties, powerful sects, and secret kickbacks, the French brought the additional complexity of one of the most strangely-assorted armies ever known to history. There were over 350,000 of them, but only about 55,000 were actually French born. They got the command positions and the desk jobs at headquarters. There were 100,000 troops of the 'Associated States' of Laos, Cambodia and Vietnam, and many more Indochinese troops actually within the French Union Forces. There were thousands of volunteers from the French colonies of Morocco, Algiers, Tunis, and Senegal. The Foreign Legion's presence consisted of about 20,000 crack troops, among them many Germans, Czechs, and other Europeans, who had been prisoners-of-war in World War II. Logistics for such a mixed group could get bizarre: for instance, live sheep were imported for the Moroccans. The varying creeds of the troops had differing rules about food.

General de Lattre, who died of cancer in France in 1952, had planned that the French Union Forces in Vietnam should undergo a process of steadily increasing Vietnamization. The French called it jaunissement or 'yellowing' as they called the Vietnamese les jaunes ('the yellow ones'). The plan was unsuccessful. Although many thousand Vietnamese did fight for the French, true Vietnamization did not take place, as the Vietnamese soldiers never got to run the show themselves, or have complete authority. Of twenty-four battalions of Vietnamese under the French, only seven were commanded by their own country-men. At the end of the war only one percent of the Vietnamese troops were commissioned officers, and only five percent NCOs.

The heart of the matter was that the French had no real desire for social change in Indochina. They did not want the camaraderie of shared messes, and dreaded having to take orders from a Vietnamese superior officer, who, they were convinced, could not 'cope' like a Frenchman. As in the French civil administration offices, there were Frenchmen at every level making decisions and giving orders, thus preventing their Vietnamese colleagues from gaining experience in these processes.

Similarly, the Vietnamization of the pro-French amphibious forces was hampered by bureaucratisation and a central office mindset. Several French government sub-committees argued back and forth between Paris and Saigon for years, with incredible pettiness and acrimony, about such matters as whether the Vietnamese river forces should be placed under the command of the army or of the navy; and should they fly the French tricolour or a flag of their own, or both, or should there be an entirely new flag for the French Union Forces. Finally in October 1954 President Diem was able to found the Vietnamese Marine Corps, but by then it was too late for them to assist the French against the Vietminh.

A French government working so slowly that it defeated its own purposes; the habitual referral to Paris for rulings on all decisions; the general reluctance to delegate responsibilities to the Vietnamese; and the belief that French rule could go unchanged: these were all factors mitigating against the process of Vietnamization. They were characteristic of the time when French power in Vietnam was drawing towards its end, and so should be judged within their own historical perspective. Awareness of the needs of people of culture other than the dominating ones was unfashionable and uncommon. Little Rock, Arkansas, was not yet famous.[2] Other colonial powers had records like the French, of delay and ambivalence in allowing natives military authority. The British, with regard to the Indianisation of the army in India between the two wars, showed a similar pattern; there were procrastinating consultations with Westminster and, particularly among old officers, dread of being commanded by Asians and sharing

---

2   *Little Rock, Arkansas, became famous in the history of the US civil rights movement in September 1957, when rioting broke out and federal troops had to be called in to support the Supreme Court ruling of May 1954, that racial segregation in the public schools and colleges was unconstitutional.*

messes with them. There was a myth prevalent that Indians would crumble under pressure. So until the outbreak of World War II Indians only had command over Indian regiments; their pay was less than that received by their British counterparts; and the status of their commissions was lower.

Around Saigon, the French used to consider the practice of sniping at natives along the bank, from a boat on the Mekong River, as just part of 'la vie sportive', an afternoon's pleasure.

The seige of Dien Bien Phu, which lasted fifty-six days and ended with the surrender of the French forces on 7th May 1954, was the scene of the most grisly and desperate fighting of the war. It revealed vividly the fatal flaws in the French military system. The bravery of individuals was wasted by poor judgment at the top level of command, and mistaken assumptions about enemy strength and tactics. Dien Bien Phu was a remote outpost in the northwest uplands of Vietnam, near the border with Laos. It was in a hollow at the end of a long river valley; so the decision to strengthen its fortifications and defend it against the Vietminh was not only contrary to the promptings of common sense, but against time-honoured military lore, which had always taught soldiers never to await the enemy in a valley. The idea of digging themselves in there instead of keeping mobile placed the French in a static, defensive posture which they were never able to shake off.

The rationale behind the decision to make Dien Bien Phu a big fortified stronghold, and begin working on it in November 1953, was the belief that the Vietminh were planning to invade Laos so that they could attack the French forces from the rear. But from the outset there was disagreement among the French commanding officers on this point. Some of them did not think that fortifying Dien Bien Phu would stop the communists from going into Laos anyway. Some were not clear as to the purpose of the project, and wondered whether they were constructing a large centre for assault troops, or a base for supplies and for men doing pacification work. The French commander-in-chief went ahead with the plan in spite of the dissenting comments.

The commander-in-chief, who had arrived in Vietnam in May 1953, was General Henri Navarre. He was a cavalry officer with no previous experience in Indochina. He hoped that at Dien Bien Phu General Vo Nguyen Giap's troops would be led into a trap. He had trenches and dugouts built, World War I style, and fortified them with wooden supports and sandbags only, as he was convinced that the communists would not have any artillery. They did, however. They brought their big guns in pieces, carried for hundreds of miles by porters on foot, some using bicycles to push their load. They assembled them hidden in thick foliage in escarpments on the slopes surrounding the fort. They hid their assault troops in deep trenches cut zigzag very close to the outer French defences.

Unexpectedly, the communists had field radio and anti-aircraft guns. General Navarre, and General de Castries, the commander at Dien Bien Phu, thought it would be feasible to supply the garrison by air. But soon after the siege began in mid-March 1954 the Vietminh had knocked out the airstrip, destroying fourteen planes on the ground there, and a Vietminh sapper had crept through sewers and emerged to wreck eighteen transport planes at a French base near Haiphong. So all supplies had to be dropped by parachute, and pilots had to get through the murderous anti-aircraft fire from the enemy lines, which brought down forty-eight planes during the fifty-six days of the siege. It was seventy-five miles to the nearest base, and only a maximum of sixty tons of matériel a day could be delivered for the sixteen thousand men in the fort. (The Vietminh troops laughed their age-old ironic Vietnamese laughter if a gust of wind blew a parachute bearing a crate of choice French wine, meant for the garrison's officers, into their lines instead.)

General Navarre, who had another campaign taking up twenty-five battalions in progress along the coast of Tonkin during the siege of Dien Bien Phu, had seriously underestimated the numbers of enemy troops gathering around the forts. They were surrounding it in ever tightening circles, as French intelligence men and scouts reported, but the general ignored their warnings.

During the siege an estimated forty thousand communist troops were fighting, while another forty thousand were engaged in various backup and supply roles. In attacks they would swarm onto the barricades in terrifying human waves, chanting over and over 'Tien Len! Doc Lap!' (Forward!

Freedom!) In the last days of the siege the French wounded could not be moved or tended, and lay with the dead where they fell. The fort became a charnel house. In the end, after two days of continuous assaults, the French ran out of ammunition and the Vietminh overran the ramparts and hoisted their flag upon them. It was 7th May 1954.

The fall of Dien Bien Phu marked the end of the war, to most of the troops, but the official cease-fire was not proclaimed until 27th July in the north, and 7th August in the south, respectively.

Only seventy-eight men of the huge French garrison escaped freely; killed or missing numbered over three thousand, and many thousands more were taken prisoner and sent off on a terrible sixty-day march to prisons and prison camps in the Red River Delta. Many died on the way. (A Czech survivor of the long march, one of the legionnaires at Dien Bien Phu, speaking in 1986 on a talk show on US public television, said that he had been treated fairly by the Vietminh, had received the same daily rice ration as his captors, and on reaching Hanoi had been returned to French officials there.)

The Vietminh lost eight thousand dead at Dien Bien Phu, and in the whole war an estimated five hundred thousand, three times more than the French. The French losses at the siege, though heavy, were not in themselves enough to end the war; but the will to fight on was gone. The troops felt no one cared about their suffering.

During the long years of the war, and particularly in the months following a communist defeat, Vo Nguyen Giap used to retreat to his remote field headquarters at Pac Bo, north of Hanoi, and use the time to plan the next offensives in great detail. Sand table models were made of the terrain in question. He would calculate exactly how many porters would be needed to supply a given number of fighting troops, how much each one could carry and how far he or she could go in a day. For the attack on Dien Bien Phu he worked out that the attackers would require one hundred tons a day of arms, spare parts, and food, and the maximum load per person was a hundred pounds. So there was a continuous line of hundreds of people working their way down the jungle trails towards Dien Bien Phu.

Behind them, driving as far as the rough roads would take them, were Chinese people manning Russian-made trucks. The People's Republic of China, proclaimed at the end of 1949 in Peking. made an agreement on 18th January 1950 with the Democratic Republic of Vietnam, giving it diplomatic recognition and in return for trade, military aid on an enormous scale, up to an estimated four thousand tons a month by 1954. There were big camps north of the border where Vietminh troops could be trained. About eight thousand Chinese advisors and technicians came to help. (The figures vary according to the slant of particular historians: French ones emphasise the magnitude of the assistance from China, whereas Vietnamese ones tend to play it down, and feel that their leaders taught Mao Tse-tung the art of guerrilla warfare, not that he taught them.)

Among the documents grouped under the title of *The Pentagon Papers*[3] was a cablegram from Douglas Dillon, US Ambassador to France at the time, to the US Secretary of State, John Foster Dulles, on 5th April 1954. The ambassador stated that General Navarre had reported that, besides the truck drivers, Chinese troops had been observed manning the Vietminh's radar-controlled anti-aircraft guns (captured in Korea) at Dien Bien Phu; they were also setting up and

---

3   *The Pentagon Papers* was the title given to a massive collection of top-secret narrative passages and related documents, outlining the rise of involvement of the US in Indochina from 1945 to 1968. It was commissioned by Robert S. McNamara, who was Secretary of Defense, in 1967. It contained 2.5 million words in 47 volumes.

On 13 June 1971 *The New York Times* began publishing a series of articles based on the Papers, but after the third article had appeared, the Justice Department obtained a temporary restraining order forbidding further publication on grounds of national security. The administration hoped for a permanent ban. But supporters of *The New York Times*, and *The Washington Post*, which had just begun producing articles based on the Papers, argued that they belonged in the public domain.

On 30th June 1971, after several days of heated controversy, the Supreme Court, on the basis of the right to a free press as stated by the First Amendment of the US Constitution, gave the newspapers permission to continue publication of the articles in question.

maintaining special telephone lines for the Vietminh, and several Chinese technical advisors were giving assistance at the Vietminh headquarters. The French, who had already tried using napalm themselves on the enemy lines, asked for US bombers, based on aircraft carriers, to help them at Dien Bien Phu. The request was refused on the grounds that it would have required the assent of Congress before it could be acted upon; but a plan called 'Operation Vulture', by which the US would drop some small atomic bombs on the Vietminh at Dien Bien Phu was discussed, and rejected. There was fear of being drawn into a war with China.

However, President Eisenhower and his Special Committee on Indochina, meeting on 30th January 1954, agreed to send two hundred US Air Force mechanics to North Vietnam to help the French, who had requested four hundred. The rather unrealistic stipulation was made, that they should only work on airfields entirely safe from capture.

The proxy aspect of the war had been clear for several years, not only because of the aid to the Vietminh flowing from the People's Republic of China, but also because of the already substantial aid to the French forces which had been supplied by the US since 1950. In the summer of that year President Truman had authorised the setting up of USMAAG (United States Military Assistance Advisory Group) in Indochina to help the French, and had also agreed to send them cash amounting to ten million dollars. More and more aid followed until the US was paying about 82% of the cost to France of waging the war. The US provided massive quantities of military hardware as well as cash; journalist and author Michael Maclear reported the amounts as follows: fourteen hundred tanks, three hundred and forty planes, three hundred and fifty patrol boats, thousands of rounds of small arms, and millions of bullets.

The Minister for National Defence in France at the time of the siege of Dien Bien Phu was Mr René Pleven. After visiting Indochina in February 1954 he suggested that negotiations for the settlement of the war be put on the agenda of the Four Power Conference which would be meeting in Geneva in April. The four powers were the USSR, the USA, the UK and France. The French government agreed; however, the Democratic Republic and the Bao Dai government members in Vietnam, and the Cambodians and Laotians, only came round to the idea of negotiating after a lot of agonising and dissension about it. Their gut-level fears were well-founded, for at the Geneva Conference Vietnam became drawn irrevocably into the orbit of international cold war power politics.

So the war with France officially drew to a close at last. To an uncanny extent the experience of the French in waging a war in Vietnam foreshadowed that of the United States in later decades. The very same gremlins haunted them: fuzziness at the top about strategy, poor co-ordination between different sections of their forces, over-reliance on mechanised gear, under-estimation of the enemy, a western mindset brought to bear on a war fought in an oriental setting, and a touching faith in the policies of 'Pacification' and 'Vietnamization'.

No wonder that in Vietnam some Americans thought that they could still see, in their mind's eye, French shadows on the grass.

A landscape near Moc Chau on the road to Dien Bien Phu (Tim Page)

CHAPTER SIX

Vietnam and System Power:
A Dialogue

Written in the form of an imaginary dialogue between a student of the US-Vietnam War, and the author, this chapter focuses on some of the characteristics of the big systems involved, and the ways in which these characteristics affected the course of events.

For instance, some of the questions raised concern the cold war as a political system – what was Vietnam's place in it? How did the CIA become deeply involved in covert operations in Vietnam? How did the American military-industrial complex achieve the power to do a lot of bombing, far in excess of the assumed needs of the situation? How did the unity of command in the PAVN (People's Army of Vietnam) differ from the divided command of the US forces? How did the somewhat messianic view of warfare held by the North Vietnamese, i.e. a grand design leading to a distant glorious goal, compare with the US approach?

Let's begin with the cold war.

I. Vietnam and the Cold War

Question:
> At the end of the last chapter, which was about the French Indochina War, 1946-54, you described how the Laotians, Cambodians, and Vietnamese dreaded going to the conference at Geneva, because they rightly guessed that they would be drawn into the orbit of international cold war politics.
>
> Could you say more about this, to explain?

Answer:
> Yes; it was a strange conference, the 'Geneva Accords' of 1954, as many of the delegates weren't on speaking terms with each other. People scurried about wheeling and dealing behind the scenes. The US delegation was forbidden to speak to the Chinese or the North Vietnamese, and the French Foreign Secretary, M Bidault, would not speak to the DRV people either.
>
> In *The Emancipation of French Indochina*, Donald Lancaster related how Mr Molotov of the USSR and Sir Anthony Eden of Great Britain, took turns at chairing the conference. Sir Anthony seemed not to be aware of what was really going on, and was outwitted by Molotov; and he squelched Pham Van Dong of North Vietnam when he complained of French harshness in Vietnam. The officials from South Vietnam trailed about, not being told anything.
>
> Major Patti, in his book *Why Vietnam?* described how sometimes delegates who weren't supposed to speak to one another in public, but had known each other previously, would meet by chance in an elevator and fall apart with irrepressible laughter, before joining their official groups with deadpan expressions.
>
> France and the USSR got what they wanted in terms of cold war politics; and for an oriental version of the same, so too did Chou En-lai, Premier and Foreign

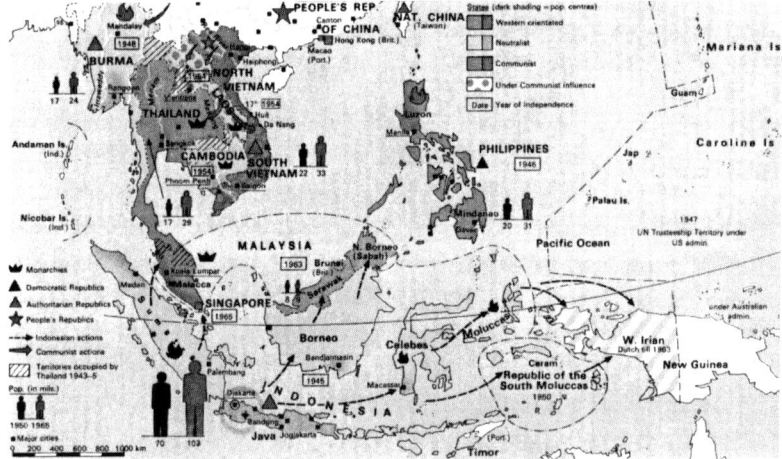

South-East Asia, 1945-65

Minister of the People's Republic of China (who also was snubbed by Sir Anthony, for being too long-winded in talking about dialectical materialism). Privately Mr Molotov agreed with M Mendès-France, Premier of France, that if he would withdraw French support from the proposed 'European Defence Community' (which was to be a western European military alliance against the USSR) he would support the partition of Vietnam at the 17th parallel, and the protection of French interests in South Vietnam.

Chou En-lai, for his part, agreed with the French not to support Pham Van Dong's claim that the resistance movements in Laos and Cambodia should be recognised. (The DRV was all right in Chinese eyes, as long as it was just a tiny buffer state on the rim of China's vastness, but it wouldn't do to let it harbour any ideas about expansion into Laos and Cambodia, and about becoming powerful in its own right.) Pham Van Dong never forgot this let-down.

So the seeds of tragedy were sown, and the Democratic Republic of Vietnam, in spite of military victory, had to give way to cold war pressures from both west and east.

Q.   It's my understanding that in spite of the scheming on the sidelines, a plan for stability in Vietnam was laid down at Geneva. Why didn't it work out?

A.   Because no machinery was put in place to enforce the rulings of the conference, which were circumvented by both sides. It had been agreed at Geneva that free elections would be held by 1956, but they never were. The partition at the 17th parallel was meant to be temporary, but was not removed till the communist victory in 1975. No foreign troops were to be allowed in the country, but the US did send more troops, giving them a semi-civvy name. Their MAAG – Military Assistance and Advisory Group – was not disbanded. They sent aid to the Vietnamese instead of to the French as formerly. The French forces left; an International Control Commission, with members from Canada, India, and Poland, was set up to see fair play but had no policing or military clout and could only complain. The members quarrelled among themselves and it was suspected that the North Vietnamese had manipulated them.

The Geneva Accords had stipulated that there was to be free movement across the 17th parallel for any people who wanted to resettle. So, many covert agents were able to move back and forth too. The US set up the Saigon Military Mission to help the government of President Diem of South Vietnam engage in covert paramilitary attacks, disinformation, and psychological warfare against the communists, who were doing the same sort of things against the South.

As a kind of insurance policy against the spread of communism in South-East Asia, the US set up SEATO, the South-East Asia Treaty Organisation, in September 1954, by which various western nations, with their oriental allies, agreed to come to the aid of each other, if any member was attacked, or 'weakened by internal subversion'.

So the cold war was off and running in Vietnam.

Q.   I've been wondering about your use of the term 'cold war'. Are you using it in a general sense, meaning veiled hostility or a hidden power plan, or does it have a more precise meaning within this context?

A.   Both sides of your question have a lot of truth in them. It is used in a general sense, but has a particular meaning in connection with US foreign policy since World War II.

The term 'cold war' had the effect of obscuring its true nature. It seems to imply that it is pacific and not really warlike, yet acts of terrorism against civilians can be part of a cold war plan, which can also include actual combat duties. Often these are undertaken sporadically by small units, as compared to large pitched battles in an openly declared war. Intelligence work plays a key role in a cold war. In Vietnam a mixed bag of counter-insurgency and pacification programs, nicknamed 'WHAM' (an acronym for 'Winning Hearts and Minds'), was part of an ongoing cold war process from the fifties to the seventies.

Cold war activities don't take place in a vacuum but are set up within a framework of military power, and have at their back the might of a powerful army. Sometimes cold war tactics have been used as a preparation for armed conquest of a given area: the 'Greater East Asian Co-Prosperity Sphere', described in Chapter 3, is an example from Japan.

Mao Tse-tung and General Vo Nguyen Giap were both strongly influenced by a Chinese general called Sun Tzu, who wrote a short book on *The Art of War*. He lived around 500 BC. It's believed that Napoleon read his book in a French translation, and was always on a winning streak as long as he followed Sun Tzu's advice, and began to lose when he forgot it. Sun Tzu said some things that sound like the cold war: e.g., that certainly it was good to win a battle, but it was much smarter to conquer without fighting. He said spies were a must for any country, to get advance information on the enemy's moves and to sow disharmony among his ranks: 'Be subtle! be subtle! and use your spies for every kind of business' (From *The Art of War*, by Sun Tzu, edited by James Clavell).

Q.   Returning to modern times, how would you describe the cold war system of US foreign policy after World War II?

A.   The cold war system of US foreign policy since WWII is usually considered to have four main aspects, all inter-connected:

1.   The concept of a Grand Area, or geo-political zone, dominated by the US not only militarily but financially as well.
2.   The idea of communism as a constant threat of crisis proportions, which if not checked would gain momentum like falling dominoes, or act like one rotten apple in a barrel infecting all the good ones, whichever metaphor is preferred.
3.   This threat requires a constant policy of 'Containment', for which is needed:
4.   Continuing expansion of a huge military-industrial complex.

Depending on the point of view, some historians feel the emphasis is wrong in this list, and the first three concepts are all meant for the over-riding purposes of No.4, the military-industrial complex.

Q.   Do you connect these ideas with President Truman?

A.   Yes, you could say he was the prime mover during his presidency, 1945-53.
     On 12th March 1947 he made a statement which became known as the Truman Doctrine. He said:

'I believe that it must be the policy of the United States to support free peoples who are resisting attempted subjugation by armed minorities or by outside pressures.'

'Free people' here mean anti-communist ones even if they were fascist; so this was a declaration that the US would be intervening anywhere to suppress communist or even mildly socialist, uprisings.
     The Truman Doctrine set US foreign policy on an anti-Russian course for several decades. Tragically,

compassion and regard for human rights were not considered relevant to the cold war framework, so weren't added to the four points listed above. So it came about that the policy of 'Containment', which sounds rather defensive and mild, was characterised by a pattern of violent intervention by the US in various countries, e.g., from Greece in 1947, through Guatemala in 1954, the Dominican Republic in 1965 and later indirectly or by proxy, in El Salvador and Nicaragua.

Q. Who first connected the phrases about the rotten apples and falling dominoes to US cold war policies?

A. Dean Acheson, Secretary of State under President Truman, explaining to congressmen why US troops were intervening in Greece in 1947, said: 'Like apples in a barrel infected by one rotten one, the corruption of Greece would infect Iran and all to the east . . .'[1]

He went on to say that the infection (of communism) would spread to Africa through Asia Minor, and to Europe through Italy and France.

Q. But I thought some of the Greek rebels were anti-Nazis and mild socialists and patriots, not all communists?

A. Yes, so I understand. President Truman, anxiously watching Russian expansion in eastern Europe, sometimes saw a Russian hand in an insurgency when maybe there wasn't one.

In cold war language 'communist' could be a label applied in a monolithic way to any person or state with ideas ranging from really Marxist to sympathy for the underdog; and a land might be called communist or considered influenced by communism if, becoming democratic and stable, it began to prosper for itself, and ceased to contribute raw materials to the Grand Area (e.g., in Chile, Dr Allende planned to nationalise the copper mines owned by US subsidiaries, with tragic results in 1973).

The dominoes you asked about were mentioned by President Eisenhower in 1954.

---

1   From a quotation in *Superpowers in Collision*, by Noam Chomsky et al.

A cartoon drawing of President Truman (David Smith)

Q.   How does what you were saying about cold war policies throw light on the origins of the US-Vietnam War? I mean, what do you see as 'the Vietnam Connection' here?

A.   I think the connection lies in Vietnam's importance as a rotten apple country in the cold war scheme of things.

In *The Pentagon Papers* there's a passage from a policy statement making this point, from the National Security Council, 1952, on 'United States Objectives and Courses of Actions with Respect to South-East Asia' (meaning Burma, Thailand, Indochina, Malaya, and Indonesia).

It states that:

'In the absence of effective and timely counteraction, the loss of any single country would probably lead to relatively swift submission to, or an alignment with, communism by the remaining countries of this group. Furthermore, an alignment with communism of the rest of South-East Asia and India, and in the longer term, of the Middle East (with the probable exceptions of at least Pakistan and Turkey), would in all probability progressively follow: such widespread alignment would endanger the stability and security of Europe.

Communist control of all South-East Asia would render the US position in the Pacific offshore island chain precarious, and would seriously jeopardise fundamental US security interests in the Far East. ' (From *The Pentagon papaers, Chapter One, The Truman and Eisenhower Years, 1945-60*).

The report stated that the loss of any country of South-East Asia to communist aggression would have critical psychological, political, and economic consequences. Pressure might be put upon Japan to become communist.

A cartoon by Toles, '*At the Vietnam Memorial*'

Q.   But these dire predictions haven't come to pass, have they?

A.   No. I suppose what I have in mind is Vietnam's perceived, rather than real, apple-rottenness, to coin a phrase; that is, the effect of Vietnam becoming communist hasn't been contagious to other countries, as imagined by the authors of this policy statement.

Q.   These cold war principles, I imagine, started off as abstractions, semantics only, if you like; how did President Truman go about making them become actual policy guidelines affecting events?

A.   By legislation – preceded and followed, as you suggest, by much discussion in think tanks in the State Department.

President Truman understood the power of bureaucracies, and knew he was going to need some, so why not make his own? (So he seems to have thought.)

So in 1947 he brought into being the National Security Act, which, with amendments later, created the National Security Council, the Central Intelligence Agency, and the National Military Establishment, later to become the Department of Defense.

In the spring of 1950 a joint think tank made up of people from the Department of State and the Department of Defense produced a famous cold war policy statement called 'NSC [National Security Council] 68.' The authors said the US ought to get started on a vast re-arming and arms manufacturing program, to be ready to stop any expansion by the USSR.

At the end of June 1950 President Truman, in an official statement from the White House, said he pledged the US to military intervention to stop further communist aggression in Asia. So, he sent troops to South Korea, money and arms to help the French in Vietnam in their war against Ho Chi Minh and company, helped to repress the communist rebellion in the Philippines, and sent the Seventh Fleet to Formosa (called Taiwan since 1945) in case it was attacked by the People's Republic of China.

At the time President Truman didn't think the job of

policing communism would take very many men.

Q. A double-barrelled question: why do you think the National Security Act was historically significant, and why did you say President Truman needed some bureaucracies?

A. He needed them for waging the cold war, for he realised that in the cold war the real winners are not heroes but bureaucrats.

Q. Hm. I'm not sure that makes it any clearer to me – would you say more about the NS Act, to clarify the issue?

A. Yes; I would say that bureaucracies are of the very essence of cold war politics: their potential for enormous power, secrecy, almost unlimited cash available, fuzzy accountability – 'Sorry sir/ma'am, not my department' (a characteristic phrase, don't you think?). All these things make them pretty impregnable.

The NS Act paved the way for the development of three powerful groups, as mentioned above: the National Security Council (for foreign policy decision-making), the CIA, and the Department of Defense. The Act set the government into a pattern of ever-increasing bureaucratisation, as each of these groups became more complex, and begot their own committees or sub-committees or various departments. The US-Vietnam War, with its fiercely competing sections of the US forces, and its huge US army bases requiring massive supplies, was a bureaucrats' war par excellence. It provided marvellous scope for making money on government contracts for arms and logistic needs of all kinds, justified by North Vietnam's role as an enemy in cold war logic.

The report 'NSC 68' gave official blessing to an immense surge, during President Truman's time, in the manufacture in the US of all and sundry arms and weaponry: guns, tanks, bombers, the lot. The DOD (Dept. of Defense) became a huge commercial set-up, and big corporations such as General Dynamics, Lockheed, and Boeing got monopoly power. President Truman ringed the world with US military bases. The interlocking needs of the big arms corporations, the

DOD or Pentagon, and the politicians became known as
the US military-industrial complex.

Q.   How did this work, and how did it affect what
happened in Vietnam?

A.   Take a break and we will get to it in the next section.

*A cartoon by Toles,
'Nicaragua is not
like Vietnam'*

II. Vietnam and the
US Military-Industrial Complex

Q.   How did the term 'military-industrial complex' originate,
     and what does it mean?
A.   I think President Eisenhower of the US was the first to
     use it, in his farewell speech at the end of his term of
     office, which lasted from 1953 to 1961. As the US econ-
     omy had become increasingly dominated by huge
     defence contracts, he gave a warning in his speech that
     the combined power of the large arms industry and the
     immense military establishment was getting out of hand and
     influencing the government too much. This three-
     cornered alliance between the corporations, the Pentagon
     and the Congress he called the military-industrial
     complex.
        It's also called the 'iron triangle', or the 'golden troika',
     I believe. Basically it's a 'You scratch my back and I'll
     scratch yours' arrangement for profit for all concerned.
     There's a revolving door system by which many officers
     in the Pentagon who have procured lucrative orders for
     a firm, receive excellent consulting positions in that firm
     when they retire. An officer who obtained, let's say, a big
     contract for a firm to build six battleships, will be
     rewarded with a handsomely paid job in that firm; and
     meanwhile congressmen who agree to vote for the pas-
     sage of legislation granting money to be spent on these
     battleships, will gets lots of funds for their campaign
     expenses from the battleship firm. It's all very cosy.
Q.   Well, what's wrong with that? Seems fair to me. People
     are being repaid for their co-operation.
A.   Yes, but unless there's some way of monitoring these big
     contracts, the system sets up a dangerous situation in
     which the people who arranged these contracts are the
     very ones who profit from them and get easy access to
     bundles of government money.

A cartoon by Oliphant, 'Can You Imagine???'

The system inevitably gives priority to profit and to the most lucrative contracts, not to the immediate needs of the fighting troops. The battleships mentioned above, for instance, might be obsolete before they are even launched; but that would be a minor consideration.

Inspection routines can get pretty sloppy, too, if the person who's supposed to be checking out a new tank or gun or what-have-you, knows that if he passes the item as OK, he'll get a good kickback from the firm producing it. The military-industrial complex is certainly strongly established and hard to change.

Q.   What makes it so unstoppable, do you think?

A.   Its hold over the American political process, both in the constituencies and in Washington.

Members of Congress know that if they're to survive politically they must make sure big defense contracts are continually steered towards the state or district they represent, not only for the sake of jobs and wealth flowing to these areas, but for the resulting contributions for their expensive campaigns. The number of jobs involved runs to thousands and thousands, because any big military contract involves the services of hundreds of sub-contractors. Since World War II whole towns have come into being in the US wherever big plants serving defense orders have been located, creating lots of spin-off jobs in the background on the supply side.

A US senator speaking recently on a television programme made very clear what power the military-industrial complex has over politics. He said that he'd always supported SDI (Strategic Defense Initiative, or Star Wars) because the project brought jobs to his constituency (Texas). He said this in a bland inoffensive way, evidently unaware that there could be anything wrong with supporting a defense project (estimated in 1983 to be costing $400 a minute), not because he thought it would provide safety for his country, but because it brought prosperity to the area where the people voting for him were residing.

Q.   I see how the MIC – as I'll call the military-industrial complex for short – works on the local scene; how does it influence events in Washington?

A.   There the pressure on members of the House to support defense projects is intense and continuous because of the power of lobbyists and PACs, or political action committees. The latter are groups of people representing special interests such as certain corporations, business or labour groups, who raise money among themselves to give to people's campaigning expenses. There's a limit set on the amount of money a PAC can give to one candidate for office, but a candidate can get money from lots of PACs at the same time. (A dairy industry PAC once gave President Nixon generous funds, so that he would agree to what they wanted: namely, to raise the retail price of milk.)

There used to be a clause in the US Code called Section 611, by which corporations having government contracts were not allowed to have PACs. This was cancelled in 1973; however, even before that, there were always lots of lobbyists for the big arms manufacturers.

How the system works is basically this way: a lobbyist gets a large fee from a corporation to lobby congressmen, making it worth their while to support some big project. (A side-effect is that big items such as helicopters get more attention than more humdrum but necessary orders, like ones for spare parts.) Lobbyists earn fantastic fees. Outside one of the committee hearing rooms in Congress there's a hallway nicknamed Gucci Gulch, because of the expensive Italian shoes the lobbyists often wear while they're milling about the hallway, waiting to buttonhole important committee members. They offer lots of perks to their clients – gourmet lunches, weekends at exclusive golf clubs, lavish parties, and extravagant Christmas gifts – you name it. They are often very knowledgeable, and provide members with well-researched, up-to-the-minute information on the matter at hand, such as details about a proposed new tank or submarine to be built.

Again, there's a revolving door element about it all: an ex-congressman has often obtained a very good position as lobbyist for a particular group or corporation because he has supported legislation, for instance, giving them tax concessions; and because of his inside knowledge of the government scene. There are thousands of lobbyists in Washington, thirty for each member of Congress, it's estimated.

Q.   All this pressure put on Congress to approve big spending for defense items – what connection has that with what went on in the US-Vietnam War? I can't really see what they had to do with each other.

A.   Oh, I think it had absolutely everything to do with how the war was fought and how the US troops lived in Vietnam; the characteristic ambience of the war, of malaise in the midst of plenty for the Americans, came directly from the power of the MIC. You see, if to produce vastly more and more arms and military supplies of all kinds, adds up to more and more profit at home, then the name of the game in the US-Vietnam War was for the big arms firms to send more and more to Vietnam, until there was much, much too much of everything.

Lobbyists with tax loopholes to defend crowd outside the House Ways and Means Committee hearing room. The hallway is named after their favorite footwear

TIME, MARCH 3, 1986

Lobbyists in 'Gucci Gulch'

Have you ever wondered about pictures you've probably seen, of US troops in the jungle weighed down with all kinds of gear? Some got footrot – a fungus – and some young men died of heatstroke with never a wound. They carried the doom-laden M16 rifle which, owing to rivalry among gunpowder firms and to fudged tests, was passed for use in Vietnam, where it would jam hopelessly. Men were found dead, crouching, as they tried desperately to fire their jammed M16s.

By contrast, their enemies often wore just black pajamas run up on an old sewing machine in a tunnel room; and perhaps they had a conical hat, and 'Ho Chi Minh' sandals made out of old tire rubber. They travelled as light as possible, even when in uniform.

Q. Hm, yes, I understand. What other instances of oversupply – or inappropriate, unhelpful provision, have you noticed in that era? – that of the US-Vietnam War, I mean.

A. The lavishly equipped US bases are one example, which I'd like to speak of again later.

Most of all, however, I think the bombing and chemical warfare carried out by the US in Vietnam illustrate the profit motive of the MIC, and its credo that 'more' equates with 'better'. The enormous amount of chemicals and number of bombs used is hard to grasp. More bombs were dropped than in World War II; there were 500 pounds of them for every person in Vietnam; twenty-one million bomb craters were made in South Vietnam alone.

There were deadly napalm and phosphorous bombs, and a large one called the 'Daisy Cutter', which, dropped from a parachute, destroyed all life over an area about the size of ten football fields. There were various kinds of fragmentation and cluster bombs used; these could split into tiny pellets that became embedded deep in the body, penetrating even a foetus in the womb.

Enormous quantities of defoliants and toxic chemicals, particularly three called Agents Orange, White, and Blue, were sprayed from planes onto the land, destroying crops and causing terrible sickness, birth deformities, and water pollution; these were dropped without discrimination, some of the chemicals falling on montagnard country.

Q. Was a deliberate effort made to bomb civilian targets?

A. It certainly seems so, particularly in the bombing of the north in the years 1965-67, in President Johnson's time.

During that period hearings were held in Stockholm and Copenhagen by the International War Crimes Tribunal. Various witnesses gave evidence about what was happening in Vietnam. The proceedings were recorded in a book called *Against the Crime of Silence*. In appendices it lists US air attacks on DRV medical facilities 1965-67, and schools attacked by the US up to the end of 1966.

Three hundred and ninety-one schools were bombed; one witness described how, when an elementary school was hit during school hours, pieces of dismembered children were spewed into the air and scattered for several hundred yards along with the debris of the building. A little girl on the way to school saw her friend's head blown off and lower bowel disgorged onto the sidewalk by a direct hit. After that she went mad and couldn't stop laughing.

Q. Oh, why are you telling me this?
A. Partly, I suppose, because I think such scenes shouldn't be forgotten and because they show only too graphically the over-kill brought about by over-supply by a dominant MIC. Do you want them sanitised?
Q. No. How many medical places were hit at that time?
A. Ninety-five medical establishments of all kinds were raided: clinics, hospitals, sanatoria, medical schools, etc.

That's a misleading figure, though, because some were bombed several times. Some places got more than one attack on the same day.

It was reported that the Hospital of Quang Binh Province was bombed 11 times, that of Ha Tinh Province 7 times, and the Hospital of Huong Khe district of Ha Tinh province was hit 8 times.

Unfortunately, it had been in the fields of education and health care that the DRV had made some improvement since 1954.

Q. I've heard about the Vietnamese lepers' town which was destroyed in the war. Where was it located?
A. It was at Quinh Lap in Nghe An Province.

The destruction of the Lepers' Town of Quinh Lap was a baffling episode in the war. Between June and

August 1965 it was bombed 39 times, with high explosive and fragmentation bombs. Dr Francis Khan reported to the Tribunal at Stockholm that among the ruins were found missile fragments, which could have been fired from a ship close to shore.

The Lepers' Town was in a very isolated and hard-to-reach location, in a narrow valley, near the sea but surrounded by hills. It was far from any target of military value, and on its roofs the Red Cross was prominently displayed. Of its 160 buildings not one was left intact, and many were pounded to rubble.

In one raid 120 people were killed and over a thousand were wounded. Nineteen died of wounds later. The surviving patients had to seek shelter in caves in the hills.

Quinh Lap had been a special place. Begun in 1957 and completed in 1959, it was known internationally as a research center for the study of leprosy, and as a model for the best possible care of lepers. An estimated 4000 lepers, of whom 1000 had been cured, had been treated there. There was a trade school, cultural centre, theatre library, hospital, church and pagoda, and service and technical buildings. But after the raids there were big craters everywhere.

Q.   How was evidence about Quinh Lap, and other 'targets', collected?

A.   Commissions of enquiry were set up internationally, from Sweden, France, Finland, Japan, and the US (on behalf on the University of California at Berkeley). There were individuals enquiring from other countries too; they and the members of the commissions visited attacked sites, and checked with local people and officials of the DRV, as to their accounts of these events. Then they reported to the Tribunal.

Q.   Could it be that the Lepers' Town was bombed 39 times by default, as it were, because nobody was counting the number of sorties against the same place?

A.   Well, perhaps there was no individual whose particular business it was to count them, so it wasn't done. Lack of co-ordination in US air command may have been a factor. On the other hand, one wonders why no one even said, 'Hey, you guys, we already bombed the lepers 38 times – are you sure we're supposed to bomb 'em one more time?'

Q. That prompts another query: I have trouble with your reference to 'system power' – as if it alone is always dominating the course of events. Don't you feel the individual has some input?

A. Oh yes I do; a system must evoke some like resonance in a person before its precepts can be put into practice – a callous system must plumb some deep well of callousness in the hearts of its members, to succeed. I'm reminded of two sayings famous in the Vietnam era: 'I want some coonskins [skins of Vietnamese] on the wall!' (President Lyndon Johnson) and, 'Let's bomb North Vietnam back into the stone age!' (George Wallace).

Yet in his book, *Notes on the Cultural Life of the Democratic Republic of Vietnam*, Peter Weiss, a German author, described his conversation with an American pilot who had been taken prisoner when his plane was shot down on a bombing mission to North Vietnam. He felt the pilot was experiencing an emotional emptiness with regard to the bombing; he had carried out a decision in which he had not been involved, and he could not visualise the people he bombed. He was immature but not truly callous.

Q. Well, he had to obey orders; what choice did he have?

A. You've put your finger on a real conflict, and controversial dilemma: does one have a duty to obey orders, however wrong one may think they are?

There were instances in the US-Vietnam War of Americans refusing to obey orders they considered excessively inhumane or dangerous. One of the men, for example, in the platoon which attacked the village of My Lai 4, shot himself in the foot so that the 'medics' would come for him and he would not have to murder any villagers any more.

One other consideration having bearing, possibly, on the repeated bombing of the Lepers' Town was the official emphasis on the US side on results which could be counted and expressed numerically – not where you dropped the bombs, but how many you dropped, might be asked – like the 'body counts' in ground combat, where it was important to show that large numbers of enemy troops had been killed.

Q.   Talking of combat, you included the CIA in your opening comments for this chapter – why was that, as it's not an army set-up, is it?

A.   No – I'll go into that in the next part of our discussion.

III. Vietnam and the CIA

Q.   Returning to my question just now, about why you think
     some part of our dialogue should be on the subject of the
     CIA: I suppose I had in mind your own question earlier
     – how did the CIA get involved in covert action in
     Vietnam?

A.   I'll have to backtrack to find an answer for that question.
         First, however, as a general statement it may be helpful
     to think of the US-Vietnam War in terms of an ongoing
     cold war process, fitting into the cold war conceptual
     framework discussed earlier. (You don't have to like the
     framework, or agree with its assumptions.) The CIA has
     been a perfect instrument for the cold war.
         You may recall that in Chapter 4 there was a reference
     to 'Wild' Bill Donovan, head of the OSS (the Office of Stra-
     tegic Services), the forerunner of the CIA. Your query
     about personalities and their input into politics domi-
     nated by big systems, certainly has a point with regard
     to Major-General Donovan. He had a very flamboyant,
     masterful personality, and he loved adventure and
     derring-do behind enemy lines. He couldn't be bothered
     with doing office work or formally training people. The
     officials in army intelligence didn't trust him and
     withheld vital information from him, so he was pushed
     towards concentrating on covert action, which appealed
     to him anyway; the consequence was, that the CIA never
     separated entirely their role with intelligence from their
     covert action work. Down the years their intelligence
     work, which they became very good at, took a back seat
     to, and was valued less than, covert operations.

Q.   What do you mean by covert work?

A.   The author Brian Freemantle, in his book, *CIA, The
     Honourable Company*, stated that an official directive from
     the Truman administration in 1948 defined covert action
     as:

'... propaganda, economic warfare; preventive direct action, including sabotage, anti-sabotage, demolition and evacuation measures; subversion against hostile states, including assistance to underground resistance groups and support of indigenous anti-communist elements in threatened countries of the free world.'

Q.   What a big mandate ... how was it legalised?

A.   By the US National Security Act of 1947, and the CIA, or Central Intelligence Agency, Act of 1949.

In the part of the National Security Act concerning the CIA, besides the clauses authorising it to correlate and evaluate intelligence, and advise the National Security Council about it, were two general phrases. They weren't noticed at the time particularly, but they enabled the CIA to grow rapidly and assume vast powers, without any clear lines of accountability to Congress.

The Act stated that the CIA could perform 'such additional services of common concern' as the NSC thought could best be directed centrally; likewise, the agency could carry out 'other such functions and duties related to intelligence', as the NSC might direct.

These open-ended clauses gave the CIA a free hand, and enabled the president, through the NSC, to get control over foreign policy and to keep many operations abroad away from public scrutiny. As the CIA people reported directly to the president, they had an advantage over other branches of intelligence, e.g., that of the Department of State, and soon superseded them.

So bureaucratic in-fighting affected the course of history. The CIA became like a government within a government as it wasn't limited any longer to reporting, but actually carried out foreign policy operations such as disinformation-spreading and pseudo-military forays abroad. There were nearly 10,000 on the staff by 1953; the agency had property far-flung over the world: houses, banks, airlines, training bases, and even a ship of its own at one time. Money was unlimited as it was considered to be a vital tool of the cold war.

Q.   How do you explain the rapid growth of the Agency?

A.   The early 1950s, a time of great expansion for the CIA, was the era of McCarthyism in the States, when fear of 'the red menace' and the power of the USSR reached panic proportions, and Senator Joseph McCarthy was accusing many people holding office in the government of belonging to communist front organisations. The author Philip Knightley, in his book *The Second Oldest Profession*, makes the point that the danger from the USSR may have been deliberately exaggerated in order to justify the vast cost of building up the hidden CIA empire.

Q. Interesting, yes, but how did what you're saying affect Vietnam?

A. Well, owing to its rapid growth, the CIA was ready and able to take part in US intervention in Vietnam at a very early stage: in 1954, in fact, at the close of the First Indochina War.

At a meeting of President Eisenhower's Special Committee on Indochina held on January 30 1954, it was agreed – you may remember from the last chapter – that some mechanics should be sent to Vietnam to help the French; in addition, some liaison officers from the US were to be sent to assist at the French HQ. Some aeroplane pilots were also to be assigned to help the French. The CIA was asked to see to the practical arrangements for them.

It's reported in *The Pentagon Papers* that, at the same meeting, Mr Allen Dulles, then Director of the CIA, made a certain request:

Mr Allen Dulles inquired if an unconventional warfare officer, specifically Colonel Lansdale, could not be added to the group of five liaison officers to which General Navarre had agreed. (From *The Pentagon Papers*, excerpt from memorandum, for the record, January 30 1954)

Q. Why do you think he wanted Lansdale?

A. Colonel Lansdale, who had been in the OSS before joining the Air Force, had become well-known for his daring, and sometimes bizarre, exploits in unconventional warfare. In the Philippines he had scattered an uprising of the Huks, a rebel communist group, by playing on local superstition. He hung the corpse of a Huk fighter on a tree and carefully punctured two holes in his neck, and drained the blood out to make it look as if he'd been killed by a vampire.

Q.   Ugh . . . What was Colonel Lansdale's official posting in Vietnam?

A.   Ostensibly he was an assistant air attaché at the US embassy in Saigon, but really he was a CIA agent. So straight away the US presence in Vietnam was marked by confusion and pretence.

Col Lansdale also muddied the trail, as it were, for the US in Vietnam, because he assumed that the North Vietnamese were fighting a guerrilla war only, and therefore should be fought with guerrilla tactics. He didn't realise that for the North Vietnamese the guerrilla fighting was part of a much larger and more deadly plan: a war of conquest. He missed this point, and passed on his mistake to President Kennedy, telling him that Vietnam was 'a cold war combat zone of great urgency'. So Kennedy placed emphasis on building up special forces such as the élite Green Berets, and stressed counter-insurgency, pacification duties, and unconventional warfare.

Q.   What sort of thing did Lansdale and the other CIA people with him do in Vietnam?

A.   Under the auspices of the Saigon Military Mission, as Lansdale's set-up was called, they did all kinds of covert work, and trained montagnards, Southern Vietnamese, and Filipinos in guerrilla warfare. Intelligence work was hardly mentioned in their plans; sabotage and 'psy-war' were stressed. Lansdale set up two groups of guerrilla fighters and undercover agents in North Vietnam under Major Lucian Conein, formerly of the French Foreign Legion and the OSS. They contaminated engine oil and wrecked maintenance shops in the bus lines and rail-roads of North Vietnam, but many of them were captured before they could do any more damage. In 1958 in Laos the CIA blew up DRV supply bases.

One of the CIA-owned airlines, Civil Air Transport,

or 'CAT', as it was called, under cover of its passengers going to North Vietnam from the south in the late fifties, used to carry guns, explosives, and agents for the CIA people in the north.

CAT's function as airborne support for the CIA's paramilitary campaigns was well camouflaged. It was registered in Washington DC as a Delaware corporation and based in Taiwan. It had another name, Air America, and subsidiary airlines. It had regular passenger flights all over the Far East and was very profitable.

Col Lansdale saw it as part of his role to help President Diem in his struggle against the huge private armies of the sects in South Vietnam, so the CIA was involved from the fifties in Saigon politics. Yet Col. Lansdale didn't agree with President Diem's various resettlement plans, such as the 'Agrovilles' and 'Strategic Hamlets'. He said he didn't believe in putting people in cages or taking them where they didn't want to go.

Q. What was the 'psy-war' you mentioned?
A. It consisted of various measures intended to spread fear of the communists and prevent people from joining them. Local superstitions were exploited by spreading the word that astrologers had foretold a tragic future for the communist leaders. Thousands of leaflets, faked to look as if they came from the government of North Vietnam, were dropped from planes on the Hanoi area. The leaflets claimed that in North Vietnam a certain code of conduct was required by the government, and there would be new restrictions on property and cash flow; they were so authentic-looking that thousands of people wanted to leave the north, and DRV currency was devalued.

CIA agents trained South Vietnamese troops to form their own propaganda units. They spread rumours and disinformation about the DRV in the villages in the southern part of communist-held territory, for instance, warning people that workers in the north were being press-ganged to go to work on the railroads in Manchuria.

Pretty soon after his coming to Vietnam in the fall of

1955, Lansdale zoomed up to the rank of Brig General, was taken from the embassy, and placed in charge of the co-ordination of all civilian and military projects of the US in Vietnam at the time, an impossible task which no one was ever able to achieve. He was at a disadvantage, too, because, like Bill Donovan before him, he was distrusted for his flamboyant, unpredictable tactics by officials in the Pentagon and Department of State.

Q. You mentioned the training of minorities which the CIA in Vietnam undertook in Lansdale's time – where was this done?

A. Besides what was done in South Vietnam, there was a wide network of bases at various points in South-East Asia, which were used by the CIA for training: Okinawa and Saipan, for instance, and several places in the Philippines. Two outfits in the Philippines, 'Eastern Construction Co.' and 'Operation Brotherhood' provided personnel already experienced in covert warfare. There was a group in Thailand, too, preparing for guerrilla fighting.

(Lansdale gave all this information in a memo to General Maxwell D. Taylor, July 1961, reprinted in *The Pentagon Papers.*)

The CIA, he reported, also supported the 'Police Aerial Re-supply Units' or PARUs, who trained montagnards in Laos. There were thirteen PARU teams, amounting to 99 men in all.

Q. Why were they in Laos? I'm not sure I see the connection there.

A. Their reason for being there was to mobilise the Meos and other montagnard people of the area around Tchepone, near the border between Laos and Vietnam, and close to communist-held land. The idea was to try to prevent the communists from penetrating the border with covert agents and supplies for the south, but the attempt was never successful. Over several years more than 40,000 montagnards were fighting as guerrillas against the DRV. There was a big CIA depot and radio HQ at a place called Long Tieng – virtually a CIA town, supplied by Air America. The montagnards also fought on behalf of the US against the Pathet Lao, who were Laotian communists backed by the DRV.

Q.   These obscure skirmishes seem so far away, so long ago; do they have some particular significance for us that you wish to draw attention to?

A.   Yes, they do, and of course they were more than skirmishes, when you think of the thousands of people involved.

I think these campaigns in Laos in the fifties and sixties are significant to us because in several ways they set a precedent, copied often, for the CIA's work in Indochina.

In the first place, they weren't called 'CIA work', but 'PEO' (Project Program Evaluation Office) affairs. PEO was the name given to the US military and advisory mission in Laos. Laos, under the Geneva Accords, was supposed to be kept neutral, so an openly military mission wasn't allowed.

From the word 'Go', as was so often true in Vietnam, everyone involved was pretending to do one thing while really doing another: pretending to be part of a civilian outfit while carrying out military and para-military acts. The CIA was not restricted by the Accords, so their work in Laos was one of many instances of their ability to evade treaties, and operate beyond the reach of law; in fact, unofficially, opium from Laos was carried by CIA planes.

In 1959, 107 US Special Forces troops, called 'White Star' men, working in teams, joined the act in Laos. Thus began the Agency's long association with Special Forces in Indochina, leading it into a strategic cul-de-sac eventually. I'll say more about this shortly.

Partly, I suppose, because of advances in anthropological studies, attitudes have changed over the years with regard to cultures unfamiliar to us, and I think nowadays we wouldn't be as gung-ho as Lansdale and company were, feeling they were doing the montagnards a favour by embroiling them in a fight that wasn't theirs, and taking them away from home. When the North Vietnamese advanced south ruthlessly in the seventies, they were left to fend for themselves, just as they had been by the French a few decades earlier.

Lastly, I think the expedition to Laos set a dangerous precedent for the CIA in that it left the impression that it was OK to have a secret private campaign all their own, without accountability for the outcome, or integrating the plan with other US campaigns in the Indochinese setting.

Q. Could you recap? I'm losing track here.

A. Yes. So far we've touched on the following points: the origin of the CIA and its basis in US law; its function in the cold war; emphasis on covert work; how it got started in Vietnam; mistakes made re nature of the DRV campaign; rapid growth of the CIA; its vast lucrative proprietary interests; training of minorities and 'psywar' in Vietnam; and the Laotian campaign beginning in the late fifties.

Q. I see – what comes next?

A. Well, there are three more aspects of CIA work in Vietnam I was going to mention in this dialogue; some more comments on their work with US Special Forces; intelligence work; and, arising from these, a general section under what I would call the Murphy's Law column.

Q. What's Murphy's Law?

A. I think Murphy said, 'Anything that can go wrong, will go wrong', so the next section will be about what went wrong, or was only partly successful, with the CIA's work in Vietnam.

The CIA's work with the US Special Forces in Vietnam was fragmented amongst a strange mixture of special projects and plans, such as 'CIDG' (Civilian Irregular Defense Groups), SOG (Study and Observation Group), Project Delta, Project Omega, and Project Eldest Son, for instance.

There were two main distinctions among them all: some, like CIDG projects, were meant to help and defend people who were loyal to the South Vietnamese government and anti-communist; others, like SOG activities (e.g., Project Delta) were directed against communists, and could range from intelligence-gathering to commando-like raids into enemy areas, and assassinations.

Money for CIDG plans came from the bottomless coffers of the CIA, while the Special Forces people carried out the work. They had what they called 'A' teams of twelve men, who would befriend a village, usually of montagnards, and help them if they promised not to harbour any Vietcong. The CIDG fortified camps, called village defence units or self-defence units as a way of circumventing the Geneva Accords' ban on setting up military bases, were set up close to a village they were ostensibly meant to defend: but often they were separated from the village by barbed wire, mines and punji stakes.

The men in the 'A' team had many skills. The teams included weapons specialists, people with medical training, radio and demolition experts, for instance. There were two of each speciality, so that the team could be divided in two if necessary. They had 'B' and 'C' teams that were similar, only bigger than the 'A' teams.

They did help the villagers by arming them and providing them with basic medical help, and gave aid with hygiene problems, such as cleaning up their water supply; but all the same, it's hard to ignore the crashing condescension involved.

Q.   Yes. Whatever was Project Eldest Son?

A.   In his book, *Vietnam the Secret War*, Kevin M. Generous described it as raids into enemy territory in order to insert rigged ammunition rounds into enemy supply dumps. When later they blew up, word was spread that the fault must lie with the inefficient Chinese manufacturers, whose work had gone to pot since the 'Cultural Revolution'.

To give some idea of the numbers of people involved in the various CIA-cum-Special Forces operations, Mr Generous estimated that, over several years, there were about 8000 indigenous persons, and 2000 Americans, involved in these projects.

Q.   Returning for a moment to a couple of distinctions you've made: 1) CIDG was for counter-insurgency work, helping friendly villagers, while SOG projects were of a guerrilla nature against hostile groups or bases; and 2) CIA people master-minded and funded the projects, but left the actual operations to Special Forces.

Have I got this right?

A.   Yes, you have; I think these distinctions are useful in a broad sense, but I should have mentioned that it wouldn't work to be dogmatic about them, because in practice there were times when these dividing lines got rather blurred.

For instance, the CIDG work with villagers often included building up a strike force of guerrilla fighters, not necessarily drawn from the adjacent village; they scouted around gathering information about enemy positions, set up ambushes, and harassed the enemy if they could.

There were always men drawn to the CIA because of their love of taking part in such missions as Project Eldest Son. There was a mystique and glamour about covert work in their way of thinking.

Sometimes CIA people and Special Forces types did each other's work; the latter could be seconded to the CIA for a particular mission, returning later to their own group.

This happened with operations conducted under Project Delta, which planned infiltration of enemy territory, surprise attacks and sabotage, and intelligence-gathering as to enemy strength. There was a Delta training school at Nha Trang, and Delta people carried out psywar and were assigned to kill Vietcong and their sympathisers in villages in South Vietnam.

In the north the location of Allied prisoners and downed airmen was sought out, and agents were dropped into North Vietnam to set up resistance groups. The operations of Delta in the north involved 450 men, and to land in enemy territory, and get out if they were lucky, they used the 281st US Helicopter Assault Company; the helicopter crews, it's reported, often slept on the choppers, which were laden down with ammunition and ready to leave any time. The information the Delta teams brought back regarding movements of enemy troops and so forth, was very useful to the regular US forces.

There were several hundred montagnard and ARVN troops working in the Delta missions. They were called 'Road-runners' (after the favourite cartoon character who always managed to survive terrible hazards?). They wore black pajamas or North Vietnamese uniforms and were dropped into enemy areas to perform acts of sabotage. A special kind of harness was lowered from the helicopters to get them out, as it was too dangerous to land.

Q. What did you mean by the psywar in the south, carried out by Delta people?

A. In 1965 the CIA and members of Special Force units tried to counteract the influence of the Nationalist Liberation Front (which was sympathetic to communists) in the southern villages. They tried to re-educate the people. If a member of the Vietcong was found, and there seemed no other means of neutralising him or removing him, he was assassinated.

After someone had been found dead, a characteristic calling card would be left where it could easily be found. It was a black card, usually, with a white eye on it. It was meant to be a warning to all communist sympathisers. President Truman had jested nearer the truth-to-be than he realised, when at a lunch when the CIA was formed, he gave guests masks and cloak-and-dagger costumes.

A witness at the International War Crime Tribunal in Copenhagen in 1967, Sgt Donald Duncan, formerly of the US Special Forces, described the above activities of the Delta organisation in South Vietnam.

Q. How about the CIA's intelligence work in Vietnam? Have you any comments to make on it?

A. Yes. The consensus of historians is that they did a good job, and that their reports on enemy strength, etc., were consistently more accurate and less rosy than those of US military intelligence in Vietnam.

The CIA realistically reported to Washington the following:

1. The number of men in PAVN (People's Army of

Vietnam) was much greater than previously estimated, and, given the difference in population
between North and South Vietnam (eighteen million
as compared to twelve million), the North
Vietnamese had a huge supply of manpower to
draw on for a very long time to come.

2. Numbers of enemy dead were considerably lower
    than previously reported.
3. Corruption in the South Vietnamese government
    made it a very wobbly ally, at best.
4. Bombing of North Vietnam and mining of
    Haiphong harbour wouldn't affect the North
    Vietnamese war effort as much as expected, because
    essential supplies, e.g., of petroleum, were dispersed
    to several different locations; matériel was brought
    overland from China; and the experience of World
    War II indicated that bombing of civilian targets had
    the effect of strengthening morale, not weakening it.
5. CIA analysts' views on Vietnam as a rotten apple
    country, or falling domino in cold war thinking,
    diverged from the official standpoint. They said that
    if all Vietnam fell to the communists, would it be all
    that disastrous for the US? They would still have
    bases in strategic places in South-East Asia, e.g., in
    Guam and in the Philippines.
6. The CIA gave warning that the PAVN would make
    a major thrust southward as in the 'Tet' offensive in
    1968, and were consistent in stating that the enemy
    had the manpower and persistence to achieve their
    goal of the conquest of South Vietnam.

Q. That's a pretty impressive track record. Why do you feel,
    then, that Murphy's Law was operating for them?
A. For many reasons.
    Regarding intelligence work: although it was good,
    back in Washington sometimes CIA reports weren't read
    – there was usually a plethora of reports to get through
    – or if they were read, they weren't acted upon. People
    hear what they want to hear, and block out unwelcome
    news. CIA reports on massive enemy manpower, and

questioning of cold war assumptions, didn't place them in the popularity business. They found it wise to play down bad news sometimes.

Q. Why did you say earlier that the work with the Special Forces led the CIA into a strategic cul-de-sac?

A. I meant that, really, it led nowhere. However much flair and dash went into a daring raid into enemy territory, and however much patient work went into befriending villagers, any successes were transient, and not co-ordinated with other US campaigns. An 'A' team might think they had secured a village and cleared it of Vietcong; but the next hour, or the next night, everything could be changed and the communists would have infiltrated it again.

A problem built into the local scene, as it were, and not the CIA's fault – though of course they got blamed when things went wrong, whatever the reason – was that many of the montagnard tribes didn't get along with the Viets. They had many old grievances against them. The Vietnamese officers, for their part, objected to the Americans giving the montagnards guns. Many of the CIDG bases strung out along the border were very lonely and hard to maintain, like the sad French forts along the De Lattre line had been in the First Indochina War.

Q. What was the attitude in Washington to the CIA's work in Vietnam with the Special Forces?

A. I don't think it was possible for people in the government to have knowledge of it in any detail, though government committees were, in theory, supposed to monitor the CIA's work. But Laos and Vietnam were far away.

Events elsewhere affected the CIA in Vietnam. President Kennedy, after the intended invasion of Cuba in April 1961 at the Bay of Pigs had failed, felt the fiasco must have been because the CIA had goofed. He began to realise that he had no control over the activities of CIA and Special Forces people far away; in 1963 their work was transferred to the supervision of the Department of Defense – that is, their work in Indochina.

Q.   You're always stressing shifts and currents, as it were, in the Washington bureaucracy, yet to me the connection isn't always clear between them and the CIA, or between the Green Beret people and their friends deep in the interior of Vietnam. How do you think the change of management, from CIA to Dept. of Defense in this case, affected them?

A.   It meant a shift of emphasis, for instance in the CIDG work with villages, from civic action to an openly military role. Instead of village defence, the aim was to build up strike forces: that is, roving groups of about 150 men, based in border camps, who would hunt down Vietcong and try to prevent infiltration of the border. Village dispensaries which had been set up were dismantled, and health workers were no longer paid.

The South Vietnamese Special Forces took charge of the whole operation. They expected the montagnards to join in, but aroused their smouldering anger by saying they had to turn in their guns to the government in Saigon, and by refusing to let them take command of any group larger than a company. The montagnards rebelled and there was some bitter fighting before a truce could be negotiated, with the help of some of the Special Forces staff who had been in the programme earlier. Patrolling the border was a failure and communists and their supplies came south more and more.

Q.   I get the impression of a lot of small, isolated groups of fighters being worn down by the constant drive to the south by the communists, and being torn apart by dissension among themselves, at a time when they were confused by the switch in command. Are there any reports available, by people who were there at the time?

A.   Yes; there's a lot of information available in *The Pentagon Papers* which, though out of print, isn't classified or restricted in any way.

There's a 'brief' – which isn't very brief – in the *Papers* sent by Ambassador Maxwell Taylor in Saigon in November 1964 to officials in Washington. He said the counter-insurgency programme country-wide was 'bogged down', and the pacification programme was deteriorating and on a downward trend, and with no support from the government in Saigon, US efforts (in unconventional warfare) were but a spinning wheel. Rather primly, he noted the South Vietnamese tendency to factionalism and lack of team spirit; and, in another memo, said that he gave orders but day succeeded day (each one hotter than the last), and nothing was done. Inertia always won over action.

Q.   Well, there's nothing particularly Vietnamese about that, is there?

A.   No; people's love of doing nothing is a difficulty built into the pursuit of any cause, however noble or ignoble, anywhere, I imagine.

Ambassador Taylor said in his brief that the forces, US or pro-US, engaged in counter-insurgency and pacification work were overwhelmed by tremendous pressure from the Vietcong, who sabotaged roads, railroads, and airfields. Meanwhile, infiltration of DRV military personnel from the north had been stepped up, and there was communist propaganda non-stop on the radio, to the saturation point. Areas in the northern part of South Vietnam, free of Vietcong a year previously, were now full of them again.

Q.   Do you have any more comments on the CIA in Vietnam of a 'Murphy's Law' nature?

A.   No, but I have some problems to mention which the CIA in Vietnam did not address, perhaps because they weren't perceived as problems at the time.

One such problem, or dilemma if you like, for CIA staff lay in the conflict between having to be both dependent and independent. At times they were expected to carry out the policy of the US administration; their involvement in the plans for the assassination of President Diem of South Vietnam is an example.

On other occasions, as in the raids into enemy country, they had to be very independent. Operating the CIA airlines, carrying out their various psywar and covert work, and training thousands of men, required agents with flair and enterprise, and rather big egos, actually. They wouldn't fit the enemy concept of the CIA as a branch of government, and the staff as civil servants.

So there was a latent conflict regarding the role of the Agency, and the extent of its independence.

Another dilemma, more of an ethical nature, is this: if you have a task to perform and you ask someone to do it for you, are you responsible for the actions of that person in carrying out the work?

Q.   This is a problem inherent in any management role and not peculiar to the CIA – the problem of how to delegate successfully – don't you think?

A.   Yes, you're right.

Regarding the CIA in Vietnam delegating their tasks, I had in mind the interrogation of prisoners. In some accounts from witnesses at the International War Crime Tribunal at Copenhagen in 1967, Special Forces people are described as standing by, or turning aside and smoking a cigarette, while South Vietnamese men tortured prisoners for information. A method of torture frequently employed was the use of electric shocks: for instance, by attaching cords from a field telephone to the prisoner's nipples or genitals.

It doesn't seem as if there was any consensus among CIA staff as to what procedures they would allow, and what forbid. I suppose if there had been rules laid down about methods of interrogation for CIA people or their agents, to many of them that would have seemed like being regimented. On the other hand, a completely laissez-faire approach opens the door to abuse.

I think that at the time of the US-Vietnam War, the CIA had not thought through the ethical implications of their work; I mean, what was their basic attitude regarding human rights, for instance? It was the feeling that this dimension of their work wasn't adequately addressed, that led them into the wilderness, politically, in the years of President Carter's administration (1977-1981), when the value of the Agency was downplayed.

Another dilemma for the CIA in Indochina was, I think, the difficulty of estimating the end results of a course of action, or its side-effects. For instance, when CIA pilots carried opium on their planes for the poppy-farmers of Laos, they could not foresee that the drug, in a deadly, potent form, would reach, and corrupt, men in the US forces in Vietnam, and that the farmers weren't going to get the huge profits involved.

Q. Don't you think the dilemmas for the CIA in Vietnam, which you've just been describing, have a universal aspect to them; that is, they're part of everyone's experience, or most people's anyway? E.g., the tension between freedom and authority; the experiences of looking the other way when one sees a wrong being committed, and not stopping it; and taking action without first trying to gauge possible results. These we can all relate to.

A. Yes, true. President Kennedy once said of the CIA that their blunders were trumpeted loudly but deafening silence covered their successes – or words to that effect.

Q. Leaving the subject of unconventional forces now, can I ask you next about the conventional ones in Vietnam?

A. Yes; let's start a new part of the dialogue on them.

CHAPTER SEVEN

Military Systems in Vietnam: The Dialogue Continued

PART 1. PAVN (People's Army of Vietnam): Some Basic Concepts

Question:

> Isn't your title for this part of our dialogue rather pedantic? What does an army need 'concepts' for?

Answer:

> Well, really, troops need them much more than you might think; how can they have any sense of purpose in fighting if they haven't conceptualised, or thought out, what they are fighting for?
>
> While it's true, as Napoleon said, 'An army marches on its stomach' (i.e., supplies are all-important in wartime) an army also marches on, or depends on, for victory, a number of intangible factors which can't be quantified, such as morale and the commanders' grasp of strategy and good organisation.
>
> These factors will be the focus for this part of our dialogue.

Q. OK – where shall we start?

A. First I'll 'brainstorm' you with the main points, so that you'll have some idea what to expect.

> 1 & 2. At the risk of being told I'm trying to re-invent the wheel, I'd like to look much further back than Marx, Lenin, or Mao Tse-tung, to trace the origins of Ho Chi Minh's and Vo Nguyen Giap's basic concepts for the PAVN. I'll take the connection

back to the writings of previously mentioned Sun Tzu, China, 5th Century BC, and General Carl von Clausewitz, Prussia, 1832. I'll describe some main points in the teachings of these authors which influenced the North Vietnamese: e.g., Sun Tzu on morale and intelligence agents; and Clausewitz on war and politics, the people in war, and the difference between tactics and strategy.

3. There are 'Three threes' in Vietnamese revolutionary warfare, so historians have said:

a) Three levels of armed forces: regular army, regional forces, and local people's militia and self-defence groups.

b) Three 'withs' every cadre had to live by: live with the people, eat with the people, work with the people.

c) Three phases of revolutionary warfare:

    i)   mainly political activity, when the enemy is strongest;

    ii)   political and military actions combined;

    iii)   final counter-offensive and all-out military thrust to victory.

4. Lenin's belief that the whole country should become a revolutionary bastion, agreed to by Giap.

5. Giap's policy with regard to guerrilla warfare differed from Mao Tse-tung's in that he used it as a tactic, not a strategy; i.e., as part of a means of fulfilling a larger plan, not the plan itself.

6. Unity of command, how achieved.

7. Methods used to involve everyone in the revolution and the war. 'Dau tranh' – name given to the struggle movement, and its meaning for the Vietnamese.

8. Giap's distant goal: conquest of all Indochina; he meant the entire territory of Laos, Cambodia, and Vietnam, and said this as early as February 1950, in a pamphlet on the subject of shifting to the phase of general counter-offensive.

That's the last point in my list.

Q. I see . . . what were you going to say about the influence of Sun Tzu?

A. His book *The Art of War,* translated into Russian long ago, is a well-known army textbook in the eastern bloc. Mao Tse-tung borrowed heavily from it for his *Little Red Book.*

The first factor essential for victory, which Sun Tzu mentioned at the very beginning of his book, was *The Moral Law,* one of five factors of crucial importance in warfare. It was very close to our term 'morale'. In the context of his writing he defined it as the devotion of men to their commander, which enables them to disregard danger in following him.

The other four factors which he said should be studied in preparing an army for war were: 'Heaven and Earth', by which he meant temporal conditions, such as the kind of country the war was being fought in; weather; role of chance in the outcome of battles; qualities of the commander; and finally, 'Method and Discipline'.

Sun Tzu, himself a brilliant general, emphasised planning and calculation and total absence of mistakes, saying that a general who wins a battle wins because he planned it carefully, so that it was fought at a time and place most favourable to him. He didn't just decide to rush into battle on impulse.

He said that it was essential to know your ground, and use local guides and spies. He distinguished no less than six kinds of terrain and nine kinds of ground, or situation, where an army might be, and gave precise instructions on the correct course of action in each case. He encouraged people to find out what to do simply by observing closely what was going on around them; for instance, he said: 'The sudden rising of birds in their flight is the sign of an ambush at the spot below' (From *The Art of War* by Sun Tzu, trans. Lionel Giles, ed. James Clavell).

Q. Funny isn't it, how even long ago people had to be told these natural things – I'm wondering if there were any parts of Sun Tzu's teaching you could pinpoint, which the Vietnamese found particularly helpful, and adapted to their own circumstances?

A.   Yes, I can think of four, but there are several others:

1.   Using the enemy's weaknesses to get victory over him. Sun Tzu said: 'The opportunity of defeating the enemy is provided by the enemy himself' (Ibid.).

This principle was applied not only in battle, but for propaganda and psychological warfare amongst foreigners. By pointing out the weaknesses and divisions in French, and later American society, the North Vietnamese were able continually to undermine support for their enemies' war efforts.

2.   Rapidity, mobility, secrecy, surprise: Sun Tzu wrote much about these qualities in an army's tactics.

3.   He stressed the importance of intelligence work. He described five different types of intelligence agents, showing how to use them in an unbeatable combination. He described why people become double agents: some are show-offs, some have been passed over for plum jobs, some were ambitious concubines – the beautiful spies of the ancient world.

4.   Sun Tzu's advice on morale and other intangible factors such as planning and strategy, was absorbed by the North Vietnamese and used in their own way to help create a background of ideas for PAVN.

Q.   How did the North Vietnamese concept of morale differ from the western one?

A.   The difference was, I think, that the North Vietnamese saw it not as a side-effect but as the most crucial factor an army needed for victory; and, instead of coming into being by chance, it could in fact be acquired and deliberately cultivated, like any body of knowledge or set of ideas. In the west good morale has sometimes been considered something nice to have, like a white Christmas, but why some units of fighting men had it and others didn't, wasn't clear.

Ho Chi Minh and Vo Nguyen Giap, however, perceived it as a profound quality based in the total spirituality of a person. In the case of their troops, they connected it with the Confucian values handed down to them, with their Buddhism and their memory of the village bodhisattvas who identified with peasant suffering, and with their reverence for their ancestors and national heroes and heroines.

The cultivation of this quality was an important part of the total revolutionary struggle movement, called 'dau tranh' by the Vietnamese. To them the term was charged with emotion, like the opening bars of the Marseillaise to French people. It was mystical and yet martial at the same time. It comprised a total plan, organised to include everyone, with a political and a military side, and many programmes. It was highly morale-raising, for the central idea was always that the people themselves were the instruments of revolutionary warfare, so everyone felt they were making a contribution towards victory, and had a sense of belonging.

Q. Did Clausewitz emphasise morale also, and was he himself a professional soldier?

A. Yes, to both of your questions: in his book, *Vom Kriege*, entitled *On War* in the English translation from the German, he stressed the importance in any army of intangible factors such as its national spirit and esprit de corps, bravery, endurance, and skill.

Gen von Clausewitz, who lived from 1780 to 1831, could be described as a professional soldier par excellence. When he was only twelve he joined the Prussian army as an ensign. He fought with the Russians against Napoleon, was captured and sent to France as a prisoner, and in later life became principal of the army academy in Berlin where he had been a student in his twenties.

(Incidentally, when Vo Nguyen Giap was a history teacher in civilian life, he had specialised in the campaigns of Napoleon.)

Q. In what ways do you feel Clausewitz influenced the North Vietnamese?

A. I'll select some of the main points in his teaching, which Giap and Ho Chi Minh made part of the background of ideas for their PAVN, I think.

As a short comment beforehand, I should mention

that Gen. von Clausewitz considered that during his army career he had seen a radical change in European society, and in the way wars were fought. In the eighteenth century, before the French Revolution (beginning 1789), war in central Europe, he said, had been between small monarchies and petty states; it was chiefly an affair set up by the cabinet and army of a state, not involving all the people; objectives were limited and there were certain conventions observed: e.g., it wasn't considered the done thing to burn the other party's villages.

'Thus matters stood when the French Revolution broke out; Austria and Prussia tried their diplomatic Art of War; this very soon proved insufficient. Whilst, according to the usual way of seeing things, all hopes were placed on a very limited military force, in 1793 such a force as no one had any conception of, made its appearance. War had again suddenly become an affair of the people, and that of a people numbering thirty millions, each one of whom regarded himself as a citizen of the State.' (From *On War* by Carl von Clausewitz, trans. Col. J.J. Graham, ed. by Col. F.N. Maude)

Numbers of troops became mind-boggling as Napoleon would hurl hundreds of thousands of men into battle at a time. It was the revolutionary fervour and patriotism of the ordinary French soldier which brought him victory, Clausewitz thought.

Q. Yet the ordinary people of France didn't really benefit from the Revolution, did they? When Ho Chi Minh first went to Paris early in this century (as I recall from an earlier chapter), he was astonished to find there poverty hardly less grinding than that at home in Vietnam.

A. True; I suppose, speaking as a professional military man, Clausewitz was observing that, besides the colossal number of his troops, Napoleon had a new weapon: the enthusiasm of the French soldiers – their nationalism, if you like. He related also that in the first decade of the nineteenth century, it became a national cause for the Prussian people, to drive the French back across the Rhine. Large sums of money were donated, thousands enlisted, and a big army was soon created.

He noted too how in Spain the war in 1808-9 became an affair of the people, whose guerrilla bands badgered and attacked Napoleon's crack troops incessantly. It was there the word 'guerrilla' – little war – was first used; the fighting wasn't only a peasants' affair, for the guerrilla soldiers were led by the clergy and nobility.

So, in answer to your previous question, on ways in which Clausewitz influenced the North Vietnamese, I would make his stress on the zeal of the people, the first point:

i) Good morale born of revolutionary zest: this was the new dimension perceived by Clausewitz as a vital ingredient in victory.
    The next three points all have to do with war and politics:
ii) The state is the supreme authority, not the army;
iii) War is not an interruption in politics, but a continuation of them, so is a normal, not abnormal, situation between states;
iv) A limited war doesn't make any sense unless there's some overriding political reason to keep it limited.

In developing this theme of war as an instrument of policy, Clausewitz wrote:

'War is nothing but a continuation of political intercourse, with a mixture of other means . . . The subordination of the military point of view to the political, is, therefore, the only thing which is possible . . .

   If policy is grand and powerful, so also will be the War; and this may be carried to the point at which war attains to its *absolute* form . . . only through this kind of view War recovers unity; only by it can we see all Wars as things of *one* kind.'

(Ibid.)

Q. The overtones are rather sinister, aren't they? He seems to be implying that war is natural, will always be going on, and he likes it.

A. Yes; I suppose, above all, he was a realist.
    Anyway, he gave very practical advice for the actual conduct of a war, which influenced the North Vietnamese.

Here are three of his main points:

v) He said it's necessary, in planning warfare, to distinguish between strategy and tactics, and to know which of your army's actions are part of your tactics, and how they differ from your strategy. There's trouble if you're not clear which is which.

For instance, in a war several 'combats', as Clausewitz called them, might be taking place: action is planned for troops on horseback in one place, and for infantry in another – these are tactics; but how such 'combats' are combined with a view to the ultimate object of the war, is part of strategy. 'Tactics is the theory of the use of military forces in combat. Strategy is the theory of the use of combats for the object of the war' (Ibid.).

Clausewitz noted scrupulously that there might be some actions in war which are both tactical and strategic in nature. But I think his point was, that a commander must be clear in his mind which is which, and what the purpose of war is.

In this connection he said:

vi) In planning hostilities the leaders of an army have to decide on what he called 'the centre of gravity' in the war, that is, their main aim, and to drive ruthlessly on to achieve it, ignoring the temptation to indulge in daring sideshows.

For instance, if your main goal is to destroy the enemy's forces, and to seize his capital city, then you have to press on with all your might to do these things, not waste time and men burning hamlets, barns, and what-have-you, far away from the main action. The battles are the key; don't kid yourself that you can win without fighting.

vii) The commanders have to be continually analysing and classifying the activities of their troops, and thinking out who does what, when, and where; they also must keep organising every action in detail, and separate in their minds the actual fighting from support services, such as the bringing forward of supplies and the care of the wounded.

Q. Regarding the distinction made between strategy and tactics, I'm wondering if you would explain the fifth point you made in your list of main points just now, viz., Gen Giap's use of guerrilla fighting as a tactic, not a strategy?

A.   Yes; he wrote extensively about revolutionary warfare. Two of his works were, in their English translations, *Banner of People's War; The Party's Military Line* (1970), and *To Arm the Revolutionary Masses; To Build the People's Army* (1972).

He saw guerrilla fighting as part of a total co-ordinated plan for revolutionary warfare, interacting with political uprisings and with campaigns by the regular army.

James Pinckney Harrison in his book, *The Endless War, Vietnam's Struggle for Independence,* quoted the following passage from *Banner of People's War:*

'. . . in the field of armed struggle and in the waging of guerrilla and regular wars, the co-ordination of guerrilla war with regular war is the most fundamental part of the art of sending all the people headlong into the fight.'

In a later work written jointly with Van Tien Dung, he stated:

'We applied both the law governing war and that governing armed uprising, and firmly grasped their interaction, and applied as well renewed co-ordination between regular and people's forces . . . ' (From *The Endless War* by J. Pinckney Harrison)

By 'people's war' Gen. Giap meant; not guerrilla warfare alone, but the total package, the whole thrust towards revolution and victory together, of which guerrilla activities were but one aspect. He agreed with Chairman Mao Tse-tung's main principles of people's war, written in 1947, but saw them only as a phase – they weren't the total picture. Mao stressed points such as: at first only attack small isolated enemy forces; keep mobile, don't worry about holding towns or territory; focus on destroying the enemy; and avoid battle unless you've got more men than the enemy, and are really ready for the fight.

   The secret of success was, again, threefold, combining, with careful timing, political action such as holding
   uprisings and demonstrations, and fighting by both
   regular and irregular forces.

Q.   Did Gen Giap agree with Clausewitz's belief that the
     state, not the army, is the supreme authority, and that
     war is an extension of political policy?

A.   Yes, he did. In an article he wrote in 1965 he stated: 'The
     military line of our party derives from and always
     follows its political line.' (Quoted in *Vietnam and
     America,* by Marvin E. Gettleman *et al*)

*Marshal Giap and his ADC. On the left is Duong Minh, Vice-Director of the
Foreign Press Centre. At the government house, Hanoi. (Tim Page)*

Q.   This is connected then with your point about unity of command, sixth in your list, I expect. What exactly do you think posed a threat to their unity of command, for the North Vietnamese?

A.   I think for them there were two possible threats, or sources of disunity and division:

i) Conflict between North and South: I mean, the leaders of the People's Liberation Armed Force, or PLAF, which was the army of the National Liberation Front of communist sympathisers in South Vietnam, might have competed with PAVN officers for authority.

ii) Conflict between party officials and army brass.

With regard to the first point, such conflict never became severe enough to damage actual combat performance, as for many years PAVN sent officers and advisors to assist their counterparts in the south, and gradually dominated them more and more, until PLAF was merged with PAVN in 1976, and ceased to exist separately. (But they'd borne the brunt in the Tet offensive, and had fought hard in many places, so they had an honourable history.)

With regard to the second point, possible conflict between party chiefs and military leaders: this was always present potentially, particularly as, over the years, the army grew to huge numbers and its officers felt themselves more and more professional. Some writers call it the 'Red versus Expert' conflict. I understand that, until the end of the US-Vietnam War, representatives of the party and those of the army managed to share authority without causing any rift, or weakening the united war effort. Two factors seem to me to have helped in this regard: the office of the Political Commissar, or Political Officer; and the presence of Party members in key positions at every level in the army. Some held office in both army and party, and so identified with both.

Dr Douglas Pike, in his book *PAVN; People's Army of Vietnam*, described the feeling North Vietnamese had for the army: it wasn't a separate official group but belonged to everybody. As Lenin had said, everyone was a soldier in a revolutionary country. To take part in revolutionary violence was part of everyone's Marxist-Leninist heritage.

Q.   What was the role of the Political Commissar?

A.   A mixture of counsellor, father figure, stern mentor, educator – he was regarded as a source of inspiration and encouragement. Writing in 1960, Gen Giap described how a local Political Commissar and army unit commander were meant to work together under a dual command system:

'Party leadership by Party committee assigning tasks to unit commander and the Political Commissar is a system that guarantees continued collective leadership . . . assures close co-ordination in operations . . . it strengthens internal unity.' (From *PAVN: People's Army of Vietnam*, by Douglas Pike)

In the years since the US-Vietnam War, various re-arrangements of this dual command have been tried, such as giving one person the combined job of both Political Commissar and unit commander; or having the unit commander report to a special military committee. But the problem hasn't gone away.

Q.   Could you say more now about the seventh point listed, that is, the methods the North Vietnamese used to involve everyone in the revolutionary war effort?

A.   Yes. I think the whole process was centered in the cadres, or local group leaders. They were often recruited through people they knew, either friends or relatives, sent for a short training course, and then, working in a village, would begin by making friends with one family, and through its members, link up with others. Thus a network of supporters would be created.

A lot was expected of the cadres and I don't think anyone without their background of poverty and Confucian obedience could ever have managed to fulfil their role. They had to keep to the injunctions of Ho Chi Minh (quoted by Peter Weiss in *Notes on the Cultural Life of the Democratic Republic of Vietnam*), who said they should be loyal to the party, should love the people, fulfil every task, and overcome all difficulties, and much else besides.

Le Duan, who became First Secretary of the Party in 1959, believed that the strength of the communists lay in their close relations with the masses, created by the work of the cadres. He too had high expectations of them, saying they should mix with the masses, set them an example by marching in the front line, should persuade and organise the masses and understand their feelings. Yet all the time they should be characterised by modesty, simplicity, and a willingness to learn from the experience of the people.

Q. It sounds as if the cadres, though drawn from the people themselves, needed to have exceptional qualities of self-denial and leadership. What about the great majority of ordinary people in the background – how did they fit into the revolutionary plan?

A. I think they had a very hard job. Many of them served in the third category of armed forces mentioned previously, the local militia and self-defence groups, yet had to do a lot of production work too. Gen. Giap wrote, in an article describing the forces' organisation, that:

'Militia and self-defense groups are extensive semi-armed forces of the labouring people who, while continuing their production work, are the main instrument of the people's power at the base.' (From *Vietnamese Studies, No. 7*, Hanoi 1965. Included in *Vietnam and America*, by Marvin Gettleman *et al*)

'Production work' could include hacking out tunnels and the Ho Chi Minh Trail, constructing and supplying bases and resting stations, growing crops, making uniforms, delivering arms – all forms of toil which a huge army needs in the background to survive.

It was some of these people the Americans used to hear laughing in the tunnel rooms as they exchanged jokes to relieve the tedium of their work. It was eerie because they couldn't see anyone and wondered where the laughter was coming from.

They also had a vital, nurturing, caring role, sheltering soldiers and workers and nursing them when they were sick or wounded.

Q.   With all that constant work to do, was there any time to spare for people to exchange ideas and discuss what the revolution was all about?

A.   Oh yes. Careful attention was paid to defining the goals of the 'struggle movement' and revolutionary process.

Truong Chinh, a member of the Polit-Buro who had been General Secretary of the party in 1940, was considered the leading exponent of Marxist-Leninist theory in the government of the DRV. He had been a journalist. When giving directions for the education of cadres, he said that they should be steeped not only in international communism, but also in the nationalism which gave the Vietnamese revolution its unique quality. They were taught that their first aim had to be victory over the imperialist invaders.

Ho Chi Minh believed that when a person developed a revolutionary mindset, this did not happen because of education in the sense of instruction, but rather by a process of consciousness-raising. Persons needed to remould themselves so that they became more aware of the sufferings of others. The revolution was an inner as well as an outer process.

Q.   How was such a change in a person brought about?

A.   There were various techniques used; some were similar to some known in social work and psychiatry in the west: role modelling, or discussing a character people could emulate as well as his or her own contribution to the revolution; and in small groups, positive use was made of the group process. By the group process, that is, the interaction between members of a group and the relationships they form, a person could gain a sense of belonging. They would get relief for their possible feeling that they had to battle their problems alone, while along the way their understanding of revolutionary ideas was deepened.

Q.   What did you mean by stating that the small group sessions were a positive use of the group process?

A.   I meant that it made a person feel good and was

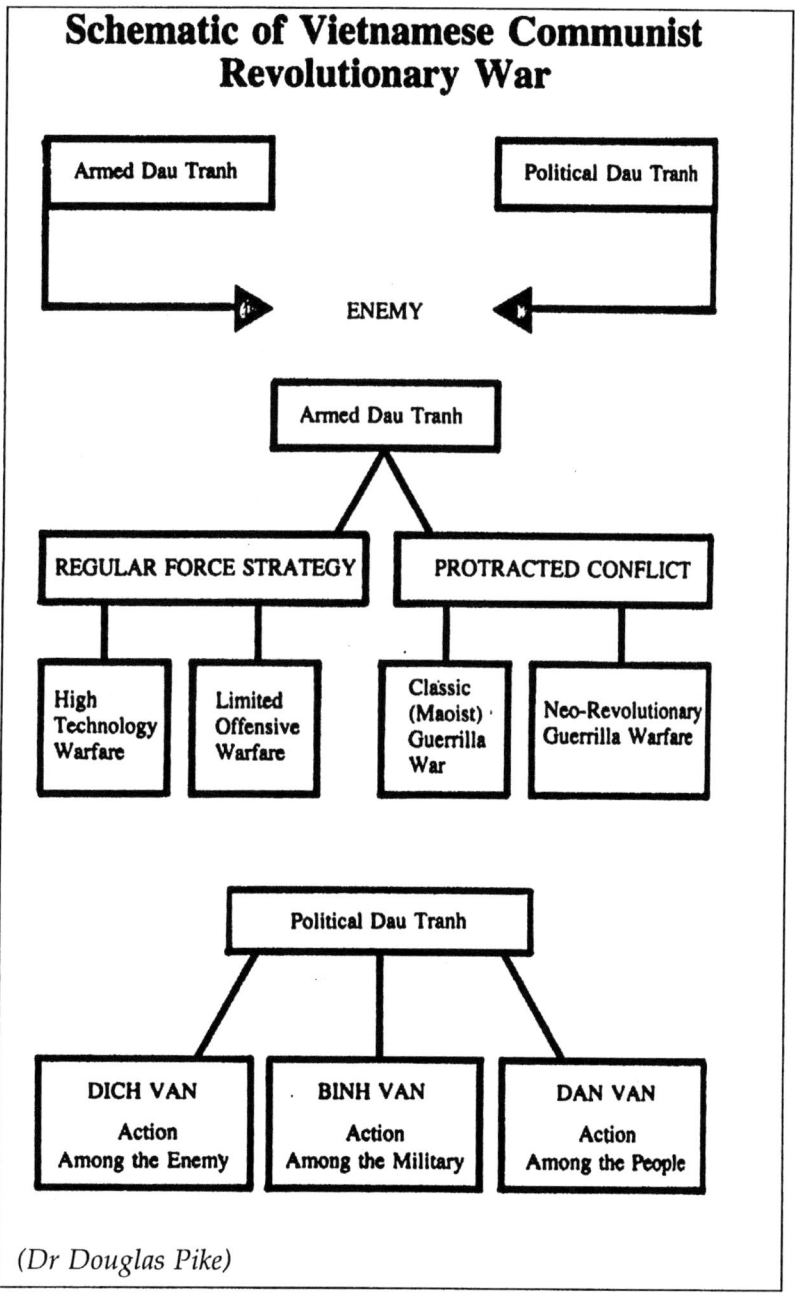

Schematic of Vietnamese Communist Revolutionary War

Armed Dau Tranh

Political Dau Tranh

ENEMY

Armed Dau Tranh

REGULAR FORCE STRATEGY

PROTRACTED CONFLICT

High Technology Warfare

Limited Offensive Warfare

Classic (Maoist) Guerrilla War

Neo-Revolutionary Guerrilla Warfare

Political Dau Tranh

DICH VAN

Action Among the Enemy

BINH VAN

Action Among the Military

DAN VAN

Action Among the People

(Dr Douglas Pike)

constructive in making them more sensitive to other people's needs, and made them think more deeply about their priorities and those of the revolution.

The US military boot camp could be regarded as an illustration of the negative use of the group process, because of the brutalising power of sarcastic DIs (drill instructors). Robert Pisor, in his book *The End of the Line: The Siege of Khe Sanh*, wrote that in his Marine boot camp he and his peers became technically proficient soldiers, but emerged 'with a diminished capacity for compassion'.

Dr Peter G. Bourne, a psychiatrist, wrote an essay entitled *From Boot Camp to My Lai 4*, which appeared in a book called *Crimes of War*. He saw a direct connection between boot camp experience and the massacre at My Lai 4.

Part of the time spent in groups in North Vietnam was devoted to self-criticism and examination, and evaluation by peers – again, a technique used in the west in the training of therapists and psychiatrists. You'd think this could be rather shattering, but on the contrary, once people felt accepted by the group, they liked it, and it strengthened their commitment to the revolutionary cause.

There were also formal lectures at least twice a week for army personnel, given by the local Political Officer for indoctrination. Probably the work with small groups, however, was a more effective way of winning and holding people's loyalty.

Q.   You're describing here methods used in communist North Vietnam, to steer and influence them to identify with the party. What was done to reach those outside North Vietnam?

A.   There were three programmes of propaganda set up for people outside North Vietnam which affected PAVN indirectly, for they paved the way for victory. They were called for short the 'van' programmes (*van* meaning 'action among'). They were:

1.   'Dich van', action among the enemy: propaganda aimed at pro-American people in South Vietnam, and at the US

government.

2. 'Binh van', action among the troops and civil servants of South Vietnam. Its pressure raised the number of desertions from the ARVN.

3. 'Dan van' was a highly organised programme of 'action among the people', that is, those of the National Liberation Front, pro-communist, to control and influence them so that they would support PAVN.

Part II
PAVN and US Forces in Vietnam:
Differences in their Situation

Q.   Is there any point in discussing this subject? Aren't the differences obvious?

A.   Well, yes, the differences are clear, but the reasons for them aren't. Tell me one which seems obvious to you.

Q.   How about the fact that the PAVN soldiers were fighting in their own country, but the US ones were far from their homeland?

A.   Exactly. You see, straightaway you've mentioned a factor in the conflict which you may think so obvious it's trite, but its implications are profound. Often the Vietnamese were fighting on, and for, ancestral land, sacred in their culture, so they had to defend it and resist its desecration to the death.

Q.   Had they any idea how long the war would be?

A.   Not exactly, but they were told to expect a long, hard war. By contrast, the US never actually declared war on the DRV. A declaration of war was considered an anachronism. But it would have given the men credibility at home, and would have made them feel they belonged in Vietnam while the war was on, instead of having to justify their presence all the time.

     Only a very small proportion of the American people took part in the conflict, whereas in the DRV everyone was totally involved.

Q.   What other differences in the circumstances of the two forces have you noted?

A.   There are several. I think they could be grouped loosely under aspects of life-style, of organisational structure, and of emotions and attitude. In reality these interact and are connected with each other.

     One big difference in life-style was that the North Vietnamese troops served till death or victory, whereas the US troops had a tour of duty not more than a year, possibly less. Internally, too, officers were sometimes moved after only a few months to a different unit, so 'unit cohesion', and strong fellowship between men and their leaders, was hard to achieve. The experience of the troops departing after a year was lost as they were continually being replaced by new ones with no experience in Vietnam.

A characteristic of US troops' life-style in Vietnam was their large number of lavishly equipped bases. These were in marked contrast to the functional PAVN bases, and rooms in tunnel complexes; US bases often had air-conditioning, fridges, showers, and concrete sidewalks; some officers had perks such as a villa at the coast and a private helicopter. The bases frequently were so huge that their upkeep absorbed thousands of men.

Q. Well, in combat their life was pretty grim, wasn't it? Should you grudge them a few comforts?

A. No, but the problem was, that after meeting base requirements for supplies, building, repairs, messing, medical and personal services, and so forth, only an estimated one man in ten was available for actual combat duties. (Some authors give a slightly higher ratio, however.)

Edward N. Luttwak, in his book *The Pentagon and the Art of War*, writing about the US troops in Vietnam, stated: 'The country gave its men to be soldiers, but the system turned them into clerks and valets, mechanics and storekeepers, in huge and disproportionate numbers'.

The trouble was, it was bad for morale, when men sweltering in the jungle on patrol, or huddled at a fire base, compared their lot bitterly with that of their peers back at base HQ.

Q. Don't you think, for the PAVN troops, the point of war – to drive out the invaders and their flunkies, to begin with – was a lot easier to grasp than it was for the American soldiers, for whom the scene was much more confused?

A. Oh yes, much more. For a start, on the US side there were three sections of the war churning along on their own momentum, without anyone trying to form any kind of connection or 'sync' one with another. There was the ground fighting, the bombing, and the mixed bag of pacification and Special Forces projects. The various intelligence groups weren't co-ordinated either.

The USSR and PRC (People's Republic of China) gave arms to PAVN, but no other allies fought beside them. But the US was fighting a coalition war. Their allies were South Vietnamese, Koreans, New Zealanders, and 'Aussies', each with their own command structure.

The US troops were fighting a limited war: that is, they weren't allowed to invade North Vietnam because of the risk of starting a war with China; but the PAVN troops could push as far south as they could manage.

To add to the complexity of the scene on the US side, every branch of the services had their own layers of officers, NCOs and supply people.

Q.   I've always associated the US-Vietnam War with helicopters – hundreds and hundreds of them everywhere, some small, some huge, with men firing from their sides and others leaping out and running into the jungle, guns blazing; yet they're really the most fragile of aircraft, and can be downed by ordinary rifle fire. How come they were used so much in Vietnam?

A.   Your question is a key one and leads us right to the heart of the US's military problems in Vietnam. There are three aspects of these problems I would like to touch on:
i.   The 'airmobile system',
ii.   The 'unified command system', and
iii.   The overlapping high command systems.

i   There was a lot of controversy about the helicopters; it was connected to, and involved, the fierce independence of each branch of the forces, and the rivalry between them. The Air Force had a monopoly on all fixed-wing aircraft over 5000 pounds weight. The Army chiefs didn't want to be indebted to the Air Force people, but wanted to have supporting aircraft of their own. There wasn't any restriction on their use of helicopters; they sent in massive orders for them, creating a gold mine for the military-industrial complex.

Gen.Hamilton H. Howze set up the 'airmobile' system, by which all the troops would have their own support, under the same command: that is, there were Air Force and Army planes, and Marine and Navy planes. Soon it came about that each branch had lots of choppers, used not only in supporting roles such as rescuing, supplying, and troop-carrying, but in actual assault and attack as well, dangerously overcrowding the airspace available.

Q.   Did the DRV have this 'airmobile' problem?

A.   No; their set-up was different altogether. Under the terms of the Geneva Accords of 1954, they were unable to add new branches to their forces, so they had the 'PAVN Air Force' and the 'PAVN Navy' – it wasn't just a question of clever semantics, because they really were all under the same administrative umbrella. The Air Force and Navy weren't considered separate bodies from the Army; if a pilot or sailor were decorated he was called 'a hero of the People's *Army.*'

Q.   I see. What did you mean by the 'unified' command system?

A.   ii   Under the Unification Act of 1949 each branch of the armed forces of the US became 'unified' – parallel, as it were – and none had more authority than the others; they had equal clout and could *not* be overruled.

This sounds very democratic, but in a time of war or crisis it was not a very effective arrangement. At the time of the US-Vietnam War, General Paul D. Harkins, whom General Westmoreland succeeded, proposed that the Army should be in command over US forces in Vietnam, but was shot down by the COs of the other branches. Yet at the siege of Khe Sanh, in South Vietnam, in 1968, the Marines, who were holding the fort, wanted their planes to provide air support, but were overruled when the Joint Chiefs of Staff favoured the claim of the Air Force to provide all supplies by air for the garrison. Because of deadly enemy fire it proved to be a thankless, dangerous task.

Q.   Where did the U.S. Joint Chiefs of Staff fit into the various command systems during the U.S.-Vietnam War.

A.   The trouble was, they didn't really fit in anywhere. Before 1958 they had been part of a direct line of command, extending from the president to the Secretary of Defense, on to themselves and then to the service chiefs; but under the Defense Reorganisation Act of 1958, the chain of command went directly from the Secretary of Defense to the service chiefs, bypassing the JCS. They were left out on a limb in an off-line position as advisors. Each member naturally had the interests of his own branch of the services at heart, so this actually had the effect of adding to the infighting, and compartmental thinking, of the forces, not lessening them (unintentionally). They had no power to monitor waste or duplication.

Q.   What did you mean by your reference to the 'overlapping' high command system?

A.   Unlike the PAVN, which came close to achieving unity of command, the US forces were unable to do so because they had so many commands in Vietnam. US Military Assistance Command, Vietnam (MACV) was included in, and under, US Pacific Command (CINCPAC), or Commander-in-Chief, Pacific. The bombing of North Vietnam was done by Strategic Air Command, but the Air Force and Army had flying missions under CINCPAC. The various 'airmobile' divisions had their own commands, as described.

So US air power, though massive in the area, was applied piecemeal.

(The end of the dialogue).

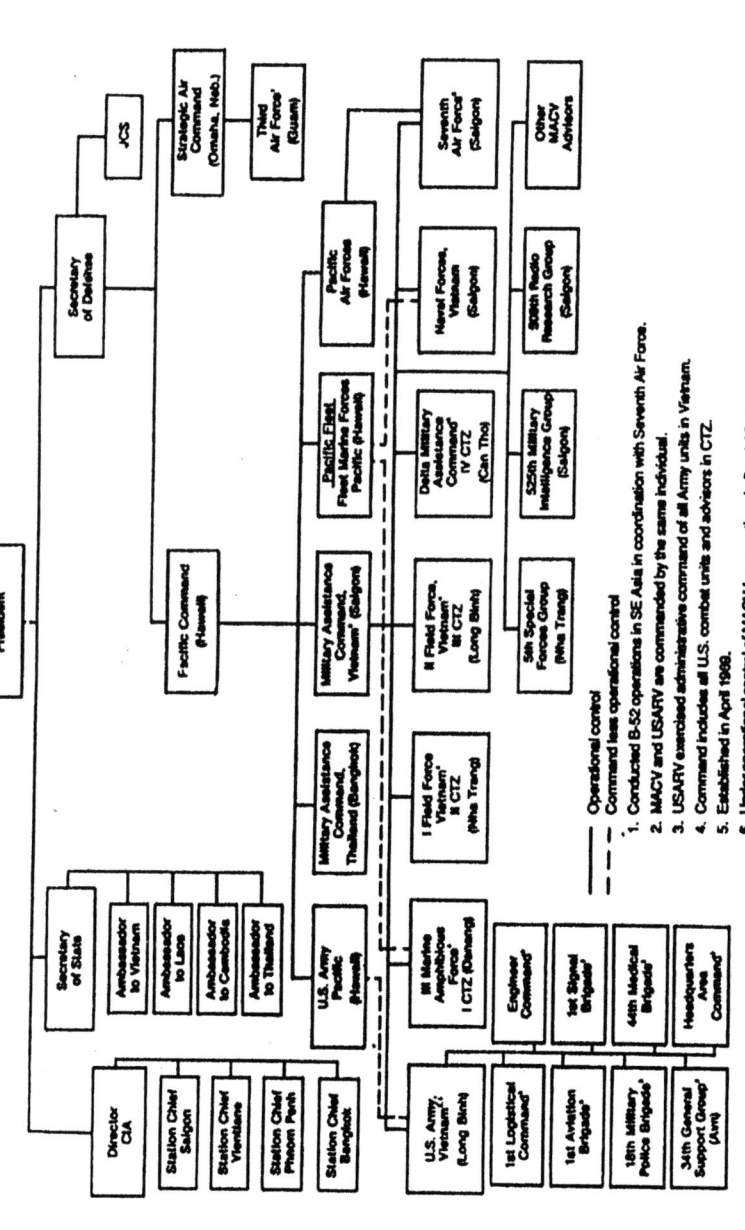

Diagram, US Command Structure in South-East Asia, 1967.
(Copyright 1984 by the University of Kentucky)

CHAPTER EIGHT

Fetishism in the US-Vietnam War: the Message from Anthropology

Officially, a deafening silence broods over the most bizarre and pathological incidents of the war. However, some of them have been recorded in a collection entitled *In the Name of America; Clergy and Laymen Concerned about Vietnam*, and in evidence given to the Russell International War Crimes Tribunal, published in book form under the title, *Against the Crime of Silence*. In autobiographical books about the war, by people who fought in it, there are some short, scattered, eye-witness accounts.

One bizarre practice was to take a body part from an enemy and keep it for a fetish. Depending on the context, the term 'fetish' can mean an object believed to have magical powers, or something about which a person may have unduly strong feelings; or an object, which though not really erotic in itself, may be sexually stimulating under some circumstances.

One fetish was for human ears. When a Vietcong soldier was killed in the jungle, one or both of his ears might be cut off and kept as trophies. If a man would or could not get them himself they could be bought for about thirty dollars apiece. Sometimes they were strung up as a decoration. They could be seen impaled on the antenna of a jeep, like kebabs.

In June 1967, in *Nation*, Desmond Smith reported that an enemy ear preserved in a bottle of alcohol was displayed in the officers' quarters at a base.

Heads were in demand, too. One officer issued his men with a kind of hunting knife called a Kabar knife, and promised a case of whisky to the first man who would bring him proof that he had used his knife against the enemy.

So a small group of soldiers went into the jungle. When the men thought they detected a movement in the undergrowth alongside the trail, one of them plunged into the bushes. There were sounds of a scuffle, and then he emerged carrying the newly-severed head of a very young Vietnamese man. Before he took it back to the CO to claim the prize, the group tossed it around to each other, with a lot of laughter and coarse comments. Only one man showed any distress. Sobbing and almost vomiting, he said: 'My God, this is an awful place! We're turning into animals!' This incident was reported in *Time*, May 1966, by Malcom Browne, and reprinted in the collection *In the Name of America*.

No objections were raised if South Vietnamese troops cut off the heads of prisoners believed to be Vietcong. Fingers were sometimes cut off and kept, as were sexual organs, but ears are most frequently mentioned as the objects of fetishist desire. A bag of dried human ears was offered to one reporter as a gift.

An incident in a raid on a village, when a man's abdomen was ripped open with a Kabar knife and his gallbladder removed while he was still living, was reported to the War Crimes Tribunal by Mr Donald Duncan, a former member of the US Special Forces, or 'Green Berets', who had served in Vietnam. The raid was carried out by members of the ARVN, supervised by the Special Forces. The man who took the gall-bladder wore it for several weeks in a little bag around his neck, and displayed it proudly to his friends, probably believing it to have aphrodisiac power.

Without actually committing this crime themselves, the Special Forces people present gave tacit approval to it by standing around and making no effort to prevent it. As so often happened during the US-Vietnam War, something highly abnormal was passed over as normal. Behaviour which would have been considered criminally insane at home, like torturing prisoners, throwing poison gas into tunnels full of people, and burning homes and rice stores, was commonplace in Vietnam in the war.

Even so, when it comes to men hoarding and fondling parts of the body cut from an enemy, it is as if we had stepped over a line and entered a new dimension of the grotesque, more horrible than anyone had ever experienced. It is as if the soldiers had said, like Satan in Milton's *Paradise Lost:*

'Farewell happy Fields
Where Joy for ever dwells: Hail, horrors, hail
Infernal world, and thou profoundest Hell
Receive thy new Possessor . . . '

One of the fallen angels, called Belial ('A fairer person lost not Heav'n', as Milton described him) summed up very well the concept of the growing banality of evil: we get so used to it, it ceases to bother us. Total evil, he said, would soon become banal to the satanic troops:

'Our purer essence . . . to the place conform'd
In temper and in nature, will receive
Familiar the fierce heat, and void of pain;
This horror will grow mild, this darkness light . . .'

(Ibid.)

There were several characteristics common to fetishist acts in the war in Vietnam, as listed below:

1.   The fetishes had no military purpose.
2.   The parts of the body were taken by males, from males.
3.   The fetish was not kept secret or private but was a public, social affair. The man who took the gallbladder, as described, flaunted it to his friends. Ears were displayed. Only one account describes a man with a fetish in solitude; he was found sitting by himself in the jungle, lovingly spraying a human ear with insect repellent. (Desmond Smith, in *Nation.* Quoted in *The Name of America)*
4.   The practice of taking fetishes was usually condoned by officers, and sometimes even encouraged.
5.   The practice was illegal under international laws of war.

The acquisition of a part of an enemy's body, to be kept as a fetish, must have been an attempt to deal with a lot of chaotic feelings. Was it a desire for revenge, after the violent death of a close friend in an ambush? It expressed the need to vent pent-up anger and fear after a long gruelling day in intense heat; hacking one's way through thick jungle carrying heavy gear, yet never getting anywhere; and constantly knowing the enemy was close, but seldom seeing him. Some men felt a need to show their peers that they were tough, and 'had what it takes', despite their own private misgivings about their courage. There was a connection between fetish-taking and poor morale; some men felt the war made no sense, that it was all pointless, and they were trapped in an insane situation.

Recent anthropological studies can throw some light on the meaning of fetishism in warfare. In Victorian times, anthropological writings would often have at least a tinge of condescending imperialism; as Kipling put it, primitive man ('half devil and half child') needed our help, and it was our duty to see that he got it, and so take up the white man's burden.

Another concept which has died very hard, was that of modern man being somehow the supreme culmination of a process of constant improvement along a continuum of progress from primitive man to ourselves. Now there are a lot of doubts about these myths of the childishness of primitive men: evidence is not being found to support them. On the contrary, recent studies reveal that the rituals performed by so-called 'primitive' tribes often expressed deep and complex emotions, not at a less developed stage than ours, but parallel with them. Chants and dances for specific occasions were important safety-valves, symbolically, for deep emotions.

Thus if a group of people, like some US patrols in the jungle of Vietnam, took what appears to outsiders to be a step over into the realm of the insane, and cut fetishist parts from the enemies' bodies, these actions could have had their own desperate logic, expressing the men's rage and hopelessness as their early idealism was lost forever.

A frustrated search for meaning, seen as a way of understanding puzzling bizarre behaviour in groups, was discussed by Dr Clifford Geertz, an anthropologist, and Dr Jonathan Miller, in a dialogue entitled *Notions of Primitive Thought*. It appeared in a collection edited by Dr Miller, called *States of Mind*.

Speaking of occult practices and strange cults, Dr Geertz

said that interest in them increased when people found that thinking rationally did not work any more. He thought that the belief that the world has no meaning can give rise to aberrant and bizarre behaviour, adding:

> 'But the attempt to try to make sense of the world, however ineptly *with whatever strange materials*, is not in itself to my mind a psychotic or pre-psychotic thing to do . . . it is the absence of some way to make sense of things that leads to the collective madness.' (From *States of Mind* ed. Jonathan Miller,)

In the larger bases and in the cities of Vietnam there were hundreds of non-combatant Americans for whom the war was not at all unbearable, as they had air-conditioned quarters, and regular meals and showers; but for the small groups of men sent on foot into enemy areas, it was a different world. They felt cut off from all normal life. Their usual values were turned upside down, and people admired a man who did something really cruel and vicious. Loyalty to the death to one's own officers, usually considered the great strength of army esprit de corps, could rapidly evaporate in the heat and terror, and the all-pervading stench of corpses that men experienced in combat zones.

In the late 1960s and early 1970s there were many incidents of assaults on US officers. They were called 'fragging' because of the fragmenting type of bullet often used. Eighty-three was the official figure quoted as being the number of officers killed in this way, but many deaths were reported as deaths in action by enemy hands, in spite of unexplained bullet wounds in officers' backs. Many officers were wounded by their own men, and bounties of several hundred dollars were offered to have some most hated officers killed.

In these circumstances morale became very low, men absented themselves from their allotted duty stations, or refused to go on particularly dangerous or brutal missions, and officers became afraid to insist on orders being obeyed. Men in small, isolated patrols had a sense of grievance, feeling they had been misled about what the war would really be like. Often their officers were not actually with them but only gave commands from helicopters, sometimes not touching down. It was hard to discern in their sorties any purposeful strategy which would have made men feel they were making good use of their combat training. So atrocities and rumours of atrocities increased.

Changes for the worse in usually law-abiding individuals when in a group, can happen in civilian settings, too. J. Patrick Wright in his book *On a Clear Day You Can See General Motors*, writing in the chapter entitled 'How Moral Men Make Immoral Decisions', described how the managing directors of General Motors refused to authorise changes in the Corvair to make it safer. This car, whose engine was at the rear, had a 'swing-axle' suspension in the first model. If driven at high speed round a sharp turn the car could flip over. While some engineers thought the suspension adequately safe, many others with long experience in building that type of car pleaded with top management to take it out of production, or at least hold it back for checking. Their requests were refused. The Corvair had been meant to appeal to the fast-driving 'with-it' young set. There were many terrible crashes, some involving members of GM executives' families. Belatedly, a rear stabilising bar was put on later models to minimise the chance of the car flipping over.

J. Patrick Wright considered the case of the Corvair to be an example of an immoral decision, made in a group by men of high personal moral standards. He stated that:

'It seemed to me, and still does, that the system of American business often produces wrong, immoral and irresponsible decisions, even though the personal morality of the people running the businesses is often quite above reproach. The system has a different morality as a group than the people do as individuals.' (From *On a Clear Day You Can See General Motors* by J. Patrick Wright)

J. Patrick Wright's last sentence, above, could have been tailor-made to describe basic policy of the involvement of the United States in Vietnam, justified by system morality, not personal morality. Loyalty to the objectives of the prevailing administration could make actions which were immoral seem moral, at least for a time. Bombing raids on Cambodia, seeming 'OK' from the perspective of an in-group around the president in Washington, were totally immoral seen in any other light. No guilt was felt about altering the numbers given of American dead, or figures of the combat strength of the enemy, if such practices appeared to be in accord with the good of the system. Whole paragraphs were cut from journalists' reports, if they were too depressing and raised questions about official policy.

Some of the writings of American men who fought in the war convey an overwhelming feeling of malaise, and sense of corruption seeping down to them from the top. Yet they could not have known much about the politics of the war; some asked themselves, were they going through all the anguish of seeing their best friends blown apart for a government which was deeply immoral? The cynicism and despair so produced could lead men to the madness of fetishism, and the caressing of severed Vietnamese ears.

Part of the Wall of the Citadel, Hue, Vietnam, with bullet marks from the US-Vietnam War

CHAPTER NINE

Vietnam and White House Power in the Nixon-Kissinger Period

After Richard Nixon became President of the US in 1969, the power of the White House, which had been increasing for several years, reached its zenith. The effect on the course of events in Vietnam was tragic. As more and more policy decisions were made in the Executive Branch without informing, let alone consulting, Congress, the war dragged on and on, wasteful and brutal, and the peace talks were inconclusive. In the Nixon years Congress played almost no role in US foreign policy, which was dictated almost exclusively by the president and his National Security Advisor, Dr Henry Kissinger (who in 1973 became Secretary of State as well).

There were many reasons why this state of affairs had come about. In August 1964, following reports that American destroyers in the Gulf of Tonkin had been attacked by North Vietnamese torpedo boats, Congress had passed the 'Gulf of Tonkin Resolution', by 416 to 0 votes in the House of Representatives, and by 88 to 2 in the Senate. The Resolution gave President Lyndon Johnson unlimited power and increased funds to escalate the war in Vietnam, and to any nation guaranteed help by SEATO (South-East Asia Treaty Organisation), assistance was promised if requested. After that, it was as if Congress looked the other way and did not feel its members could query foreign policy affairs. They were habitually more concerned with domestic matters, and with promoting the interests of the regions where their constituents – who had voted them into office in the first place-were residing.

Yet a considerable abdication of power had taken place. According to the Constitution, Congress has the right to declare war and to appropriate the funds needed to fight it; and it can impeach and remove a president from office. But a president cannot impeach or remove members of the Congress. A president can veto legislation passed by Congress, but the veto can be over-ruled if two-thirds of both the House of Representatives and the Senate vote that way.

Ultimate authority, when the chips are down, rests therefore with the Congress. However, with regard to the armed forces, the framers of the Constitution intended that there should be a dynamic give and take between the president and the Congress, as the president was named Commander-in-Chief of the army and navy, yet the Congress was meant to monitor and check what went on. Section 8, Article One of the Constitution states that: 'The Congress shall have power . . . to raise and support Armies . . . to provide and maintain a Navy; to make rules for the Government and Regulation of the land and naval Forces . . . '

Fine, in theory; but it is hard for the Congress to regulate or govern policies its members do not know very much about. On most of the main features of President Nixon's foreign policy in Indochina, such as the Vietnamisation of the armed forces, the invasion of Cambodia, the visit to China, and the increased bombing of North Vietnam, no open dialogue took place. Congress suffered from a chronic shortage of up-to-date information. There were not enough people whose job it was to ferret out data and get feedback, and far fewer facilities to do it with: e.g., fewer computers, office staff, and rooms than were available in the Executive Branch.

Even when the members of Congress did try to monitor the various committees and sub-committees of the Executive Branch, they got into a rather circular activity, as they could only report on the information given to them, not on what was left out; it was like asking the fox for news of the chicken coop.

Dr Kissinger, whose appointment as National Security Advisor did not need to be ratified by the Senate, did not have to report to the House. Following the lobbying process set up by the Department of Defense, persons called 'Congressional liaison agents', in large numbers, were sent instead. Offices were provided for them, so that outposts of the Executive Branch grew up within the very halls of Congress. These agents would funnel selected data to the House and Senate committees, which by 1970 had increased to three hundred and five, if one counts sub-committees, as compared to only thirty-four in 1946.

During the Nixon administration this bureaucratisation of Congress was paralleled by a similar process in the Executive Branch, where inter-agency groups and committees multiplied. In February 1973 Senator Muskie complained to the director of the Office of Management and Budget, set up in 1970 in the Executive Branch, that the administration was spoon-feeding Congress only 'the info you decide we ought to have, in the way you decide we ought to have it and at the time you decide we ought to have it.'[1]

Similarly, the House Rules Committee reported that members felt that unelected bureaucrats, virtually forming a fourth branch of government, were taking over the prerogatives of Congress, and allocating billions of dollars in funds wherever they pleased.

The main reason for the growth of the National Security Council and other executive agencies was basically to do with internal power politics. They were meant to mask an autocratic situation, and enable the President to receive advice suited to his wishes in policy-forming, leaving massive bureaucracies such as the Department of State and of Defense on the sidelines, while going through the motions of appearing to include their staff in decision-making processes.

There has probably never been a time in the history of the US when a balance, satisfactory to everyone concerned, was achieved between the power of the presidency and the other two branches of government. Over the generations power fluctuated between them. Not intending to create a source of conflict in which people thought in terms of 'Us' against 'Them', the Founders of the Constitution of the US had in mind a president and a Congress complementing each other: the president with executive power, able to act speedily if need be; and the Congress able to deliberate more slowly on the matter in hand.

A precedent for increased executive power was set by

---

1   From *Who Runs Congress?* by Mark Green with Michael Waldman

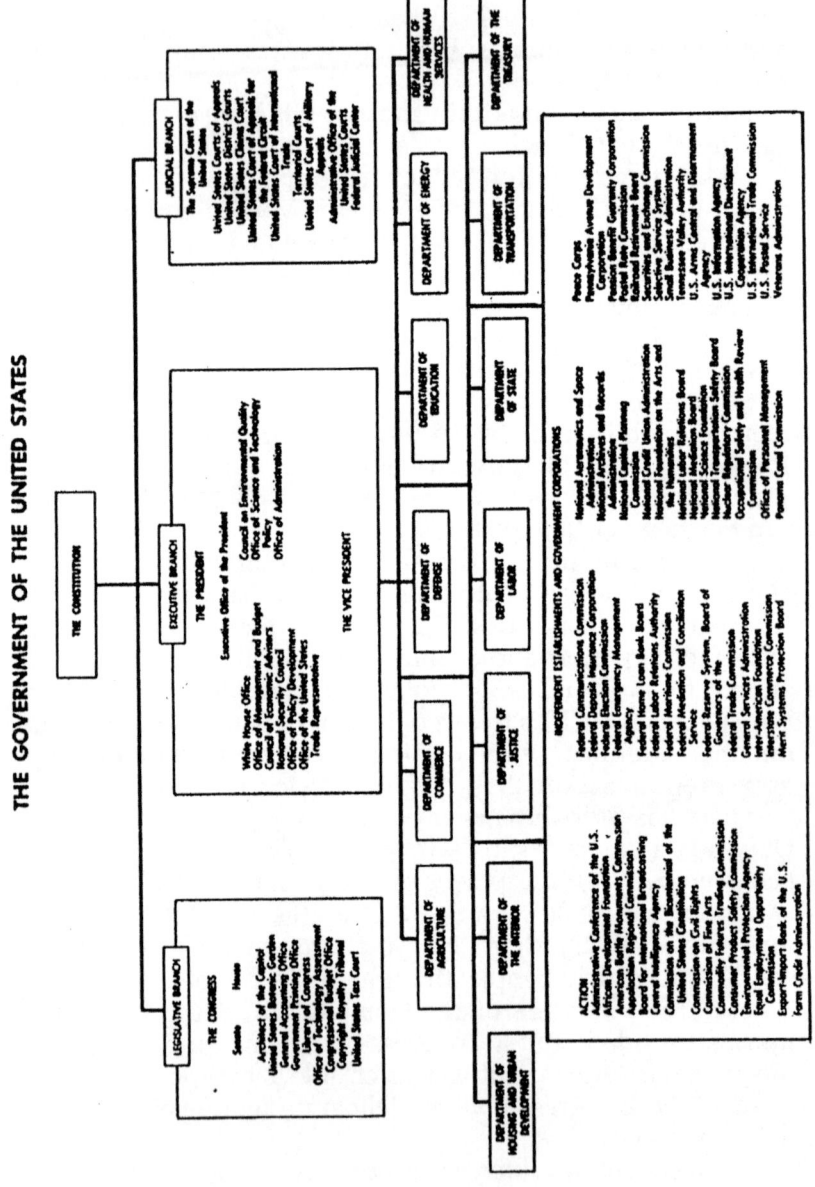

THE GOVERNMENT OF THE UNITED STATES

From the US Government Manual

President Lincoln who, early in the Civil War, declared martial law, suspended habeas corpus, called up thousands of troops and spent large sums of money without waiting for Congress to convene so that he could get the members' agreement. They just gave their approval afterwards. Through long periods in the nineteenth century, however, the Congress, not the president, took the lead in bringing in new laws, and the president was expected to approve what was done, not give advice beforehand.

After the assassination of President William McKinley in September 1901, Theodore Roosevelt became President, and because of his forceful personality, his office became more dominating. In his presidency, Franklin D. Roosevelt greatly increased the power of the president, and in 1939 reorganised the Executive Branch, expanding it to include more agencies and staff, thus laying the basis for the complex system that was in place in the US-Vietnam War era in the White House; and then, in the Vietnam period, President Lyndon Johnson continued the process of keeping power in the White House by excluding Congress from major decisions, and being secretive and misleading about the real price the country was paying for the war: not only financially, but also in terms of numbers of Americans dead and wounded.

President Nixon represented, in his outlook, the high point in the rise in presidential power. He did not see the presidency as a sharing of power, but believed that, in the last analysis, the president was above the law, and did not have to account to anyone for his actions. When, during an enquiry, he was asked in 1973 to explain why he had agreed to let the CIA, for a certain time, open mail belonging to US citizens, he stated:

'It is quite obvious that there are certain inherently governmental actions, which if undertaken by the sovereign in protection of the interest of the nation's security, are lawful, but which if undertaken by private persons are not . . . it is naive to attempt to categorise activities a President might authorise as 'legal' or 'illegal' without reference to the circumstances . . . ' (From *CIA, The 'Honourable' Company*, by Brian Freemantle).

President Nixon never actually signed an authorisation for

the mail to be opened, and later withdrew his verbal agreement.

Soon after Dr Kissinger had become National Security Advisor for President Nixon late in 1968, he began work on a plan, based on the structure already in place, to reorganise the roles of the National Security Council and of the Advisor, in such a way that control of foreign policy would pass totally to the Executive Branch.

The fate of thousands in South-East Asia hung on the bureaucratic changes in Washington, as the centre of gravity for foreign affairs decisions shifted to the White House, and in practice Dr Kissinger became chief of state for national security, taking over not only the formulation of policy but its conduct as well. The Secretaries of State and of Defense, and even some members of the NSC were not kept informed always.

In December 1968 Dr Kissinger asked Morton Halperin to prepare a paper for him on the application of systems analysis methods to help the president in sorting information, and making decisions, on foreign policy issues. Morton Halperin, whom Dr Kissinger had known at Harvard, had been working in the Office of International Security Affairs in the Department of Defense.

There were many committees spawning paperwork for the president to read, as Lyndon Johnson found when in 1966 he tried to find a neater way of reviewing recommended policies; he set up the Senior Interdepartmental Group, chaired by the Under-Secretary of State, called the SIG. Reporting to the SIG were five Interdepartmental Regional Groups, called IRGs, whose function was to offer a wide range of policy options to the president regarding various regions of the world.[2] These arrangements, however, did not alter the situation in which members of the Department of State, not the National Security Advisor or the National Security Council, chose what questions would be asked, what issues explored, or data provided, on foreign affairs. The system nurtured conservatism and maintenance of the status quo.

In Morton Halperin's plan the IRGs were retained and re-

---

2   From *Uncertain Greatness,* by Roger Morris

named Interdepartmental Groups; but they were to be responsible to a new committee called the Review Group, over which
Dr Kissinger presided. Its members were senior representatives of various government agencies. Dr Kissinger used to
send the Interdepartmental Groups National Security Study
Memoranda, or NSSMs, as they were called. These gave
guidelines on the issues on which they had to prepare reports.
They did this under the supervision of members of Dr
Kissinger's staff, who, if satisfied with the work, gave the
reports to the National Security Council for discussion. Then
the president could make a decision based on the choices put
before him, and it was only after such a discussion that the
Under-Secretary of State could monitor the decision, at a
committee meeting where sat – you guessed it – Dr Kissinger.
The Review Group chose the agenda anyway.

The lines of communication all circled back to Dr Kissinger.
President Nixon told him: 'OK, but you'll have to get it past
Rogers,' meaning, he would need the consent of William P.
Rogers, Secretary of State, for the plan. Dr Kissinger obtained
this. Melvin Laird, Secretary of Defense, asked Dr Kissinger to
have the CIA represented in the system, to which Dr Kissinger
agreed, although he pointed out that it had been correct to
exclude the agency at first, as it was not a policy-making
group.

Roger Morris, in his book *Uncertain Greatness*, which relates
Dr Kissinger's rise to power, recalls that within a year of his
taking office he was chairman not only of the Review Group,
but in addition he presided over the Verification Panel concerning arms control strategy, the Washington Special Actions
Group for crisis management, the Vietnam Special Studies
Group, and the Defense Program Review Committee. The
Joint Chiefs of Staff came to feel that he usurped their role, and
thought that his assistant, Colonel Alexander M. Haig, Jr, was
listened to with more respect than General Abrams and other
more experienced serving commanders in the field.

The new plan set up by Dr Kissinger began a major change
in the traditional role of the National Security Council and the
Advisor for National Security. They ceased to be advisors only
and became involved in carrying out policies. When President
Truman created the Council under the National Security Act

of 1947, it was stated in the Act that:

> 'The function of the Council shall be to *advise* the President with respect to the integration of domestic, foreign, and military policies relating to the national security, so as to enable military services and the other departments and agencies of the Government to cooperate more effectively in matters involving the national security.'

In successive administrations the size and importance of the National Security Council varied, according to the preferences and working style of each president. President Eisenhower enlarged it and used many committees, but after some time began to think there were too many people involved. So President Kennedy reduced the staff of the Council to only twelve professionals. President Johnson also preferred to work with just a small council, and he liked speed and informality above all, which of course could lead to the neglect of proper record-keeping. Under President Nixon the Council was once more much enlarged, up to fifty professionals by 1970, plus the attendant committees. So the National Security Council was very much the expression of each President's way of operating, and was usually not in the limelight, and not subject to checking by the Congress.

Similarly, the National Security Advisor, or the Assistant to the president for National Security Affairs, as he was called at first, had traditionally kept a low profile. President Eisenhower created the position in 1953, and under him the Advisor was the chief executive officer of the Council, and was not a policy-making person. The Advisor was meant to be an 'honest broker' for the president, impartially informing him on the options available to him in foreign policy affairs, and the various points of view about them. However, as noted in *The Tower Commission Report* of 1987, if the president relied too much on the help of his National Security Advisor and excluded his cabinet, there could be friction and the loss of advice from some experienced people. The Secretary of State was, by tradition, the president's spokesman for foreign affairs. If the National Security Advisor took over this role, as Dr Kissinger did long before becoming Secretary of State as well in 1973, some problems would be inevitable. There would be confusion about the president's foreign policy; it would be hard for the NSA to be really objective and to avoid thinking of his work in terms of personal triumphs or disasters for himself; and people would query the legitimacy of a one-man-band operator for the whole nation.

Dr Kissinger was careful to defuse criticism by holding press conferences at which selected information was given out, and by favouring some Congressmen with private interviews. But the basic, institutionalised flaw in the system of government, enabling unelected figures to control enormous power, remained unchanged.

This flaw made possible the dragging out of the US-Vietnam War for years and years, while attempts to make an end were limited to negotiations by Dr Kissinger or Colonel Haig almost exclusively. No alternative approaches were tried or other people brought in, no innovative moves, such as asking President Thieu of South Vietnam, or even Le Duc Tho of the North Vietnam Polit-Buro himself, to Washington for a conference. The country seemed locked into a gruelling round of 'peace talks' alternating with renewed bombing of North Vietnam, very much in isolation, without any international resources for conciliation being brought to bear on the situation.

A lot of what was happening was kept secret; there was some justification by precedent for this, as the National Security Advisor by tradition was supposed to manage crises for the president promptly and privately. In addition, President Nixon was by nature very careful about confidentiality and fearful of possible breaches in it. So during his office the White House was wired up with more technology than it had ever been: it was full of hidden bugs, cameras, listening devices and so forth. In hindsight they seem Kafka-esque and unnecessary. The effect was to increase the insulation of the White House from the real world outside, and in particular from the horror of life in Vietnam at that time. What was going on inside the White House seemed more pressing and more exciting. President Nixon devised what he called his 'Madman Theory', thinking that if he were described as irrational and given to violent mood-swings, the North Vietnamese might quickly make concessions to the US.

Two illegal actions in which the administration was

implicated fitted in very much with the above scenario: first, the burgling of the office of the psychiatrist attending Daniel Ellsberg, who had leaked *The Pentagon Papers* to the New York Times; and secondly, the Watergate Affair – 'the poisonous afterbirth of Vietnam', as Andrew St George put it – when members of a Republican party group were caught trying to remove electronic bugging devices from Democratic Party campaign headquarters in a building called Watergate.

President Nixon's visit to China was innovative, certainly, but it was based on old cold war thinking. Dr Kissinger planned the trip, which took place in February 1972, because he thought that a rapprochement between China and the US might cause a cooling in relations between the USSR and China, and then both of them would reduce their aid to the North Vietnamese. They might put pressure on the latter to hold back their advance in South Vietnam to give time for the U.S. forces to withdraw, and to delay their final takeover of the South until after President Nixon's term of office had run out.

However, at that time neither the People's Republic of China nor the USSR changed their policy of sending help to North Vietnam. But there was much applause at home for the China visit; it was clever politically, appeased the left-wing critics, was well-covered on television, and was a refreshing change from McCarthyist harangues about the evils of communism. The pretence that Taiwan was the only 'real' China was dropped.

Dr Kissinger had wider concerns too; he had visited Chou En-lai in confidence several times to prepare for the visit, and saw that there might be some advantages for the US if he could indirectly bring about some guarded hostility between the USSR and China, and figuratively drive a wedge between them. The idea was to keep them both guessing as to the US's real intentions; the USSR might fear being isolated as a result of a new cosiness between China and the US, which would make them more amenable to accepting Dr Kissinger's plans for détente: there were various possibilities, in theory.

Meanwhile, the North Vietnamese protested to the People's Republic that they were betraying the cause of national liberation by welcoming the American president to China; while on the American side, the Chinese seemed to be helping

Vietnam in order to increase their own power. The Chinese for their part saw Vietnam through the prism of an oriental cold war logic: she was a useful buffer state against western imperialism.

Behind the rationale for getting at Hanoi via Peking and Moscow, which now seems a tortuous route, was the cold war monolithic perception of communism as the same everywhere; universally evil; and needing to be contained. US foreign policy with regard to Vietnam lacked any feel for other driving forces making up the Hanoi version of communism, such as fierce nationalism and Confucian principles.

In the cold war view of foreign policy, which President Nixon and Dr Kissinger had in common, decisions were made, and issues seen as important or unimportant, according to their relevance to the struggle for supremacy between the great powers. It was imperative to keep inviolate for the US a vast geo-political area, or sphere of influence. What mattered was the gamesmanship, in which Laos and Cambodia, or Vietnam for that matter, were not actual places where real people laughed and cried, but were more like bargaining chips to be used to the best advantage in a much bigger design outside their borders.

Dr Kissinger had two main theories, closely connected, on which to base his strategy for foreign policy: they were 'linkage', and the balance of power. In the Arthur K. Salomon Lecture on *Continuity and Change in American Foreign Policy*, given on 19th September 1977 at the Graduate School of Business Administration, New York University, Dr Kissinger described the concept of linkage as: 'the suggestion that we would design and manage our (foreign) policy with a clear understanding of how changes in one part of the international system affect other parts'.[3] He said that perception of linkage was synonymous with an overall strategic view, and that in an interdependent world the actions of a major power have consequences beyond the issue or region immediately concerned. Dr Kissinger also noted that Americans often had trouble with the idea of linkage because of their 'water-tight compartments' habits of thought, brought on by a highly

---

3   From *For the Record, Selected Statements, 1977-80*, by Henry Kissinger:

departmentalised system of higher education and a fragmented government bureaucracy. Linkage could be a patriotic way of thinking; Dr Kissinger stated during the course of his lecture at New York University that: 'Displays of American impotence in one part of the world, such as South-East Asia or Africa, have a direct effect on our credibility in other parts of the world, such as the Middle East' (Ibid.). (The term 'credibility' in this context probably has the connotation, of 'other nations' perception of our power'.) It was essential, Dr Kissinger said, to maintain the geo-political balance around the world. To him, this global balance of power was supremely important. One had to give up everything for it.

His comments on this subject and on war, in some extracts from *A Conversation with Walter Laqueur*, in *The Washington Quarterly*, January 1978, under the main title, *The Lessons of the Past*, are revealing. They throw some light on his baffling ability to be involved in the long-drawn-out suffering in Vietnam without being destroyed by it, (unlike President Lyndon Johnson, for instance). He thought that a foreign policy based on pure balance of power is very difficult to conduct, and requires a total commitment to the national interest on the part of the statesman.

Drawing on analogies from Napoleonic times, Dr Kissinger reasoned that the sovereignty of the state being all-important, war, if engaged in, should be an integral part of the planning for the national interest, not something the nation drifted into in an ad hoc way, with romantic patriotism. As General von Clausewitz himself had felt before him, he felt too that war was a rational political act, and a normal, not abnormal, situation between states, so there was no need to feel guilt or depression about it. Dr Kissinger's use of the theory of the balance of power did not address, however, the ends-means dilemma – does the end justify the means? For instance, North Vietnam was bombed to get 'peace'; and the Roman Catholic Cathedral at Hue was ruined in the process of 'saving western values', according to cold war thinking.

When President Nixon was running for office in 1968, he said that he had a secret plan to end the war in Vietnam, and several months later he revealed it. It became known as the

'Nixon Doctrine', and meant 'I will send arms, not men'. The plan was twofold: to cut down the numbers of US troops in Vietnam unit by unit, gradually phasing out the draft; and to swell the ARVN (South Vietnamese forces) to more than double their previous numbers, providing them with an enormous store of arms, supplies, and vehicles. The plan was called 'Vietnamisation'.

This was the old French 'Jaunissement' writ large; and in the end, in spite of brave fighting by some individuals, and temporary small victories in some areas, the result of the policy was no better than it had been in the fifties. It was really a strategy for withdrawal, and part of a cold war containment policy, but the containment was to be done at arm's length, as it were, by a client state.

Politically it was very successful at home, but only for the time being, however. It was recognised that the existing draft system had penalised men of limited education who could not win deferment by enrolling in university courses. From the end of 1969 the numbers drafted were lowered until at the end of January 1973 there were no more draft calls, and the US military presence in Vietnam was an all-volunteer force. In his book on American foreign policy entitled *Rise to Globalism*, Stephen E. Ambrose stated that by spring 1972 the number of American ground-troops had fallen to 70,000 from 540,000 present there four years earlier; deaths of Americans in combat had been reduced to one a day from three hundred a week. The steady stream of coffins draped in the flag and flown home to remote small towns and big cities of America, had dwindled to a trickle at last.

The huge orders for military gear of every kind needed for Vietnamisation assured President Nixon of the continuing support, through their enormous profits, of the big corporate arms manufacturers, and kept employment high in arms production and associated fields. So the policy, while unsatisfactory from a military point of view, was very satisfactory for the US military-industrial complex.

George Esper, writing in *The Eye-witness History of the Vietnam War, 1961-75*, described how millions of dollars were poured into training programmes for the South Vietnamese, whose forces increased to more than a million men by the end of 1969. They got, he said, a huge arsenal of '700,000 M16 rifles, 600 pieces of artillery, 30,000 grenade launchers, 10,000 machine guns and thousands of vehicles, including trucks, tanks, armoured personnel carriers, helicopters, planes and jets'. Entire military bases were handed over to the South Vietnamese, and no less than two hundred and forty-two US Navy river craft, used for patrolling the waterways of the Mekong Delta, were also given to them. Vietnamisation brought many problems in its train. The full gravity of its effect at home, causing increased inflation and an economy too dependent on defence orders, would not show until the time ahead when President Nixon's time in office would be long since over.

There were many immediate difficulties on the scene in Vietnam. After the bases were handed over to the ARVN many were stripped of all moveable items and looted. There was a lot of catching up to do and not enough time allotted in which to do it, as the South Vietnamese were used to having the Americans take command, do the planning, and take charge of logistics. There were many difficulties arising from the language barrier, particularly in training them in particular skills, such as flying and maintaining a helicopter. The basic trouble, however, with regard to the ARVN in learning new skills was not lack of ability, but lack of motivation. Unlike the North Vietnamese, who had a cause they passionately believed in, the soldiers of the south had no real incentive to follow the Americans into the deep jungles of Laos, Cambodia, or their own central highlands, and get killed or wounded therein (or at best, get bogged down there during the monsoon). On the contrary, they had a strong disincentive to going because they could make much more than their meagre pay by staying around Saigon and profiting from the black market. (There was once, on paper, a whole ghost battalion of phantom phoney soldiers, drawing US pay but never seeing any action because in reality they were all in Saigon busy trafficking.)

Graft and corruption were paramount; they always had been part of the way of life in Saigon, but with the glut of goods of all descriptions sent to the country under the Nixon Doctrine, the opportunities for illicit business were multiplied many hundred times over. Everyone, even government officers of high prestige, had some covert line of business on the side. Large objects such as trucks could disappear without trace. In South Vietnam the idea that war is an extension of commerce in another form took on a new cynicism.

General Bruce Palmer, Jr, in his book *The 25-Year War: America's Military Role in Vietnam*, described as one of the problems in dealing with corruption, the balkanisation of South Vietnam. The Republic was divided for administration into no less than forty-four provinces. The provincial chiefs had military as well as political control, and had their own armies, called regional forces. Then each province was subdivided into districts with their own pecking order of district chiefs, village chiefs, and leaders of part-time local militia. Vietnamisation brought apparent prosperity, but it was artificial, as most people did not produce any food or goods by their labour, but were directly or indirectly paid by the US for services of many kinds: as maids, pimps, secretaries, translators, and shoeshine boys, for example.

The Vietnamese people, true to their Confucian background, place loyalty to family and friends first on their list of priorities, and in the US-Vietnam war period saw nothing strange about hiding a friend or relative in South Vietnam who was one of the Vietcong; and they happily sent hundreds of bicycles, motor-bikes, radios, typewriters, and other useful items (meant for the ARVN by the US) off to the communists, cutting out as many middlemen as possible. Westerners found this collusion hard to understand; but after all, the South Vietnamese had never defined the North Vietnamese as 'the enemy'.

One corps of ARVN had a very inspiring, charismatic leader named General Do Cao Tri. Under him the soldiers fought very well, but in 1971 he was killed in a helicopter crash in Cambodia. After that his men had no heart to go on fighting, and many of them gave up and went home. They were very attached to their homes and families, and would desert in droves if expected to stay with a long campaign far from home. Besides their shrewd knowledge of just how dangerous the wild lonely parts of the country were, they had a deeper reason: in their culture, true self-fulfilment lay, as noted earlier, in joining their ancestors at last in the family burial ground. There would be a loss of identity and immortality if one's corpse lay rotting alone in some deep canyon of the Laotian or Cambodian jungle.

As they characteristically saw situations in personal terms, the officers of the ARVN would often hoard supplies from US meant for their whole unit, only dispensing them to a few individuals as favours. The habit of interpreting events in personal ways took a grim turn when, from 1968 to 1971, the Phoenix Programme was operated in South Vietnam by the National Police Field Force, and the Provincial Reconnaissance Units or PRUs. These were paramilitary government agents, whose numbers had more than doubled under the Vietnamisation policy. The programme was connected unofficially with the CIA, but officially was under 'CORDS', an abbreviation for 'Civilian Operations and Rural Development Support', which was a US agency for pacification.

The purpose of the 'Phoenix' programme was to destroy the powerful unseen network of communist infiltration in the south, but it got out of hand. Many of the agents acted like secret police, killing and torturing indiscriminately, and others considered the programme gave them license to settle old vendettas and private scores, and to engage in systematic extortion. Thousands of people were killed, the estimates of their numbers varying from 20,000 up to 40,000. These grisly figures illustrate how a project which seemed to make sense in theory, became in practice very hard to monitor, and did not turn out as expected because there were variables, like the Vietnamese very personalised view of life, which had not been considered.

The PRUs were hardly better than legalised criminals, and in fact many were believed to have come straight from jail into the program. While they did catch many communist agents, their savage methods had the opposite effect to the one intended, and made people want to join the 'Front' (that is, the National Liberation Front with the Vietcong) and their sympathisers more than before. The old Taoist 'law of reversed effort' was fulfilled again.

The PRUs worked closely with some American naval special-warfare units called the SEALs, a name short for 'Sea,

Air and Land Units.' Instead of having a stabilising effect on the society into which 'Vietnamisation' was introduced, they unintentionally heightened the atmosphere of bizarre banditry which characterised South Vietnam. They pushed the concept of counter-insurgency close to that grey area where sane behaviour begins to slip over into insane. They went native, crawling in and out of swamps in the Mekong Delta, wherever there were communist strongholds. They blacked their faces and wore black pajamas. Some of them took 'speed' to escalate their sensory awareness, and carried a drug which would make them incoherent for twenty-four hours if captured, giving their companions time to switch to a new code, and to change plans, if required.

The Phoenix programme provoked killings in revenge, adding to the unrest in South Vietnam in the late sixties and early seventies. President Thieu drafted every able-bodied man between the ages of eighteen and thirty-eight into the armed forces or the police. In 1970 he decreed that high schools and universities should be militarised, and closed them while students went to compulsory military lectures and training exercises. The resulting riots and demonstrations were savagely put down. The Buddhists revolted again, and once more one of them burned himself to death in protest. President Thieu appeared more and more to be as much a dictator as President Diem had been back in the fifties and sixties. Taxes were increased, prices rose, and as the flow of dollars began to level off with the departure of many US troops (though many pseudo-military advisors remained), it was hard to make enough to live on.

Meanwhile, from the point of view of the leading American military officers in Vietnam, life was hard too, as they often received orders from the White House, or the Secretary of State, which clashed with the orders sent from the Joint Chiefs of Staff; and they were expected, with greatly reduced numbers of troops, to have the same amount of action going on as before, and as many, if not more, fighters in the air and aircraft carriers ready at sea, as they had before Vietnamisation.

Between 1969 and 1972 President Nixon carried out four new projects in Indochina: the bombing of North Vietnamese 'sanctuaries' across the border in Cambodia in 1969, the invasion of Cambodia in 1970, the invasion of Laos in 1971, and the mining of Haiphong harbour in 1972. He had in mind the 'Madman Theory'; if he could display a tough and ruthless US administration, he thought, the Chinese and Russians might be more cautious in aiding the DRV, and the US would be in a stronger position in their negotiations with Hanoi.

The sanctuaries were secret bases for the communist forces, in the jungle on the Cambodian side of the border west of Saigon. There were secluded places to hide and rest, radio centers, medical stations, and caches of rice and guns. The most important of the sanctuaries was the 'COSVN' or Central Office for South Vietnam, which was located on an old plantation called the Mimot Plantation, in the Cambodian jungle, in an area called The Fish-Hook. There the border curved to the east into Vietnamese territory, forming a rather hook-shaped bulge. The US commanders believed that it was here the Vietcong leaders planned their campaigns and prepared to mass their troops to invade South Vietnam; and, if they could destroy their headquarters, many American men would be saved and the war shortened.

This was the rationale for *Operation Menu*, as the bombing of Cambodia begun on 18th March 1969 was called. It continued for fourteen months; over thirty-six hundred air raids were made, with an estimated cost to the US of four billion dollars. The raids had code names: the first was called *Breakfast*, as it had been planned at a breakfast meeting. Then others were dubbed *Lunch*, *Dinner*, and so on, as if the whole episode were imaginary, and just part of a game or play. Over a hundred thousand tons of bombs were dropped from B-52s flying invisibly at very high altitudes. How many thousands of Cambodians died, no-one ever knew.

The raids were no secret to the Vietcong, who got very accurate warnings beamed to them from Russian trawlers stationed off Guam. The planes were mostly based at Anderson Air Force Base there. But in Washington *Operation Menu* was kept as secret as possible. The pattern, or configuration, of those who were informed and those who were not graphically showed the divisive, emasculating effect of the tight control on information kept up by the White

House: polarising everyone; setting Congress against the administration and the 'desk job' military in Washington against their peers in action; and adding to the adversarial tone which prevailed, instead of lessening it. Deputy chiefs of staff at the Pentagon were informed about the bombing, but their counterparts in the field were not. The chief officers of the US Air Force, and members of congressional committees relevant to the war effort, for the most part, were not told; nor were some of the army intelligence people in Saigon.

Secrecy, suspicion and ambivalence were widespread. When news of the raids was first made public, about two months after they started, by a Pentagon correspondent writing for the New York Times, suspicion that one of them might be the source of the 'leak' fell upon Morton Halperin and two other members of the National Security Council staff. Their telephones at home and in their offices were bugged but no incriminating comments were revealed.

When some members of congressional committees wanted to discuss the raids after they had become public knowledge, some of their chairmen would not allow these discussions to take place, as they approved of the bombing anyway. As they had suggested the bombing of COSVN in the first place, the Joint Chiefs of Staff knew of the raids (but when they spoke of bombing the sanctuaries, they may have envisaged one sortie only). Their Chairman said at the time that he would be prepared, if necessary, even to deny that the raids ever took place. The computerised records of the bombers' flights were disguised by means of dual reporting.

The bombing raids across the border into Cambodia were studiously ignored by Prince Norodom Sihanouk, who was the ruler of Cambodia at the time. By skilful diplomacy he had managed for several years to keep the war in Vietnam from spreading to his country. He allowed the Vietnamese communists to get supplies through the port of Sihanoukville in the south (now called Kompong Som). He let the People's Army of Vietnam march and set up bases on Cambodian territory along the frontier. In March 1970 Prince Sihanouk was deposed while he was away by Marshal Lon Nol, who, supported by the US government, led a militarist revolt and fought against the communist Khmer Rouge, who at that time were backed by Prince Sihanouk. After this coup d'etat Sihanoukville was no longer open to the PAVN.

In Washington there were varying perceptions as to the nature of the enemy headquarters, COSVN. Some people said it never was an actual place; the CIA representative stressed its mobility, saying that it was more like a system for 'Distant Early Warning', than an actual building. Thomas Powers, in his book *The Man Who Kept the Secrets; Richard Helms and the CIA*, related how receiving stations just inside Cambodia, near the border with Vietnam, were getting the warnings from the Russian trawlers about the approach of the bombers. They were relayed to them from Hanoi. A receiving station could actually consist of just a few men in a truck with radio equipment, heavily camouflaged and concealed in the jungle. In a moment they could switch off and speed away, leaving no trace behind. So the CIA people advised that any attempt to invade the Cambodian junge and destroy the COSVN, which was under consideration, would fail because it was on the move all the time.

But at first Dr Kissinger and his staff on the National Security Council, using western imagery, had constructed reality on their own hypotheses, and imagined the COSVN to be like a big American military base, a large complex of solid buildings, lots of concrete everywhere, secret underground offices with phones and filing cabinets; there would be sleeping quarters and messing facilities too, they thought.[4] However, Melvin Laird, Secretary of Defense, told them that it would not be as elaborate as that, but said they would probably find large supply dumps.

The reality was not quite like any of the above, though the CIA people got close. Truong Nhu Tang, the Minister of Justice in the Provisional Revolutionary Government, a resistance group in the south who supported the northern communists, described the COSVN in his book *A Viet Cong Memoir*. (Co-authors were David Chanoff and Doan Van Toai.) In 1978 Truong Nhu Tang defected to Paris, sad and disappointed because of the arrogant treatment the southern communists had, he said, received at that time from the northern victors. It

---

4   Ibid

A cartoon drawing of the White House with guns (David Suter)

was not, he felt, at all as Ho Chi Minh had intended. He said that the essence of the COSVN was always its people, although it was in fact an actual place. It was a leadership group, carrying out the orders of the North Vietnamese command, and making a link between the northern and southern communists, or their supporters, in the south. There was a small permanent staff at the centre but most of the time the members were away on the missions assigned to them. Hidden by the triple canopy of the jungle, down a winding trail, the COSVN was a peasant hut that at first glance looked like other huts along the trail. The only sign that it was a place of importance was the guarded checkpoint at the approach; but when close, one could see bunkers and tunnel entrances alongside the hut. It was located only a few miles away from the bases set up in the jungle on the Vietnam side of the border, for three other resistance groups.

These groups were the National Liberation Front, or NLF; the Provisional Revolutionary Government, known as the PRG; and the Alliance for National, Democratic, and Peace Forces. They illustrated the pluralism and subtle variations in South Vietnamese society, as membership in them could be interchangeable, and a person could belong to any or all of them at the same time. Yet they were not all identical. The NLF was the oldest. It had begun to take shape late in 1958 as a political group resisting President Diem's repressive rule. The Provisional Revolutionary Government was the structure set up by the NLF in 1969, forming a shadow government in the jungle, in preparation for the expected time when President Thieu and the Americans would be gone, and they could take up their share of power. They worked closely with the Alliance, in which were united various nationalist groups of South Vietnam, representing certain categories of people, such as religious or ethnic groups, and others set up for university students, youth, and women. Their members wanted independence, but were not as far left as some members of the NLF and the PRG. These groups worked with the COSVN in planning their strategy for the eventual takeover of the South.

In spite of the near-starvation, snake bites, and malaria, Truong Nhu Tang looked back on his years in the jungle as a time of joy and brotherhood which was never to come again. Even then, however, there were signs, in discussions with their northern comrades, that they were a lot more doctrinaire, and had drifted further away from Buddhist values, than the southerners.

At the time of the bombing raids not many of them were killed because of the efficient warning system. The pounding and roaring of the attacks was utterly devastating, however, leaving many people very ill, deaf, and with shattered nerve systems. They escaped northwestward down jungle trails in pouring monsoon rain, to places deep in Cambodia where new bases with medical care were set up. Any huts or bunkers in the path of the bombers vanished completely, and only huge craters were left where they had been. The COSVN was destroyed during the invasion of Cambodia, but by then it had been deserted for two months.

The invasion of Cambodia by US and South Vietnamese forces took place between May and July, 1970. The role of the Joint Chiefs of Staff in it was very slight, and it was almost entirely master-minded from the White House. The commanders in Vietnam only had two days to prepare for it.[5] The trouble was, they were far advanced into the phased with-

---

5   Reported in *The Twenty Year War: America's Military Role in Vietnam,* by General Bruce Palmer.

drawal and repatriation of thousands of American troops, in accordance with Vietnamisation orders. By July the monsoon had started, bogging everyone down; however, large quantities of supplies had been captured, bases destroyed, and casualties inflicted. The North Vietnamese were driven back up the Mekong River about sixty kilometres, to Phnom Penh. Their losses caused a delay in their next attack, so the invasion appeared a success when viewed in terms of immediate gains; but its later results were actually damaging to the US and South Vietnamese forces.

During the months before the invasion of Cambodia anti-war feeling had been escalating in the US. The media had made public in the autumn the story of the massacre at My Lai 4, and Premier Pham Van Dong of the Democratic Republic of Vietnam had sent to Congress an open letter to the American people, urging them to put pressure on their president to bring the American presence in Vietnam to an end. Although the anti-war movement was at first associated with radicals among students, hippies, and men who had served in Vietnam, after a time it was supported by Wall Street lawyers, clergy, Harvard University faculty members, and suburban housewives; in fact, by a mixture of people of many different backgrounds.

Even in the White House, approval for the invasion of Cambodia was not unanimous. When Dr Kissinger told some of his aides about it, four of them resigned. They were Anthony Lake, Laurence Lynne, Roger Morris, and William Watts. Anthony Lake and Roger Morris had tried to present an alternative policy – negotiate now instead of later, to save lives – but President Nixon and Dr Kissinger did not take it up.

In the fall of 1969 there were big riots, camp-outs, and demonstrations outside the White House. A solid block of people would link arms across the road and, swaying as they sang, would chant for hours:

> 'Ho ho, Ho Chi Minh,
> The NLF is gonna win';

and other couplets such as:

> 'One two three four,
> Richard Nixon [or Tricky Dicky] stop the war.'

The crowd carried anti-war placards, and waved Viet Cong flags.

President Nixon thought that it would make a very telling point in a speech, to state that the COSVN would be destroyed. Although Dr Kissinger tried hard to dissuade him from mentioning it because of the lack, at the time, of hard evidence for its location, or even its existence as an actual building, he went ahead anyway, and made it the main thrust of his speech to the nation on television on 30th April 1970. He claimed that Cambodia had asked for the assistance of the US, and that the lives of thousands of Americans in South Vietnam were threatened by the hordes of North Vietnamese troops massing in the sanctuaries on the Cambodian border. He said: 'This is not an invasion of Cambodia'.

A few days later, on 4th May Ohio National Guardsmen fired on students at Kent State University who had been demonstrating for several days against the war. Two men and two women were killed and eleven wounded. Yet the Guard was not supposed to use live ammunition except as a last resort, and it should have been in the men's pouches, not already loaded into their guns. Hundreds of colleges closed in protest.

After a time the anti-war movement died down, as fewer Americans were killed; but as Ho Chi Minh had himself foretold, the war was, in part, won for him on Pennsylvania Avenue. (A few days before his death on 3rd September 1969, he wrote a reply to a letter from President Nixon thanking him for it, and saying that he desired a just peace, but pointing out that the first step towards it must be the withdrawal of all US troops from Vietnam. He said that an outline of the procedure for a settlement had already been drawn up by the NLF; and while he was angry at the destruction of his country, and the huge numbers of Vietnamese dead and wounded, he grieved also for the American dead.)

Some historians believe that the invasion of Cambodia, in the end, actually hastened the defeat of the US in Vietnam. Congress tried hard to limit any further trigger-happy expansion of the war by the Executive Branch. Funds were cut off for more combat activities in Vietnam, and ground troops and advisors were not allowed to operate in the lands bordering Vietnam.

(still several platoons went regardless into the forbidden areas, where bombing continued ruthlessly.) The Cooper-Church Amendment to the 1970 Defense Department Appropriations Act stipulated that none of the funds appropriated under the Act should be used for American infantry to fight in Cambodia, Thailand, nor, by a subsequent clause, in Laos. Troops had to be out of Cambodia by July.

The Gulf of Tonkin Resolution, which had given President Johnson carte blanche to escalate US active combat in Vietnam, was repealed. (President Nixon said he didn't need it anyway. The Gulf of Tonkin Incident, in which North Vietnamese were alleged to have attacked US shipping, turned out later to be a carefully orchestrated piece of misinformation to further the Americanisation of the war.)

The War Powers Resolution, which became law as the War Powers Act on 7th November 1973, was an attempt to make sure that, if the US went to war with another country, it was as a result of the collective and joint judgment of the president and the Congress that it was the right course. Particularly, if no declaration of war had been made, as with the war in Vietnam, the Act stated that within 48 hours of the beginning of fighting, the president had to submit detailed reports on the reasons for the combat, numbers of men involved, where it was taking place, and so forth. Copies of the report had to go on the same day to the Speaker of the House, the President of the Senate, the Committee on International Relations of the House, and the Committee on Foreign Relations of the Senate. The president was to submit further reports regularly as long as hostilities continued. The fighting could go on for a maximum of sixty days, but after that congressional permission had to be obtained to continue it up to thirty days at the most. There were further instructions as to what should be done if Congress was not in session when fighting broke out, or if the Senate and the House of Representatives could not agree on whether or not to allow an extension of hostilities.

It sounded as if the authors of the act were already sensing that the system of government was too complex to enable them to get a simple 'yea' or 'nay' speedily on going to war; and in fact, in spite of the above-mentioned limit-setting, the War Powers Act was difficult to enforce, and proved to be a paper tiger which was out-manoeuvred later, and had little effect on curbing White House power.

The invasion of Cambodia, besides causing a big outcry in the US and making Congressmen begin to realise how much power had slipped away from them, had two other results unfavourable to the Washington administration. Since supplies could no longer come to the North Vietnamese via Sihanoukville, they had to modernise the Ho Chi Minh Trail and the bases alongside it, as it was, now more than ever, their lifeline. Troops, and war matériel of all kinds, passed down it from the north, and there was a constant flow in the 1970s of traffic going northward from South Vietnam, too, bringing supplies covertly obtained. In the north there were links with the Trail, by rail and road, leading into southern China. From there supplies passed into North Vietnam from the USSR, and from China, too. So, curiously, the PAVN did eventually have bases, fully built up, barrack-like, very much as some of the National Security members had imagined the COSVN to be.

As this modernisation of the Trail and its bases provided a very vital background from which men and stores could be made ready for an assault on the south, the White House people felt they had to organise an invasion of Laos in February 1971, to cut the Trail in the area of Tchepone. This was another indirect result of the invasion of Cambodia. It did not stop the flow of supplies from the north, however.

In the late 1950s the Trail was a series of steep winding jungle paths, which it took people many months to travel. Many died on the way, succumbing to malaria, dysentery, snakebite, or attacks by wild animals such as tigers and leopards, who still roamed there then. Truong Nhu Tang, in his book *A Viet Cong Memoir*, estimated, that by 1974 nearly a hundred thousand men and women had been living and working continuously on the Trail for years. It had become a complex network of interconnected hard-surfaced two-lane roads, busy with mechanised traffic all the time. As soon as part of the road was bombed, the workers bypassed the crater if it could not be filled in, and laid down detours around it. Bridges and pontoons over streams were constantly repaired or replaced if hit. As well as the large bases which provided everything needed for an army on the move, there were spaced out along the Trail workers' camps where they could eat and sleep, camouflaged by the jungle. They even had visits from singers, musicians, and actors now and then.

The invasion of Laos in February 1971 must have given the field commanders of US forces in Vietnam that *déja vu* feeling, that surely they had been through the same situation already. It resembled the invasion of Cambodia in that there was very short notice given, the people on the spot did not know much about the plan until the last minute, and the initiative and enthusiasm for it came mostly from the White House. Coolnesses, rivalries, or divisions in Washington and in the US military command, affected the project. Melvin Laird, the Defense Secretary, and then Col Alexander Haig, Assistant to Dr Kissinger, the National Security Advisor, made separate visits to Vietnam and came up with separate assessments about the invasion, instead of getting together about it.

General Bruce Palmer, Jr, in *The 25-Year War*, relates how the North Vietnamese found out about the invasion ahead of time and were able to prepare their troops and all anti-aircraft defences, because personnel at US military headquarters leaked the news to the Saigon press; so it was common knowledge before the official memos about it came through.

Called 'Lam Son 719' after a battle famous in Vietnamese history, the invasion was a re-run in other ways beside those mentioned: US Special Forces, with CIA people, had made many unofficial incursions and raids across the border into Laos, since the 1950s. The old base at Khe Sanh, full of ghosts from the terrible siege which had taken place there in 1968, being on a strategic road close to the border, was reopened as a supply depot and co-ordinating HQ for aircraft.

There were major differences, however, between this invasion and the Cambodian one. As the use of US ground troops and advisors outside Vietnam had been forbidden by Congress, the whole basis of the planning was that South Vietnamese troops, advancing into Laos along low ground, would take the brunt of the fighting, while their flanks would be protected by other detachments on the surrounding high ground. These would be made up of South Vietnamese air-borne, ranger, and marine battalions brought to the scene by helicopters. Aerial support was not prohibited, nor was long-

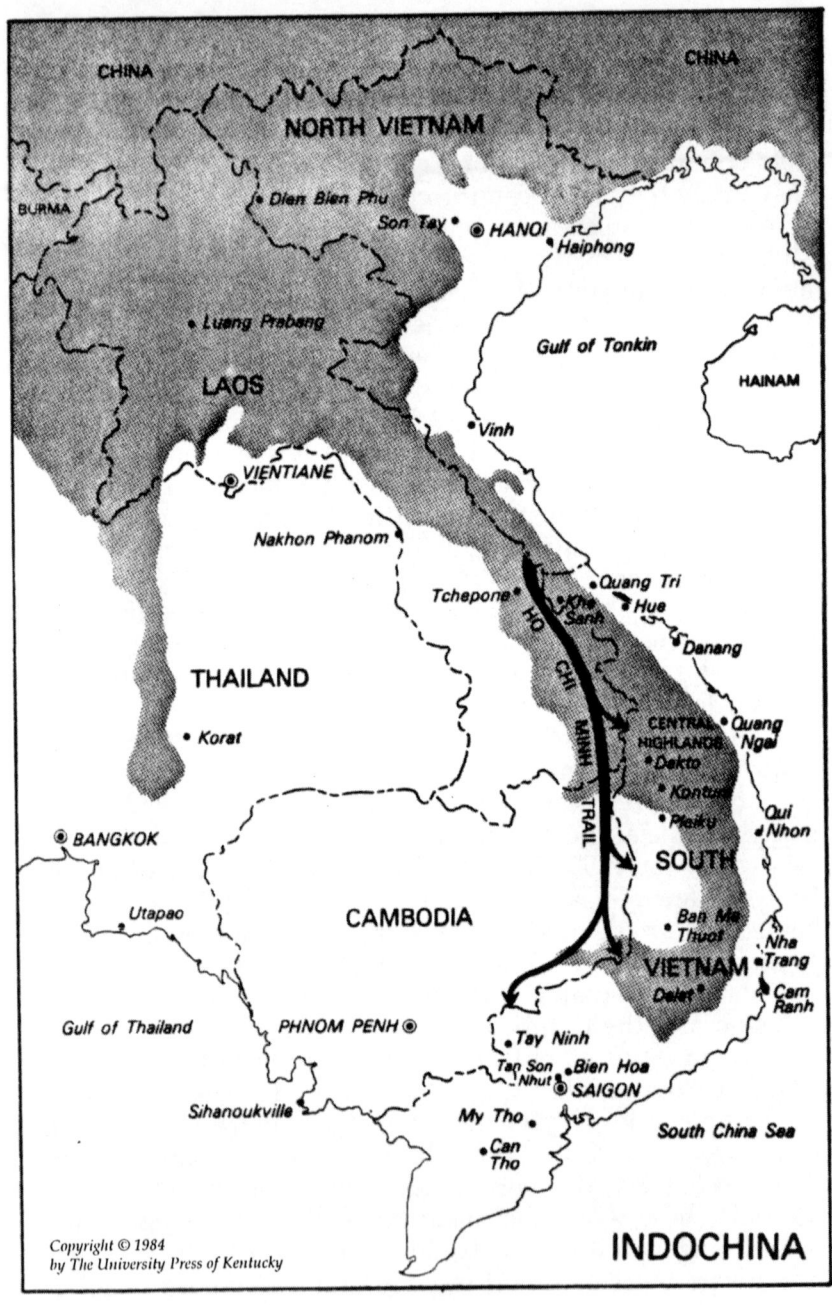

range artillery fired from the Vietnam side of the border.

But bad weather, and language difficulties between US pilots and South Vietnamese people guiding them into their assigned positions, ruined these plans. In the hilly jungles it was hard to find landing places for the helicopters. Spaces had to be hacked out for them. They often had to fly very low because of mist and driving rain, becoming easy targets for anti-aircraft fire. Over a hundred were brought down and many more damaged. Seven fighter-bombers were also lost; about a hundred US pilots and crew members were killed or were missing in action, and there were many wounded. Because of the rain the ground became a morass. It was difficult to keep up as planned with supplying the troops from the flanks, and taking away the dead and injured. Messages from pilots were often misunderstood. The North Vietnamese had tanks, heavy artillery, surface-to-air missiles, and outnumbered the ARVN two to one. (The CIA reported more 'copters lost than the army did.) Then after little more than a month, President Thieu decided to withdraw his troops, and there followed several days of grim fighting as the Americans tried to get them away by helicopter, while the North Vietnamese made tighter and tighter rings round them. Enemy losses were estimated by US officials to be very high, in the thousands; but the ARVN suffered even more. Some battalions lost about two-thirds of their men, while others, according to some historians, were almost entirely wiped out.

The invasion helped to delay the next major communist offensive, but the general public in the US did not think of that as, horrified, they saw pictures on TV of the small-boned, incredibly youthful South Vietnamese soldiers clinging to, or falling off, the skids of rapidly rising helicopters meant to rescue them.

In Washington, men who had fought in Vietnam, who had formed a group called 'Vietnam Veterans Against the War', staged mass demonstrations, and gathering at the steps of the Capitol, stripped off their medals and flung them over the barricade set up to keep them out of the building. However, one of them, John Kerry, was allowed to address the Senate Foreign Relations Committee, and was able to point out how cynically the ruling 'no ground troops to be deployed outside

Vietnam', had been circumvented in Laos. The letter of the law was kept, but the US crews in the helicopters killed just as effectively as the ARVN did on the ground; in fact, they were probably more deadly.

Short though it was, this incursion into Laos showed many of the hallmarks of US action in Indochina at the time. From the White House there were unrealistic expectations of high performance, regardless of factors such as problems of terrain and of weather, and hardships of local people. Security was poor, making leaking of information in advance easy. Helicopters are fragile and easily brought down (actually comparatively few were lost in proportion to the number deployed). There were problems in co-ordinating aircraft under different commands, and across different cultures. There was a big difference, too, in being a member of PAVN and feeling a sense of mission, and being one of the ARVN, compelled to fight.

In May 1972 Haiphong harbour was mined and bombed with undue overkill and deadly precision by US 7th Fleet and Navy and Marine aircraft. But as supplies to the North Vietnamese were coming continuously overland from the north, from the USSR and China, the attacks did not have much effect on the course of the war.

For twelve days in December 1972 the Nixon administration carried out saturation bombing of North Vietnam. The programme was known as 'the Christmas Bombing'. In one area one mile long by half a mile wide, 100 bombers and 500 fighter-bombers dropped 100,000 bombs. Twenty-six planes were lost, ninety-three men were killed or missing, and thirty-one were taken prisoner. Michael Maclear, in his book *Vietnam: The Ten Thousand Day War*, reported that one of the captured pilots, speaking in front of a foreign news camera, said that he was surprised at the lack of military targets in the area he was hitting.

The Christmas Bombing and the continuous bombing of other areas of North Vietnam as well which took place during the Nixon era, set back Vietnam's economy for years and years, but did not shatter communist morale; on the contrary, it played into the DRV's hands by hardening world opinion against the Americans' actions. Their propaganda was done for them. Meanwhile, the big arms corporations went laughing all the way to the bank, for the bombing was very profitable for them. While it was going on, the USSR and China carefully looked the other way.

Some people have considered that the Christmas Bombing caused the DRV to come more quickly to a settlement with Dr Kissinger; but others thought it made no great difference, and was seen as a public relations manoeuvre, a last big dramatic act of savagery before the Americans completed their withdrawal.

The 'peace' talks between Dr Kissinger and Le Duc Tho of North Vietnam, and between Dr Kissinger and President Thieu of South Vietnam, with Col. Haig also sometimes going to bat there on his own, went on and on and round and round for years. There was a surreal quality about them, as if everybody were talking to each other under water. The meaning of apparently familiar words could change with different speakers. Dr Kissinger evidently often felt as if he was trying to grasp a jellyfish which was always slipping away from him, as he said at a press conference on December 16 1972:

> 'We cannot do that [get closer to an agreement], if every day an issue is settled a new one is raised, [then] when an issue is settled in an agreement, it is raised again as an understanding and if it is settled in an understanding, it is raised again as a protocol.' (From *Vietnam, A History in Documents*, ed. Gareth Porter)

There was bafflegab and stalling on both sides. The various participants each had different perceptions of the real situation in Vietnam, and brought different mindsets to the talks. The North Vietnamese saw no need to hurry, as to them the talks were just a phase in the long-term plan for the DRV: the federation by conquest of all Indochina. Dr Kissinger, still with the cold war idea of containment of communism in mind, did not realise at first that the DRV would dare to insist that their troops were to be stationed in South Vietnam, and that there were to be no US troops there at all. He appeared to visualise the status quo continuing unofficially, with large numbers of para-military US advisors, and lots of munitions for the ARVN.

President Thieu was quite unrealistic. He thought American support for his régime would continue indefinitely. Long after the communists were already in South Vietnam, in hundreds of thousands, he stated in a broadcast speech that they would never be allowed to enter the hamlets and villages, but would be driven back everywhere. He was one of the last to know that Dr Kissinger would agree to their presence in return for the release of US prisoners, so naturally he had a sense of grievance. He refused to consider giving a coalition government, which had been proposed to accommodate the claims of the southern communist supporters and some neutral groups, a voice in the nation's affairs.

The members of the PRG and the National Liberation Front had representatives at some of the conferences. They mis-read the intentions of the northerners. When the Party Secretary-General, Le Duan, spoke of national concord and reconciliation, they thought that, for sure, this phrase meant that there would be a coalition government in which they would be prominent; and people, such as the conscripted soldiers, who had supported President Thieu because they had to, would be pardoned by the communists after the Americans had gone. (But it turned out that there was to be only one government, from Hanoi, and the conscripts were sent to re-education camps along with the collaborators.)

For their work at the peace talks Le Duc Tho and Dr Kissinger were offered the Nobel Peace Prize jointly, but Le Duc Tho refused his share because, as he said, there was no peace.

At first in the talks the communists had said that President Thieu had to be removed from office, but after a time they dropped this demand because they realised that, once the Americans had gone and had ceased to provide aid, his position would be untenable anyway. They were well aware that Dr Kissinger was in a very difficult position: if they were occupying South Vietnam, the US forces had gone home, and support for the war was disappearing in the States, what did he really have going for him? They realised that the proposal to retain US 'advisors' in South Vietnam was a covert way of keeping up a military presence there, and saw that President Thieu's

despotism had the effect of driving more people into their
ranks. They used, among others, the two techniques of 'fight
and talk, talk and fight', and 'separate and isolate'. The latter
seemed like the old Roman dictum,'Divide and Conquer'. The
North Vietnamese were thinking of it in terms of separating
President Thieu and Dr. Kissinger from their means of
support, US troops and money in Vietnam, and public opinion
in the US.

A COSVN Directive dated January 19 1973 stated:

> 'We must closely combine political struggle with armed struggle and
> legalistic struggle, using political struggle as the base, armed
> struggle as support, while bringing into full play the legalistic effects
> of the agreement.' (From *Vietnam, A History in Documents*, ed. Gareth
> Porter)

Le Duc Tho spun out the talks long enough so that when the
final offensive took place, the dry season had come.

President Nixon resigned his office on 9th August 1974,
when he was threatened with impeachment because of his
part in the Watergate Affair. But the Nixon Doctrine of export-
ing arms, not men, lived on and flourished like the green bay
tree.

During the Nixon administration, and in President Ford's
time, arms sales by the US multiplied astronomically. Saudi
Arabia and Iran were particularly good customers, while
Israel did a lot of trade in arms, too, besides receiving generous aid from the States. There were close ties between President
Nixon and the large arms corporations. In his book, *The Arms
Bazaar* Anthony Sampson reported that the Northrop company paid 150,000 dollars into President Nixon's campaign
expenses, and described how a Saudi Arabian middleman,
Adnan Khashoggi, who was a friend of the Saudi royal family,
contributed a million dollars to his 1972 election campaign.
There were large sums from other Arabian sources, too. Representatives of General Dynamics, and Lockheed, which President
Nixon bailed out of near bankruptcy in 1971, had large orders
through Khashoggi, who was also a friend of Bebe Rebozo, an
associate of President Nixon. These orders, creating thousands
of jobs, counteracted criticism of the administration for a while.

So the military-industrial complex often dictated foreign

policy, rather than foreign policy being the guide for the complex. The Nixon era illustrated the peaking both of White House power and the hold of the big arms corporations on the government: the logical conclusion of cold war rule.

After President Nixon had left, Dr Kissinger, who continued to be Secretary of State under President Ford, made one last try to get more money from the Congress to help President Thieu, and when he failed, realising South Vietnam was a lost cause from his point of view, he may have believed that Saigon was bound to fall (as it did on April 30 1975).

It is possible that, looking ahead to fresh cold war alignments in the future, he saw a possible advantage in keeping China anxious because the USSR had bases in Vietnam (as he guessed they would). So, leaving Saigon aside, he turned his attention to fresh tasks in foreign policy.

By contrast, to the Vietnamese communists the day of final victory was one never to be forgotten. General Van Tien Dung, who had been General Vo Nguyen Giap's Chief of Staff at Dien Bien Phu, described the scene in Saigon and its surroundings, as everywhere a sea of people rushed out to greet the oncoming troops, embracing each other, waving flags and singing. Strewn along the sides of the roads were the relics, as he put it, 'of a reactionary political doctrine that had unraveled', guns, artillery, uniforms, vehicles, and boots hastily discarded in flight. He wrote:

'This historic and sacred, intoxicating and completely satisfying moment was one that comes once in a generation, once in many generations. Our generation had known many victorious mornings. But there had been no morning so fresh and beautiful, so radiant, so clear and cool, so sweet-scented, as this morning of total victory.' (From *Our Great Spring Victory: An Account of the Liberation of South Vietnam* by General Van Tien Dung, trans. J. Spragens Jr., in the New York Monthly Review Press, 1977. Quoted in the anthology, *Vietnam and America*)

POSTSCRIPT

Once more, a student of Vietnamese affairs is having a dialogue with the author.

Question:
In the book you've described how various big systems and groups have affected the course of history, and changed people's lives; what difference, if any, do you see now? Are they more, or less powerful than they were in the US-Vietnam War period?

Answer:
It seems to me that any system or group which was big at that time is bigger than ever now.

Looking east first, the People's Army of Vietnam, for instance, is now one of the world's largest standing armies, ranking fourth or sixth, depending on what categories of armed persons you include in the tally.

The oriental faiths and schools of thought are stronger than ever in the east, and more and more people are becoming drawn to them in the west, as an offset to our pervading consumerism and fast lane life-style. In Vietnam I have seen very ornate pagodas, often with statues of Quan Am.

Q.   How about western systems?

A.   The process of bureaucratisation has escalated greatly; e.g., the CIA and the Executive Branch of the US government are both larger than ever now. In his time President Reagan added thousands of persons to his payroll, and increased CIA funding over and above inflation allowance.

The 'Iran-Contra' scandal of the 1980s, in which secret arms deals were made with Iran and profits sent to the Nicaraguan Contras – millions disappearing without trace en route – showed that it's still hard for the US Congress to find out about, let alone monitor, CIA and NSC operations. They carry out policy, while their original mandates, of reporting and advising only, are ignored.

Q.   You mentioned the Washington 'PACs'; how are they doing?

A.   The PACs, or Political Action Committees, have more power than ever. Legislation to curb them has not been successful. Some Congressmen are creating their own, on the basis of 'If you can't beat 'em, join 'em.'

Q.   What about the US military-industrial complex you described? Is it still as powerful?

A.   More so than ever, many thousand times over, I think.

Arms dealers prosper as never before. While some US forces bases are being closed, many are being enlarged and renovated, and of course there are always strong local objections to a base closure, because of the revenue to the district.

Some critics and commentators on military matters

consider that the Gulf War has justified the huge military-industrial complex, but others feel that it's only seemed to do so, and has left massive problems unsolved. One critic (Jonathan Power) predicted the aftermath of the Gulf War would bring 'the Grandaddy of all Vietnams' in its train. For the Kurds this prophecy has come true.

As for the Gulf War banishing the 'Vietnam Syndrome', that is, fear of being bogged down in a long hard land war: again, opinions are divided. Some people feel that it was banished to a large extent because of the speed of the operation, and the technical expertise of the US forces; others think that the campaign in the Gulf did not really prove that another war such as the US-Vietnam War couldn't happen again.

Q.   It's clear that morale in the US forces received a great boost from the Gulf War. Do you think they still have the same internal problems as you related that they had, when in Vietnam?

A.   No. Since the Vietnam years the US forces have undergone major restructuring. The lack of unity of command, the inter-service rivalries, and under-educated officers, problems noted in Vietnam, are mostly in the past now.

Educational requisites for recruits are higher, and training more intellectually challenging, than they used to be. There was a vital change made when, under the Goldwater-Nichols Reorganisation Act of 1986, the Chairman of the Joint Chiefs of Staff became the sole military advisor to the president, putting him back into the direct line of command, as he had been before 1958. During the US-Vietnam War he had been on the sidelines, as it were, as head of the various service corps, which had the effect of fragmenting authority, as you may recall from previous comments.

Within the Pentagon itself much 'house-cleaning' has been achieved in recent years, regarding stricter controls on the testing of all armed forces equipment, and on its pricing. The groundwork for this was laid by a group called the Pentagon Whistleblowers, who worked on a project to expose fraud in defence contracts. It was called 'The Project on Military Procurement.' Dinah Rasor, in her book *The Pentagon Underground*, describes how the Whistleblowers faced hostility and dismissal for a long time, but did at last gain recognition, and caused some cases of corruption and fraud to be brought to court.

Q.   Have you any comment to make on the situation of the US-Vietnam Vets?

A.   Yes. The US-Vietnam Vets have received some compensation, though not an adequate amount, for damage to themselves and their families allegedly caused by exposure to the chemical Agent Orange. Two administrative changes militate in their favour: the continuing inquiry into the effects of Agent Orange is no longer conducted internally by the Veterans' Administration only, but has passed to other civilian agencies; and the head of the Vets' Administration now has cabinet status.

Q.   Have you heard anything about the Vets who were at My Lai?

A.   Yes. Lt Calley, Jr, is employed in his father-in-law's store. The others, like many Vietnam Vets, had a lot of trouble finding work after the war. Mostly they just got casual labour, part-time, or for short periods. One was living

A Street in My Tho, Tien Giang Province, Vietnam.

under a bridge in Pittsburgh with his girlfriend, when she shot him in a quarrel.

It's estimated that several hundred US Vietnam Vets still live alone in the forests of the Pacific Northwest of the US, while some have found reclusive homes in Hawaii. The number of suicides among Vietnam Vets is believed to be very high.

Q. I imagine this to be true, don't you, particularly if you include deaths which might not have been considered suicides at first, such as those automobile-'accidents', where the drivers were driving when heavily impaired?

A. Yes, I agree.

Q. How do you think Vietnam is faring now internationally?

A. Well, I think Vietnam has had a bad press in the west for a long time, and news reports have been slanted against her. For instance, Vietnam is usually cited as an aggressor in Cambodia, but there's no mention of the Khmer Rouge as an aggressor in Vietnam.[1] For several years in the 1970s Pol Pot's forces repeatedly crossed the southern border between Vietnam and Cambodia, threatening the Vietnamese Mekong Delta area, and brutally forcing nearly half a million people from their homes. When negotiations proved useless, then the Vietnamese government decided to cross over into Cambodia and drive Pol Pot back. The threat the Khmer Rouge poses to Vietnamese security has largely been ignored in the west.

Vietnam hasn't received any credit for withdrawing from Cambodia as requested. The longsuffering Cambodian people, whose opinion, it seems to me, is seldom sought or quoted, dreaded the departure of the Vietnamese troops, for they knew that without them nothing stood between them and Pol Pot. (China has aided Pol Pot, as a proxy way of fighting Vietnam.)

We hear very little in the west about the aid provided to Cambodia by Vietnam, in the way of goods e.g., rice seed, cement, and plastics; help of a technical nature; and in the construction of dispensaries and radio stations, and repair of bridges and roads.

Q.   What's needed is access to several varied sources of information on Vietnam, don't you think?

A.   Yes.

Q.   Are there countries seeking to trade with, and invest in, Vietnam at present?

A.   Yes, several countries are looking her way for investment opportunities, and some joint ventures in business are being negotiated. Oil and other minerals, fishing and sea food processing, for example, are some of the types of resources and trade which may be developed there, by other Asian nations and Europeans, for instance by the Germans. A French film company is there at present, making a film about the Siege of Dien Bien Phu. The national flair for small businesses and individual

---

1   See *Punishing The Poor: The International Isolation of Kampuchea*, by Eva Mysliwiec, Oxfam, 274 Banbury Rd, Oxford OX2 7DZ, UK.

entrepreneurship is shown in the family-run market stalls, laden with attractive food, and the countless small street-side cafés, where people sit for hours with their friends and watch the passing crowd. In small riverside yards there's boat building and welding going on. Vietnamese lacquer work is very fine.

There's a chronic lack of capital for road repairs, new buses, trucks, and for new large car and truck ferries on the vast rivers, vital for the freight and transport requirements of the country. However, shiny new motorbikes abound.

My hope is that soon Vietnam will be seen as she really is and not as a pawn of great powers: then the economic boycott may be lifted.

I understand that recently US State Department officials have announced their intention to start a dialogue with their opposite numbers in Vietnam.

The road between Hue and Da Nang, Central Vietnam

SELECTED
BIBLIOGRAPHY

Ambrose, Stephen E., *Rise to Globalism, American Foreign Policy*, 1938-1980. vol 8 of *The Pelican History of the United States*. Harmondsworth: Penguin Books, 1980.

Archer, Jules, *Ho Chi Minh, Legend of Hanoi*. New York: Macmillan, 1971.

Associated Press and George Esper, *The Eye-Witness History of the Vietnam War, 1961-75*. New York: The Associated Press, 1983.

Bechert, Heinz, and Vu Duy Tu, *Buddhism in Vietnam*, from *Buddhism in the Modern World*, edited by Heinrich Dumoulin. London and New York: Macmillan, 1976.

Bloch, Maurice, *Marxism and Anthropology, The History of a Relationship*. Oxford: Oxford University Press, 1985.

Capra, Fritjof, *The Tao of Physics*. London: Flamingo Books, 1983.

Chomsky, Noam, with John Gittings and Jonathan Steele, *Superpowers in Collision*. Harmondsworth: Penguin Books, 1984.

Chomsky, Noam, *Turning the Tide: The US and Latin America*. Toronto, Black Rose Books, 1986.

Churchman, C. West, *The Systems Approach*. New York, Laurel Books, 1979.

Clausewitz, Carl von, *On War*. Trans. by Col. J.J. Graham, 1908, ed. by Col. F. N. Maude. Harmondsworth, Penguin Classics, 1985. (From *Vom Kriege*, 1832.)

Cousins, Norman, *The Pathology of Power*. New York and London, W.W. Norton, 1987.

Croizart, Col. Victor, *The Brown Water Navy, The River and Coastal War in Indo-China and Vietnam, 1948-72*. Poole, Dorset, UK Blandford Press, 1984.

Cronin, Thomas E., *The Swelling of the Presidency*, from *Watergate: Its Effect on the American Political System*. ed. by David C. Snafell. Cambridge MA, Winthrop.

Deacon, Richard, *Kempei Tai, A History of the Japanese Secret Service*. New York, Berkley Books, 1985.

Duffet, John, ed., *Against the Crime of Silence*, Proceedings of the Russell International War Crime Tribunal. New York, Clarion Books, 1968.

Dumoulin, Heinrich, ed., *Buddhism in the Modern World*. New York: Macmillan, 1976.

Dournes, Jacques, *Minorities of Central Vietnam*. London, The Minority Rights Group, 1983.

Engels, Friedrich, and Marx, Karl, *The Communist Manifesto*. New York, Pocket Books, 1964. (From 1848; see Marx, Karl)

Esper, George, see Associated Press.

Fallaci, Oriana, *Interviews with History*. Boston, Houghton Mifflin, 1976.

Fitzgerald, Frances, *Fire in the Lake*. New York, Vintage, 1973.

Freemantle, Brian, CIA, *The 'Honourable' Company*. London, Michael Joseph Ltd, 1983.

Gabriel, Richard A., *Military Incompetence: Why the American Military Doesn't Win*. New York, Hill and Wang, 1985.

Generous, Kevin M., *Vietnam, The Secret War*. London, Bison Books, 1985.

Geertz, Dr Clifford, *Notions of Primitive Thought*, from *States of Mind*, ed. by Dr Jonathan Miller. London: Methuen, 1983.

Gettleman, Marvin E., ed., *Vietnam: History, Documents and Opinions on a Major World Crisis*. Greenwich, CT: Fawcett, 1965.

Gettleman, Marvin E., with Jane Franklin, Marilyn Young, and H. Bruce Franklin, *Vietnam and America: A Documented History*. New York, Grove Press Inc., 1985.

Goldston, Robert, *The Vietnamese Revolution*. New York: Bobbs-Merrill, 1972.

Government Manual, USA 1986-7, Office of the Federal Register and National Archives and Records Administration; published by the Superintendent of Documents, Government Printing Office, Washington DC.

Green, Mark, et al., *Who Runs Congress?* (intro. by Ralph Nader), New York, Dell, 1984.

Halberstam, David, *The Best and the Brightest*. New York, Fawcett, 1972.

Harrison, James Pinckney, *The Endless War: Vietnam's Struggle for Independence*. Toronto, McGraw-Hill, 1983.

Herr, Michael, *Dispatches*. New York: Alfred A.Knopf, 1977.

Hersh, Seymour, *My Lai 4: A Report on the Massacre and its Aftermath*. New York, Random House, 1970.

In the Name of America: Clergy and Laymen Concerned about Vietnam. Library of Congress. 68-21064.

Karnow, Stanley, *Vietnam: A History*. Harmondsworth, Penguin Books, 1983.

Kidron, Michael, and Dan Smith, *The War Atlas, Armed Conflict, Armed Peace*. London and Sydney, Pan Books, 1983.

Kinder, Hermann, and Werner Hilgemann, *The Penguin Atlas of World History, Volume Two, from the French Revolution to the Present*. Harmondsworth, Penguin Books, 1985.

Kissinger, Dr Henry A., *For the Record: Selected Statements, 1977-1980.* Boston and Toronto, Little, Brown and Co., 1981.

Knightley, Phillip, *The Second Oldest Profession: The Spy as Patriot, Bureaucrat, Fantasist and Whore.* London and Sydney: Pan Books, 1987.

Lancaster, Donald, *The Emancipation of French Indochina.* Oxford, Oxford University Press, 1961.

Lao Tzu, *Tao Te Ching.* Trans. by D.C. Lau. Harmondsworth, Penguin Books, 1984.

Luttwak, Edward N., *The Pentagon and the Art of War: The Question of Military Reform.* New York, Simon and Schuster, 1985.

Maclear, Michael, *Vietnam: The Ten Thousand Day War.* London, Methuen, 1981.

McLellan, David, ed., Marx: *The First Hundred Years.* London, Fontana Paperbacks, 1983.

Marx, Karl, and Engels Friedrich, *The Communist Manifesto,* 1848. trans. by Samuel Moore from the German. New York, Simon and Schuster, 1964.

Mascaro, Juan, trans. from the Pali of *The Dhammapada, The Path of Perfection.* Harmondsworth, Penguin Books, 1983.

Messimer, Dwight R., *Pawns of War: The Loss of the USS Langley and the USS Pecos.* Annapolis, MD, Naval Institute Press, 1983.

Morris, Roger, *Uncertain Greatness: Henry Kissinger and American Foreign Policy.* New York, Harper and Row, 1977.

Owens, Robert G., *Organisational Behavior in Schools.* Engelwood Cliffs, NJ, Prentice-Hall Inc., 1970.

Page, Tim, *Ten Years After: Vietnam Today.* New York, Alfred A. Knopf, 1987.

Palmer, Alan, *The Penguin Dictionary of Twentieth-Century History, 1900-1982.* Harmondsworth, Penguin Books, 1983.

Palmer, General Bruce Jr., *The 25-Year War: America's Military Role in Vietnam.* Lexington KY, University of Kentucky Press, 1984.

Patti, Archimedes, *Why Vietnam? Prelude to America's Albatross.* Los Angeles, University of California Press, 1980.

Pentagon Papers, The, as published by the New York Times. New York, Bantam Books, Inc., 1971.

Pike, Douglas, *PAVN: People's Army of Vietnam.* Novato, CA, Presidio Press, 1986.

Pisor, Robert, *The End of the Line; The Siege of Khe Sanh.* New York and London, W.W. Norton, 1982.

Porter, Gareth, ed., *Vietnam, A History in Documents.* New York, New American Library, Inc., 1971.

Powers, Thomas, *The Man Who Kept the Secrets: Richard Helms and the CIA.* New York, Simon and Schuster, 1981.

Pratt, John Clark, ed., *Vietnam Voices: Perspectives on the War Years, 1941-1982.* Harmondsworth, Penguin Books, 1984.

Rasor, Dina, *The Pentagon Underground.* New York, Times Books, a division of Random House, 1985.

Rust, William J., and the Editors of US News Books, *Kennedy in Vietnam: American Vietnam Policy, 1960-1963.* New York, Scribner's, 1985.

Sampson, Anthony, *The Arms Bazaar.* New York, The Viking Press, 1977.

Shawcross, William, *Dr Kissinger Goes to War,* article in Harper's Magazine, May 1979.

Smith, Dan, see Kidron.

Smith, Huston, *The Religions of Man.* New York, Perennial Library, Harper and Row, 1965.

Summers, Col. Harry G. Jr., *On Strategy, A Critical Analysis of the Vietnam War.* New York, Dell Publishing Co., 1982.

Sun Tzu, *The Art of War. c. 500 BC,* trans. by Lionel Giles, 1910, ed. by James Clavell. New York, Delacorte Press, 1983.

Truong Nhu Tang, with David Chanoff and Doan Van Toai, *A Viet Cong Memoir*. New York, Vintage Books, a division of Random House, 1985.

Tower Commission Report, The. New York, Bantam Books & Times Books, 1987.

Toffler, Alvin, *Previews and Premises*. New York, William Morrow and Co., 1983.

Vu Duy Tu, see Bechert, Heinz.

Weiss, Peter, *Notes on the Cultural Life of the Democratic Republic of Vietnam*. London, Calder and Boyars, 1971.

Wright, J. Patrick, *On a Clear Day You Can See General Motors*. New York, Avon Books, 1979.

Zaehner, R.C., *A New Buddha and a New Tao*, from *The Concise Encyclopedia of Living Faiths*, ed. by R.C. Zaehner. Boston, Beacon Press, 1967.

ACKNOWLEDGEMENTS

BARTHOLOMEW, a division of Harper Collins Publishers Ltd., the map of SE Asia from the Reader's Digest *Great World Atlas*: 12 Duncan St Edinburgh EH9 ITA.

Bell Helicopter Textron Inc., PO Box 482, Fort Worth, Texas 76101: photograph no. 32 from *Military Helicopters*, by Michael J. Gething, of 3 Bell UH-ID Iroquois Helicopters in Vietnam.

British Broadcasting Corporation (BBC), 35 Marylebone High St., London W1M 4AA: a quotation from an essay by Dr Clifford Geertz in *States of Mind*, with permission from BBC Enterprises Ltd.

Cassell, plc, Villiers House, 4/47 Strand, London WC2N 5JE: From *Brown Water Navy*, by Col. Victor Croizat, USMC, Retd.: a map of the French Administrative Divisions of Indochina, a photograph of the interior of the Cao Dai Temple at Tay Ninh, and two photographs of French troops in Vietnam, in 1950 & 1952 respectively.

Doubleday and Co. Inc., 666 5th Avenue, New York NY 10103: 5 small maps from The Penguin *Atlas of World History*, Vol.II, by Hermann Kinder & Werner Hilgemann.

Dournes, Jacques, Chemin de Peyremale, 30140 Anduze, France. A photograph of Böhnar children, and a quotation of part of a poem, from *Minorities of Central Vietnam*, by Jacques Dournes.

Little, Brown and Co, Publishers, 34 Beacon St, Boston MA 02108: some quotations from *For the Record* by Dr Henry Kissinger.

Grateful acknowledgement is hereby made to Dr Henry A. Kissinger for the use of quotations from his book entitled *For The Record*, copyright 1981, Dr Henry A. Kissinger.

Multimedia Product Development Inc., Suite 724, 410 South Michigan Avenue, Chicago IL 60605: quotation from *On A Clear Day You Can See General Motors* by J. Patrick Wright. Copyright © 1979 by J. Patrick Wright. Published by Wright Enterprises. Reprinted with permission of Multimedia Product Development Inc.

Page, Mr Tim, 2 Fairbourne Heath Cottages, Windmill Hill, Ulcombe, Nr Maidstone, Kent ME17 1LP, UK: 2 photographs, from his book *Ten Years After: Vietnam Today*. The pictures are of Marshal Giap, and of a landscape near Dien Bien Phu.

Patti, Major Archimedes, Ste 310, 480 Versailles Place, Longwood, Fla 32779. A photograph of Ho Chi Minh proclaiming Independence, from *Why Vietnam? Prelude To America's Albatross*.

Penguin Classics, Harmondsworth, Middlesex, UK UB7 ODA: some quotations from the *Dhammapada*, translated by Juan Mascaro, and from Tao Te Ching, translated by D.C. Lau.

Presidio Press, Ste. 300,505B San Marin Drive, Novato CA 94945: USA a diagram, *Schematic of Vietnamese Communist Revolutionary War* reprinted with permission from *People's Army of Vietnam*, by Douglas Pike ©.

Smith, Mr David E., 18 Beckwith Road, Dulwich, London UK SE24 9LG: a cartoon drawing of President Truman, which appeared in *The Manchester Guardian Weekly*, March 2, 1986.

Suter, Mr David, PO Box 1538, Amagansett, New York 11930: a cartoon drawing of the White House with guns, from the May 1979 issue of *Harper's Magazine*.

Time Magazine, a photograph of lobbyists in *Gucci Gulch* by Terry Ashe, *Time Magazine*, 1968, New York NY 10020.

Universal Press Syndicate, 4900 Main St Kansas City, MO 64112: 2 cartoons by Tom Toles and 3 by Pat Oliphant. Toles Copyright 1983 and 1986 The *Buffalo News*. Reprinted with permission of Universal Press Syndicate. All rights reserved. Oliphant Copyright 1985, 1987, and 1990. Universal Press Syndicate. Reprinted with permission. All rights reserved.

University of Kentucky, 663 South Limestone, Lexington, KY 40508-4008: USA a map of Indochina showing the Ho Chi Minh Trail, and a chart of US Command Structure in Southeast Asia, 1967, both from *The 25-Year War; America's Military Role in Vietnam,* by Gen Bruce Palmer Jr. Copyright © 1984 by the University Press of Kentucky.

Vietnamese friends who graciously agreed to appear in some photographs: Ms Nguyen Loan Thu and Mr Nguyen Choang.

The author wishes to thank the above-named for their material.

INDEX

References to maps and illustrations are in italics

A

B

Boeing Corporation, 113
Bourne, Dr Peter G., 158
Browne, Malcolm, 168
Buddha, Siddharta Gautama, 17, 25, 29-33, 36
Buddhism, 17, 24, 28, 29-35, 147
Buddhism, Mahayana and Theravada branches of, 33
Buddhism, Union for Study of, 34
Buddhist Home Contemplation Movement, 27
Buddhist Revolt, the, xxv, 35
Buddhists, World Fellowship of, 28
Bureaucracy, concept of, the, xxvi, xxvii

C

Calley, Lt W., Jr., xv, xxi
Cambodia,
        11, 33, *38, 86*, 94, 105, *105*, 144, 172, 188, 189, *202*, 214
    bombing of, 192, 193, 196
    invasion of, 192, 196-201
Cao Dai sect, the, 24-26, 27, 50, 51, 53, 69, 84, 93
Carter, President J.E., 140
Castries, Gen. Christian de, 97
Central Intelligence Agency (CIA), xxvi, 13, 36, 103, 113, 124, *178*
    origin and function in cold war; 125-128
    covert work in Vietnam, 128-30
    work in Laos with montagnards, 130-32, 136
    in Vietnam with Special Forces, 132-36, 137
    intelligence work in Vietnam, 135-7
    role conflicts and ethical dilemmas in, 138-41
    gained representation on National Security Council, 179
Central Office for South Vietnam (COSVN), 192-6, 198, 200
Champa and the Chams, 8, *9*, 13
Chiang Kai-shek, 74, 80, 82n
China, Nationalist, 51, 68, 83
China, People's Republic of, (PRC), 82n, 99, 100, 105, *105*, 112, 162
Chou En-lai, 104, 105
Christmas bombing, (see Nixon)
Churchman, C. West. xix, xx
CIA (see Central Intelligence Agency)

D

E

F

G

H

I

J

K

Kempei Tai, xxiv, 53, 54, 69, 70
Kennedy, President John F., xxiii, 24, 128, 137, 141, 181
Kent State University, 198
Kerry, John, 203
Khashoggi, Adnan, 207
Khe Sanh, 158, 165, 201, 202
Khmers, 8, 12, 33
Khmer Rouge, 193, 214
Kipling, Rudyard, 170
Kissinger, Dr. Henry:
    National Security Advisor and Secretary of State;
                175, 181
    re-arranged committees in Exec. Branch of govt.;
                180, 181
    visit to China with President Nixon; 184
    linkage theory; 186
    balance of power theory; 186
    had ideas in common with Clausewitz; 186
    aides resigning over bombing of Cambodia; 197
    peace talks, 205, 206, 207
Knightley, Phillip, 127
Kublai Khan, 3
Kuomintang, the, 51, 68, 74

L

Laird, Melvin, 181, 194, 201
Lake, Anthony, 197
Lang Son, 70
Lansdale, Maj. Gen. Edward G., 127-131
Laos, 13, *38, 86,* 90, 96, 105, *105,* 144, 185, 188
    US Special Forces and CIA in; 129-132
    invasion of, 192, 200-4, 202
Lao Tzu, 17, 35
Lattre, de, Gen. J. de Tassigny, 87, 89, 94
Lattre, Line de, 87, 89, 137

M

N

S

T

U

V

W

Y